MARRIAGES

Of

CAMPBELL COUNTY, VIRGINIA

1782 - 1810

93 - 860

CAMPBELL COUNTY COURTHOUSE
Built 1845

Piedmont Photo Crafts, Forest, Va.

Marriages
of
Campbell County
Virginia

1782-1810

Compiled by

Lucy Harrison Miller Baber

and

Hazel Letts Williamson

Baltimore

GENEALOGICAL PUBLISHING CO., INC.

1980

Originally published: Lynchburg, Virginia, 1971
Copyright © 1971 by
Lucy Harrison Miller Baber and Hazel Letts Williamson
All Rights Reserved
Reprinted, by arrangement,
Genealogical Publishing Co., Inc.
Baltimore, 1980
Library of Congress Catalogue Card Number 79-56412
International Standard Book Number 0-8063-0879-6
Made in the United States of America

Sponsored

by

BLUE RIDGE CHAPTER

National Society Daughters of the American Revolution

The sponsoring of this book
is a part of the observance of the Chapter's
Seventy-fifth Anniversary

ASSOCIATES IN RESEARCH

Louise Ann Blunt

Lucile Slate Enright

Nell Gardner Kimlin

Elizabeth Bailey Norman

Bess Sydnor Thompson Rucker

ACKNOWLEDGMENTS

We are deeply appreciative of the Blue Ridge Chapter's decision to sponsor the publication of our book. We also gratefully acknowledge the sustained support, interest, and encouragement of our Regent, Mrs. Richard F. Hawkins, during whose administration the research and assembling of data for this book was done as the Chapter's Genealogical Records Committee project.

As Co-Chairmen of this Committee, we want to give special recognition to our five so-called, "associates in research", members of the original Committee of seven, who gave dedicated service journeying to the Courthouse to help decipher and abstract the documents, or to the library to check out various references. When the time came, they also helped with the indexing, organizing of mailing lists or assumed responsibilities in connection with book sales. These able associates were: Louise Ann Blunt, Mrs. O. B. Enright, Jr., Mrs. Donald W. Kimlin, Mrs. Chester R. Norman, and Mrs. J. Eldon Rucker.

When the necessity arose in the later stages of this project for additional help, the Committee was expanded to include five very capable new members: Mrs. J. J. Bowman, Mrs. Louis R. Funai, Jr., Mrs. R. Vaughn Harper, Mrs. Russell Nolan, and Mrs. Albert E. Simms. Other members of the Blue Ridge Chapter, although not actually serving on the Committee, gave specific support in one way or another to this project. May we thank: Ruth H. Blunt, Dr. Roberta D. Cornelius, Mrs. Daniel Bowman, Mrs. L. T. G. Hyatt, Mrs. William N. Nelson, Mrs. Paul D. Oakey, and Mrs. Charles G. Patterson, Jr.

Our grateful appreciation to The Honorable William W. Sweeney, Judge Sixth Judicial Circuit of Virginia, for his general concern and a number of very constructive suggestions. Judge Sweeney also arranged for a reproduction of the excellent picture of the Campbell County Courthouse which is so much admired on the walls of his Judicial Chambers. The original photograph was taken by Ernest Eldridge of Piedmont Photo Crafts, Forest, Virginia, whom we thank for the courtesy copy for our book.

We genuinely appreciate the ready assistance and numerous courtesies extended to us on the occasion of our many visits to the Courthouse by Mr. H. E. Bennett, Clerk, and Mrs. Margaret Nichols, Deputy Clerk, of the Campbell County Circuit Court. Mr. Walter Haberer, Executive Secretary of Campbell County, was also most cordial.

The compilers are sincerely indebted to Mr. George H. S. King, F.A.S.G., of Fredericksburg, Virginia, and to Mr. J. Frederick Dorman, F.A.S.G., of Washington, D. C. Both have been more than kind in giving general guidance and in directing us to specific sources. We also appreciate Mr. Dorman's willingness to give scrutiny to our final compilation and (we hope) thereby at least partially rescue us from mistakes of fact or interpretation.

We are indebted to the Rev. Dr. C. FitzSimons Allison, Professor of Church History, Episcopal Theological Seminary, Alexandria, Virginia, for clarifying for us certain points in Ecclesiastical Law, and for citing relevant sources for our own background information. The Rev. J. J. Bowman of College Hill Baptist Church, Lynchburg, also helped us gain a better understanding of certain points in question which we appreciated.

The staff at our local Jones Memorial Library was ever ready to help resolve our reference problems. Our warmest gratitude to: Mrs. Josephine B. Wingfield, Librarian, Mrs. Harry E. Skelton, Mrs. George T. Adams, Jr., Delores Swanson, and Mrs. William J. Hubbard. (Mrs. Adams and Mrs. Hubbard, incidentally, are Blue Ridge Chapter members.)

Our research also took us to the Virginia State Library where we found the usual willingness to be helpful. For taking time to answer innumerable questions or to seek out source material, we particularly want to thank: Mr. Milton C. Russell, Head, Reference and Circulation Section, General Library Branch; Dr. Louis H. Manarin, Archivist; Mr. John W. Dudley, Ass't. Archivist, and Mrs. Jewell T. Clark.

We are grateful to Douglas Summers Brown of Emporia, Virginia, the recognized authority on Quakers of our area, who added particularly to our knowledge and understanding of South River Quakers in particular and Quakers in general.

We certainly appreciate the consideration of Katherine Elliott, South Hill, Virginia, in passing on to us the benefit of her wide experience in the publishing of genealogical books.

We were fortunate in having the services of two very efficient typists: Mrs. James L. Epperson who had the tedious job of doing the preliminary copy, often from long-hand drafts; and Mrs. S. Wirt Yates who strove painstakingly for perfection in the typing of our final copy.

A very special kind of thanks goes to two people: Charles G. Baber and Raymond H. Williamson, our husbands. 'Twas Raymond who, among other things, devised that ingenious Quaker Migration Chart, Appendix C; and Charles who "systematized" us in our struggle to cope with the over-whelming amount of detail. Both husbands displayed infinite patience in putting up with our long time preoccupation with the past.

L. H. M. B.

H. L. W.

CONTENTS

Acknowledgments vii

Preface xi

The Beginnings of Campbell County xiii

Section I - About the Courthouse Records   2
              Key to Abbreviations and Symbols   6
              Marriage Bonds of Campbell County................   7

Section II - About Quaker Marriages 109
              Quaker Marriages of Campbell County.............. 110

Appendix A - Overview of Legal Requirements................... 120

Appendix B - Officiating Ministers 123

Appendix C - Quaker Migrations 125

Index 127

ILLUSTRATIONS

Campbell County Courthouse .... Frontispiece

Map of Campbell County   x

Replica of Marriage Bond   5

Chart of Quaker Migrations   126

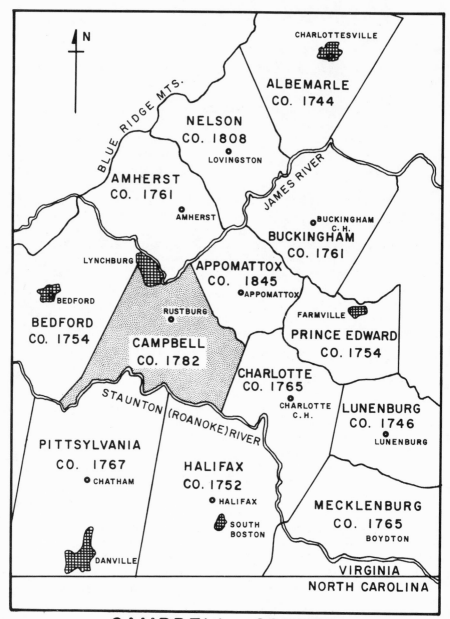

CAMPBELL COUNTY
AND NEIGHBORING COUNTIES
WITH
- PRESENT DAY BOUNDARIES
- COUNTY COURT HOUSES, THUS: ●
- COUNTY FORMATION DATES

PREFACE

The research and assembling of data relative to these marriages has been a two year project of the Genealogical Records Committee of Blue Ridge Chapter, Lynchburg, Virginia, National Society Daughters of the American Revolution. It was done in accordance with one of the objectives of the National Society which is the preservation and making available of historical and genealogical records.

Because of our interest in presenting a comprehensive listing of Campbell County marriages, it was necessary to consult two distinct sources of information which are presented in this book in two separate Sections:

Section I - Information about the approximately 1250 marriages found in the Campbell County Courthouse records for the period 1782 through 1810, taken from the original marriage bonds, consents, and ministers' returns.

Section II - Data concerning about 50 Quaker marriages which took place during this period at the three Campbell County Quaker Meeting-houses: South River, Seneca, and Hills Creek. We found no marriage bonds or ministers' returns at the courthouse for these marriages. Our prime sources for this Section were photostatic copies of original Quaker records at the Virginia State Library, Archives Division.[1] Included in our listing are the names not only of the bride, groom, and parents, but also extensive lists of witnesses. These names have been published previously in James Pinkney Bell's out-of-print book, Our Quaker Friends of Ye Olden Time, (Lynchburg, Virginia 1905.) We checked the names and marriage dates in Bell against the original data, and gained sufficient confidence in the degree of his completeness and accuracy so that his book was used as our source for the names of the witnesses. The few inconsistencies found in these two sources have been noted.

In working with the courthouse and Quaker records, our curiosity led us to further research which resulted in the following three Appendixes included herein:

Appendix A - A chronological summary of the basic provisions of the early marriage laws of the Colony and of the Commonwealth of Virginia.

Appendix B - A list of the ministers who performed these Campbell County marriages, with their denominations and places of residence.

Appendix C - A chart showing Quaker migrations to and from Campbell County, by region and by decade.

The information presented in this book has been fully indexed. In addition to listing and indexing the names of the marriage principals, we have given similar treatment to the names of the bondsmen, parents, witnesses, and ministers. Variations encountered in the spelling of names are also included.

Certain data in this book have been published previously.[2] Some of these books are out-of-print, and others are not too readily available. However, much of the material in this book is the result of original research heretofore unpublished.

We believe Marriages of Campbell County 1782-1810 will be valued by historians and genealogists as well as by people with just an interest in their Campbell County forebears, because for the first time primary and secondary sources have been pulled together into a single carefully re-searched volume. The comprehensive index and explanatory material have been assembled with the user very much in our minds.

We recognize that there may be some errors in this compilation. These we regret, and urge that you call them to our attention, citing some primary proof for the submitted correction.

Lucy Harrison Miller Baber

Hazel Letts Williamson

Lynchburg, Virginia
February 1971

1. Virginia State Library Acquisition No. 19869
    Friends' Records, South River, Bedford County, Va. Register 1757-1857.

    Virginia State Library Acquisition No. 19872
    Friends' Records, South River, Bedford County, Va. Proceedings of Monthly Meeting 1757-1797, Vol. 1.
     The above two volumes are negative photostats made from
     original volumes lent to the Virginia State Library by the
     Society of Friends, Baltimore, Maryland, January 29, 1927.

2. Bell, James Pinkney, Our Quaker Friends of Ye Olden Time, (Lynchburg, Virginia 1905).

    Brown, Douglas Summers, Lynchburg's Pioneer Quakers and Their Meeting House, (Lynchburg, Virginia 1936).

    Clarkson, Thomas, A Portraiture of Quakerism, v.2, (New York 1806).

    Early, Ruth H., Campbell Chronicles and Family Sketches 1782-1926, (Lynchburg, Virginia 1927).

    Fawcett, Marion Asher, Historical Sketch of Campbell County, Virginia, (Brookneal, Virginia 1963).

    Hinshaw, William Wade, Encyclopedia of American Quaker Genealogy, v.6, Virginia, (Ann Arbor, Michigan 1950).

    Lane, Mrs. John E., Regent, Colonel Charles Lynch Chapter NSDAR, "Register of Marriages in Campbell County, Virginia from 1782 to 1800," Daughters of the American Revolution Magazine, v.64, pp. 505-11, 1930.

THE BEGINNINGS OF CAMPBELL COUNTY, VIRGINIA

The period of these marriage records, 1782-1810, was a time of change and transition in the nation, in Virginia, and in the lives of people in Campbell County; transition from war to peace; transition from the status of a group of separate British Colonies to that of an independent nation (the "Critical Period in American History"); transition from a loosely organized government under the Articles of Confederation (1781) to a clearer federal unity under the new Constitution of 1789; transition of the bookkeeper's "money of account" from the Virginia colonial pounds, shillings and pence to Jefferson's decimal dollars and cents; transition of Campbell County from frontier to farm land; and transition from marriages which were legal only when celebrated in the church "established" for centuries, to legally valid marriages in churches of various denominations. In such a yeasty time, small wonder that we find a few lapses in the courthouse records, occasional incomplete marriage returns from the ministers, and a general emphasis on virtues other than disciplined writing and spelling.

Campbell County came into being in substantially its present geographical form when in 1782 it was split from Bedford County.

Between 1779 and 1781, several petitions from Bedford County residents had been sent to the Virginia General Assembly asking that Bedford County be divided into two counties. The proposed separation was not without opposition, for other petitioners were against separation. However, in 1781, a petition containing the signatures of three hundred residents urging division had been sent to the General Assembly, where it was favorably acted upon in November. The new county came into being in February 1782. The stated reason for the division was that Bedford County was seventy miles long and thirty-five miles wide, so that it was a hardship on the tax collectors who were unable to complete their assessments in the required time, not to mention the hardship on the citizens who must travel long distances to reach the courthouse.

The name for Campbell County was suggested by Patrick Henry. His sister Elizabeth had married General William Campbell, the "hero of King's Mountain" -- a decisive battle in the Revolution. General Campbell had died in September 1781, shortly before the successful petition creating Campbell County.

The first court for the new county of Campbell was held at the home of Micajah Terrell on 7 February 1782. The following Gentlemen Justices were sworn into office at this time: Samuel Hairston, Richard Stith, Charles Lynch, John Ward, John Callaway, John Fitzpatrick, Francis Thorp, John Hunter, Robert Adams, Jr., James Callaway, John Talbot, George Stovall, Jr., William Henderson.

The governmental structure of this newly created county also included the following with their deputies or assistants:

Robert Alexander, Clerk
Harry Innis, Attorney-at-Law
Francis Thorp, Sheriff
Richard Stith, County Surveyor
James Callaway, County-Lieutenant, the highest military office

In April 1783, Jeremiah Rust donated fifty acres of land on Fish Dam Road for a county seat. Around this grew up a village which became Rustburg.

This new county, Campbell, was formed from land successively within the boundaries of several older, larger counties whose areas had been reduced by a series of divisions. Earlier court records concerning events before 1782 within the boundaries of present-day Campbell County may be found at Bedford County Courthouse. Still earlier events, before 1754, are recorded in the courthouses of Lunenburg, Brunswick, Surry, Isle of Wight, Albemarle, Goochland, and Henrico Counties.

Of more probable concern to a present-day searcher is the loss of important Campbell County territory to the Town or City of Lynchburg in some eleven annexations, beginning in 1805. Thus most Lynchburg court records before 1805 remain in Campbell County Courthouse or a parent county courthouse. Also, small areas of Campbell County territory were lost to Appomattox County in 1848 and 1858.

SECTION I

MARRIAGE BONDS OF CAMPBELL COUNTY

1782-1810

ABOUT THE COURTHOUSE RECORDS

Section I in this book is primarily a compilation of data
abstracted after careful examination of the original marriage bonds,
consents, and clerk's recordings of ministers' returns found at the
Campbell County Courthouse, Rustburg, Virginia.

The Campbell County marriage bonds (one of which is reproduced
herein) and the associated papers at the courthouse cover the period
from 1782, when Campbell County was formed, to 1853, when the new
series of marriage registers was introduced in Virginia.[1] Because
of the tremendous number of these papers, it was deemed advisable
that we limit this initial undertaking to just the period 1782-1810.

To avoid confusion, it should be noted that there are at Campbell
County Courthouse, in addition to loose bonds and consent papers, two
separate and distinct volumes of marriage records relating to the
1782-1810 period.

The first volume, a small leather-bound book with the title,
Register of Marriages C C C in gold letters on the outside, is actually
a book of the original entries of ministers' returns as recorded by the
clerk. For each marriage, it contains the names of the groom, the
bride, the officiating minister, and the date of the marriage. It
appears to have been re-bound in recent years. In the rebinding the
top line on some of the pages has been covered by the binding, making
it difficult to decipher and in some cases impossible. Consequently
we may have missed a few items. We will hereinafter refer to this
book as the original Register.

The second book of marriage records relating to this period is a
much larger leather-bound volume with the title, Marriage Register,
No. 1, 1782 to _____ . This volume is currently in use at the courthouse, and appears from its fabric to have been compiled in recent
years from information taken from the marriage bonds, from consents,
and from the ministers' returns in the original Register. For each
marriage, there is listed the name of the groom, the bride, and the
date of the marriage bond; also in most cases the names of the bride's
parents and the officiating minister appear. This is one of the
volumes on microfilm (reel 36) in the Archives Division of the Virginia
State Library. It is arranged alphabetically by husbands' names, and
an index to females appears at the end of the volume. This book will
hereinafter be referred to by its title, Marriage Register No. 1, 1782____ .

If a marriage is listed in the original Register of ministers'
returns, we may be very certain that the marriage actually took place -
even though in a few cases no corresponding bonds were found at the
courthouse. Some 45 per cent of these marriage bonds have no corresponding entries in the original Register; it is highly probable
that these marriages also took place.

Although we were able to examine this original Register, not even a sample seems to have survived of the papers on which the ministers made their returns to the clerk. Hence, we do not know the format or procedures used by the ministers in making their returns. It would appear from the large number of bonds on which no returns were found that, in spite of the possible heavy fine for not reporting marriages, the ministers were quite casual about making returns and the law was not vigorously enforced.

Undoubtedly the manner in which some of the ministers made their returns influenced the clerk's recordings in the original Register. There are some entries with incomplete or missing dates. A few entries are recorded twice or even three times. The sequence of entries is seldom strictly chronological; in an extreme case, for example, the entry for Patrick Lamb and Nancy Truitt, 17 October 1810, follows an entry for 1814. We checked entries through 1817 to pick up stray recordings of marriages through 1810. There is an occasional entry date for a minister's return earlier than the date of the corresponding bond and consent; in such cases we rechecked the dates for possible transcribing errors. To cite another example, the minister's return date for the marriage of John Baber and Sally Moorman is actually recorded as 24 March 1790, about three months before the date of the bond and consent, 13 May 1790.

For the benefit of those not too familiar with the early marriage laws of Virginia, the marriage bond was a prerequisite to the issuance of a marriage license. The bond had to be filled out by the county clerk, signed by the bondsmen, and attested by the clerk before the license could be written. The bond's apparent purpose was to prevent illegal marriages from occurring.

The bonds were usually signed by two bondsmen. In most instances one of these was the prospective bridegroom, and the other a friend or a family connection of the bride or groom. A written parental or guardian's consent was required if either principal were under twenty-one years of age. However, if the bride's father was a bondsman, no separate consent was necessary since his signature on the bond implied his approval. Many of these consents, handwritten on odd scraps of paper, have been preserved with the bonds to which they relate. The signatures on these consents are invaluable in resolving questions of identity when more than one person of the same name was living in the county. (For a detailed discussion of these early marriage laws see Appendix A).

In these abstracts we have included family relationships only when such relationship is stated in the body of the marriage bond or in the consent papers. The fact that a bondsman has the same last name as the bride does not necessarily prove relationship, although it suggests it.

Race or color has been recorded in these abstracts only when such was indicated on the original records, and in each case the wording as it appeared thereon has been transcribed.

In cases where difficulty was encountered in deciphering information in these original papers, other court records such as Court Order Books, Will Books, and tax records were consulted.

While most of the Campbell County bonds adhered to a $150 bonding sum, we encountered a number in the amounts of $400, $500, $2500, and one as high as $4000. This seemed interesting and significant, but we have been unable to determine the reason for this variance. One reason might be that the law required that licenses be issued in the county where the bride usually resided, and if the bridegroom lived outside this county, or if the clerk had reason to believe that the bridegroom might move out of the county, or if he were insolvent, the clerk was required to take bond of such person or persons with good security in the county to pay all fees accruing due.[2] We made a spot check on these high-dollar bonds and found only one person who fit any of these categories.

At some time in the past, persons working with the Campbell County marriage bonds have written in pencil on the outside of each bond their interpretation of the name of the bride and the year the bond was issued. These names and dates are in agreement with the records in Marriage Register No. 1, 1782-___. However, on a very few of these bonds pencil-dated 1795 and 1805 we have interpreted the year of issuance to be 1791 and 1801. Ministers' returns recorded in the original Register bear out our interpretation which we base on the manner in which the clerk wrote the numeral "1" on the bond. Where we know this situation to exist we have included both dates in these abstracts, e.g. 1791:1795 and 1801:1805. We have included two dates in other cases where the two dates appear on the bond and an associated paper and could not be resolved.

We have included the clerks' names, which appear on the bonds, only when they appear in other than their clerkship capacity. The majority of the Campbell County marriage bonds for this period were issued by Robert Alexander, Clerk of Campbell County. Occasionally bonds were issued by the deputy clerks, J. Alexander, W. Alexander, A. Austin, J. Patrick, and D. Bullock.

Robert Alexander became clerk at the time the county was formed in 1782, and served in that capacity until his death in 1820. He had previously held the position of deputy clerk in Bedford County under Clerk James Steptoe. It is interesting that the Alexander family through father, son, and grandson, held the position of Campbell County Clerk for almost one hundred years.

1. Acts of Assembly 1852-53, p. 40.
2. 3H 445, 1705.

REPLICA OF MARRIAGE BOND

KEY TO ABBREVIATIONS AND SYMBOLS

*   placed after the bride's name indicates she gave her own
           consent to the county clerk for the marriage.

(b)   bondsman.

(w)   witness.

M.R.   minister's return recorded in the <u>Register of Marriages</u> C C C
           (original <u>Register</u>) See page 2.

2<u>H</u> 55   an example of the coding used for references taken from
           Hening, William Waller, <u>The Statutes At Large being a</u>
           <u>Collection of all the Laws</u> of <u>Virginia</u>; 13 volumes,
           (Richmond, Virginia 1809-1823). The first number (2)
           indicates the volume number; <u>H</u> indicates Hening; 55 indicates
           the page number in the volume.

1<u>S</u> 132   an example of the coding used for references taken from
           Shepherd, Samuel, <u>The Statutes At Large of Virginia ...being</u>
           <u>a Continuation of Hening</u>; 3 volumes, (Richmond, Virginia
           1835-1836). The first number (1) indicates the volume
           number; <u>S</u> indicates Shepherd; 132 indicates the page number
           in the volume.

p.   page.

pp.   pages.

v.   volume.

Bell   Bell, James Pinkney, <u>Our Quaker Friends of Ye Olden Time</u>,
           (Lynchburg, Virginia 1905).

A

ACREE, DAVID and Rhoda Thurman, bond 8 April 1797. Consent by Richard
    Thurman, father of the bride. David Acree (b) and Richard Thurman (b).

ADAMS, DAVID and Peggy Gregory, bond 8 August 1803. Consent by John
    Gregory, father of the bride. David Adams (b) and John Gregory (b).
    M.R. 18 August 1803 by Henry Brown lists John Adams as the groom.

ADAMS, JOHN and Sally Arnold, bond 1 October 1807. Consent by James
    Arnold, father of the bride. John Adams (b) and William Adams (b);
    John Goodman (w) and William Addams (w).

ADAMS, THOMAS F. and Nancy Epperson, bond 7 January 1809. Consent by
    Little B. Epperson, father of the bride. Thomas F. Adams (b) and
    Joseph Epperson (b); Richard Epperson (w), Samuel Epperson (w) and
    Joseph Epperson (w). M.R. 7 January 1809 by Edmund Johns.

ADAMS, WILLIAM and Patsey Arnold*, bond 24 May 1805. William Adams (b)
    and John Goodman (b); John Goodman (w).

AKERS, JOHN and Agnes Bryan, bond 6 February 1783. Consent by John
    Bryan, father of the bride. John Akers (b) and Andrew Bryan (b);
    John Bryan, Jr., (w) and Andrew Bryan (w).

AKERS, WILLIAM and Polly Haraway, bond 17 March 1798. Consent by Chas.
    Haraway, father of the bride. William Akers (b) and John Haraway (b);
    John Haraway (w).

AKIN, JOSEPH (batchelor) and Ann Dudgeon (spinster)*, bond 7 July 1784.
    Consent certified by Thos. Moore. Joseph Akin (b) and John Patrick,Jr.
    (b).

ALEXANDER, THOMAS and Elizabeth Buckner, bond 18 July 1791. Thomas
    Alexander (b) and John Mason (b). M.R. __July 1791 by Charles Cobbs.

ALFORD, JOHN and Mary Brown, bond 28 July 1786. John Alford (b) and
    Will Brown (b).

ALLEN, HARTWELL and Sarah Calloway, bond 14 April 1806. Hartwell Allen (b)
    and John Calloway (b).

ALLEY, PETER (batchelor) and Jane Hundley (spinster)*, bond 5 February
    1788. Consent by guardian not named. Peter Alley (b) and John
    Alley (b); Peter Alley (w), Tuck Staples (w) and Teen Hundley (w).
    M.R. 7 February 1788 by Joshua Worley.

ALLMOND, WILLIAM and Susanna Hamersly*, bond 14 February 1808. William
    Allmond (b) and David Jones (b); David Jones (w).

ALMOND, RHEUBIN and Molly Lucas, bond 13 March 1809. Rheubin Almond (b)
    and James Hurt (b).

ANTHONY, MARK and Sarah Henry Tate*, bond 15 May 1795. Mark Anthony (b) and Jesse Tate (b); Jesse Tate (w). M.R. 24 May 1795 by Anderson Weekes.

ARMISTEAD, WILLIAM and Mary Lewis Cobb, bond 9 June 1806. William Armistead (b) and Robert Cobb (b).

ARMONETT, JACOB and Susannah Winfrey, bond 4 September 1793. Consent by Charles Winfree, father of the bride. Jacob Armonett (b) and Wm. Hines (b); John Winfree (w) and James Hines (w). M.R. 5 September 1793 by Obadiah Edge lists the groom as Jacob Amorett, and the bride as Susannah Winfry.

ARRINGTON, ADLER and Patsy Wood, bond 4 November 1796. Consent by John Wood, father of the bride. Adler Arrington (b) and William Roper (b); Edmond Wood (w) and William Roper (w). M.R. __November 1796 by Charles Cobbs.

ARRINGTON, CHARLES and Sally Rosser, bond 9 December 1810. Consent by William Rosser, father of the bride. Charles Arrington (b) and John Arrington (b); John Rosser (w) and John Arrington (w). M.R. 9 December 1810 by Edmund Johns.

ARRINGTON, DANIEL and Elizabeth McIver, bond 11 January 1802. Daniel Arrington (b) and James McIver (b). M.R. 14 January 1802 by Henry Brown.

ARRINGTON, JOHN and Patty Rosser, bond 28 December 1793. Consent by Pleasant Rosser, father of the bride. John Arrington (b) and Pleasant Rosser (b); Alexander Clark (w) and Jonathan Rosser (w). M.R. 12 January 1794 by Menoah Lesley.

ARTHUR, BONABUS and Elizabeth C. Mason, bond __ 1806. Bonabus Arthur (b) and Martin Mason (b).

ARTHUR, WILLIAM and Catherine Mackey, bond 27 September 1794. Consent by Robert Alexander, no relationship stated. William Arthur (b) and John Morison (b); John Morison (w). M.R. 30 September 1794 by Menoah Lesley.

ASHER, JOHN and Betsey Tanner, bond 12 April 1808. Consent by Benjamin Tanner, father of the bride. John Asher (b) and Mathew Tanner (b); James Tanner (w) and Benjamin Tanner (w). M.R. 17 April 1808 by Obadiah Edge.

ASKEW, WILLIAM and Elizabeth Dixon, bond 4 January 1790. Consent by Susanna Dixon, mother of the bride. William Askew (b) and James Wilson (b). M.R. 7 January 1790 by William Flowers.

AUSTIN, JAMES and Catherine Patrick, bond 3 December 1792. Consent by John Patrick, father of the bride. James Austin (b) and Edmond Patrick (b).

AUSTIN, WILLIAM and Lockey Thompson, daughter of John Thompson, bond 26 August 1806. William Austin (b) and John Thompson (b).

B

BABER, JAMES (batchelor) and Milly Arthur (spinster), bond 13 May 1785. James Baber (b) and Peter Claywell (b).

BABER, JOHN and Sally Moorman, bond 13 May 1790. Consent by Charles Moorman, father of the bride. John Baber (b) and Benjamin Haden (b); John Moorman (w) and Benjamin Haden (w). M.R. 24 March 1790 by James Kenney.

BAGBY, WILLIAM and Elizabeth Johnson (Miss), bond 12 November 1803. William Bagby (b) and Charles Johnson (b).

BAILEY, JAMES and Mary Ann Mosley (Moseley)*, bond 12 May 1802. James Bailey (b) and Cornelius Powell (b); B. Wily (w) and Cornelius Powell (w).

BAILEY, JAMES and Nancy Harvey, bond 29 May 1804. Consent by William Harvey 48, father of the bride. James Bailey (b) and Richard Harvey (b); Thomas Harvey (w) and Richard Harvey (w).

BAILEY, JONATHAN and Sally Botelar, daughter of Thomas Botelar, bond 9 January 1809. Jonathan Bailey (b) and Thomas Botelar (b). M.R. 26 January 1809 by Samuel Davidson lists the bride as Sary Butlar.

BAILEY (BAILY), NUNNERY and Peggy Stephens (Stevens), bond 18 July 1808. Consent by Robert Stevens, father of the bride. Jacob Stephens (Stevens) (b) and Nunnery Bailey (b); Jacob Stevens (w) and Lewis Robertson (w).

BAILEY, ROBERT and Lucy Smith. M.R. 6 January 1789 by James Hurt.

BAILEY, THOMAS and Temperance Bailey, bond 21 April 1794. Consent by William Bailey and Marah (?) Bailey. Thomas Bailey (b) and Richard Driskill (b); Sarah Bailey (w), Richard Driskill (w) and Toby Bailey (w). M.R. __April 1794, by Charles Cobbs.

BAILEY (BEALEY), WILLIAM and Penelop Pulliam (Pullam), bond 3 August 1786. Consent by Iseam Pullam, father of the bride. William Bailey (b) and Samuel Poe (b); Wm. Bealey (w) and E_?__ Pullam (w).

BAKER (BABER), DOUGLAS and Sarah Steel, bond 23 August 1788. Consent by Alex. Steel. Douglas Baker (Baber) (b) and John Steel (b).

BALDWIN, ZEBULON of Lynchburg and Susannah Miller, bond 22 April 1795. Consent by John Miller, father of the bride. Zebulon Baldwin (b) and Thomas Moorman (b); Thomas Wiatt (w) and Thomas Norman (w).

BANGHAM, BENJAMIN and Lucy Moorman, bond 13 November 1797. Benjamin
Bangham (b) and Achillis Moorman (b). M.R. 28 December 1797 by
James Mitchell.

BARBER, WILLIAM and Jane Watkins, bond 24 September 1796. Consent by
Moses Watkins. William Barber (b) and John Pugh (b); John Pugh (w).
M.R. 2 October 1796 by William Flowers.

BARNARD, TIMOTHY and Jane Gibson (Miss*), bond 13 October 1794. In the
consent E. Smith certifies she is of age. Timothy Barnard (b) and
Joseph Ferguson (b); Elisha Smith (w) and Joseph Ferguson (w).
M.R. 18 October 1794 by Menoah Lesley.

BARNS, SAMUEL and Tabitha Hanks. M.R. __November 1793 by Charles Cobbs.

BARRACK, MOORE and Susannah Garrett, bond 20 May 1807. Consent by John
Garrett, father of the bride. Moore Barrach (b) and Elijah Garrett (b);
James St. Clair (w) and Elijah Garrett (w). M.R. 21 May 1807 by
William Peters Martin lists the groom as Moore Barrox.

BARRICK, RUSSELL and Polly Timberlake*, bond 7 February 1804. Consent
by Polley Timberlake and John Timberlake, father of the bride.
Russell Barrick (b) and Samuel Johnson (b); Richard Timberlake (w)
and Samuel Johnson (w). M.R. 9 May 1804 by William Peters Martin
lists the groom as Russell Barracks.

BARRICK, RUSSELL and Rhoda Frith*, bond 11 September 1809. Russell
Barrick (b); Mathew Thompson (w) and Samuel Thompson (w).

BARTON, ELIJAH and Sally Kenney (Kenny), bond 28 May 1796. Consent by
James Kenney, father of the bride. Elijah Barton (b) and Elijah
Reeder(?) (b); Elijah Reede (w) and John Porat(?) (w). M.R. __ 1796
by James Kenny lists the bride as Sally Kenny.

BASS, JOSIAH, JR. and Betsy R. Walker, ward of Peter Bass, bond
11 November 1794. Josiah Bass, Jr. (b) and Peter Bass (b).

BAUGHN, HENRY and Patsy Whitlow, bond 29 April 1805. Consent by Henry
Whitlow who states "both of legal age." Henry Baughn (b) and William
Whitlow (b); Andrew D. Whitlow (w) and William Whitlow (w).

BAUGHN, RICHARD and Anne Jones, bond 12 May 1798. Consent by Benjamin
Jones, father of the bride. Richard Baughn (b) and Thomas
Alexander (b); Thos. Alexander (w), Thomas Smith (w) and William
Walker (w). M.R. __ May 1798 by Charles Cobbs.

BAYLIS, JOHN, JR. and Ruth Turnley, bond 15 December 1794. Consent by
James Turnley. John Baylis, Jr. (b) and James Turnley, Jr. (b);
James Turnley, Jr. (w) and William Trigg (w).

BECKHAM, WILLIAM and Sally Rector, bond 26 April 1783. Consent by Gan
Rector, father of the bride. William Beckham (b) and John Turner
(b); Thomas Butler (w).

BELL, JAMES and Sarah Patty *, bond 4 September 1794. James Bell (b)
and Benjamin Conifax (b); Benjamin Conifax (w) and _?_ Angel (w).
M.R. __ 1793 by James Kenney lists the birde as Sarah Paty.

BELL, JAMES and Dorothy Bybee, bond 19 December 1807. Consent by Edward
Bybe and Anne Bybe, parents of the bride. James Bell (b) and
Radford Conifex (b); Radford Conifax (w). M.R. 22 December 1807 by
James Warner lists the bride as Dorothy Bybee.

BELL, WILLIAM and Sarah Wilson, daughter of James Wilson, bond 11 April
1801. William Bell (b) and James Wilson (b). M.R. 15 ____ 1801
by Henry Brown lists the bride as Sinah P. Wilson.

BERNARD (BARNARD), BENJAMIN and Lucy Candler, bond 14 October 1805.
Consent by James Candler, father of the bride. Benjamin Barnard (b)
and Daniel Candler (b); Daniel Candler (w) and Lucy Candler (w).

BERNARD, JOSEPH and Martha Smith, bond 16 August 1790. Consent by
Elizabeth Whitlow(?), mother of the bride. Joseph Bernard (b) and
William Bernard (b); William Bernard (w) and P. Smith (w).

BLACK, JAMES of Prince Edward County and Peggy Irvine, bond 28 January
1793. James Black (b) and John Irvine (b). M.R. 31 ____ 1793 by
William Mahon.

BLACK, WILLIAM and Catherine Cock, bond 19 August 1805. Consent by
Thomas Cock, father of the bride. William Black (b) and Smith Kent
(b); Robert E. Kent (w) and Smith Kent (w).

BLAKE, WILLIAM and Elizabeth Burton*, bond 15 May 1804. James Both (b)
and William Blake (b); William Dazelwood(?) (w) and James Both (w).
M.R. 5 May 1804 by William Peters Martin.

BLAKEY, PLEASANT and Sally Patteson, bond 31 December 1792. Consent by
Obadiah Patteson, father of the bride. Landis Patteson (b); James
Patteson (w) and James Patteson (w).

BLANKENSHIP, ARCHIBALD and Prudence Condray, M.R. 8 October 1794 by
Menoah Lesley.

BLANKENSHIP, BENJAMIN and Jane Harrold, bond 8 April 1786. Consent by
Gillard Harold and Phelia Harold. Benjamin Blankenship (b) and
Hudson Blankenship (b); Alexander Clark (w).

BLANKENSHIP, ELIJAH (bachelor) and Judith Snow (spinster), bond 5 January
1787. Consent by John Snow. Elijah Blankenship (b) and John Snow, Jr.
(b); J. Patrick (w).

BLANKENSHIP, HENRY and Nancy Potter, bond 4 January 1792. Henry Blankenship (b) and Augustine Potter (b). M.R. 6 January 1792 by Menoah
Lesley.

BLANKENSHIP, JESSE (bachelor) and Mary Mann (widow)*, bond 13 September
1786. Consent by Ison Blankenship, father of the groom. Jesse
Blankenship (b) and Thomas Massie (b).

BLANKENSHIP, LEVI and Polly Williams, bond 6 December 1808. Levi
Blankenship (b) and William Mullin (b).

BLANKENSHIP, ZACHARIA and Edith Blankenship, daughter of Hudson Blankenship,
bond 25 July 1794. Zacharia Blankenship (b) and Hudson Blankenship (b).
M.R. ___ August 1794 by James Kenney.

BLOXSOM, RICHARD and Polly Murrell, bond 24 September 1803. Consent by
Thomas Murrell, father of the bride. Richard Bloxsom (b) and
Thomas Murrell (b); James Russell(?) (w). M.R. 24 September 1803
by Henry Brown

BOAZ, EDMUND and Rhoda Connifax, daughter of William Connifax, bond
14 January 1794. William Connifax (b) and Edmund Boaz (b). M.R.
16 January 1794 by William Flowers lists the bride as Rhoda Cannifax.

BOAZ, RUSSELL and Penelope Candler, bond 11 November 1805. Russell Boaz (b)
and William Candler, father of Penelope Candler (b).

BOBBIT, HUMPHREY and Lucy George* free Negroes bond 4 December 1785.
Lucy in her consent calls the groom Humphrey Bobson. Achillis
Douglas also gives consent stating that Lucy "formerly the property
of John Lynch." He also gives the name of the groom Humphrey
Bobson. Humphrey Bobbit (b) and Frank Freeman (b); Joseph Hackett
(w) and Charles Eastins(?) (w).

BOLAY, JOHN and Rebeckah Rector, bond 11 December 1797. Consent by Jane
Rector, mother of the bride. John Bolay (b) and William Boteler (b);
William Boteler (w) and Jacob Beteler (w).

BOND, GEORGE and Patsy Kivel*, bond 10 October 1802. George Bond (b)
and Charles Moorman (b); Charles Moorman (w) and Charles Johnson (w).
M.R. 13 October 1802 by Henry Brown lists the bride as Patsy Kneel.

BOOKER, PETER and Nancy Fowler, bond 14 April 1804. Consent by Jno.
Fowler, Jr., father of the bride. Christopher Fowler (b) and
Peter Booker (b); William Fowler (w) and Christopher Fowler (w).
M.R. 14 April 1804 by William P. Martin.

BOTELER, HENRY and Kesiah Oglesby, bond 4 November 1796. Consent by Mary
Oglesby, mother of the bride. Henry Boteler (b) and William Boteler (b);
Edward Oglesby (w) and William Boteler (w). M.R. 15 December 1796 by
William Flowers.

BOTELER, WILLIAM JR. and Sarah Cunningham, bond 9 December 1799. William
Boteler (b) and Murrell Cunningham (b). M.R. 26 December 1799 by
William Flowers lists the groom as William Butler.

BOWES, RUSSELL and Penelope Candler, bond 11 November 1805. Russell Bowes
(b) and William Candler, father of the bride (b).

BRADFIELD, JOHN and Hannah Reeder*, bond 20 November 1798. John Bradfield
(b) and James Boaz (b); Andrew Milburn (w).

BRADLEY, COLLINS and Lucy Johnson, bond 5 April 1792. Collins Bradley (b)
and John Johnson (b). M.R. __ 1792 by Menoah Lesley.

BRADLEY, STEPHEN and Margaret Dickey, bond 14 April 1806. Consent by
Edmond and Jean Dickey, parents of the bride. Stephen Bradley (b)
and Samuel Dickey (b); Samuel Dickey (w) and James Dickey (w).
M.R. 24 April 1806 by William Flowers, Jr. lists the bride as
Margaret Dicky.

BRADLEY, WILLIAM and Nancy Grey, bond 9 November 1795. Consent by John
Bradley who certifies "Nancy Grey is above 21 years and has neither
parents or guardian in this country." William Bradley (b) and John
Bradley (b). M.R. __ 1796 by James Kenny lists the bride as Nancy
Gray.

BREWER, JOHN H. and Fanny Warwick(e), bond 26 June 1799. Consent by James
Warwicke, father of the bride. John H. Brown (b) and Benjamin A.
Winston (b); Thos. Lawson (w) and Benjamin A. Winston (w).
M.R. __ 1799 by Samuel Mitchell lists the bride as Fanny Warrick.

BRIANT, ELIJAH and Lucy Key, daughter of Jacob Key, bond 3 June 1803.
Elijah Briant (b) and Jacob Key (b).

BRICKEEN, JOHN and Perthenia Adams, bond 24 February 1810. Consent by
John Adams, father of the bride. John Brickeen (b) and John Adams,
Jr. (b); Solomon Claywell (w) and John Adams, Jr. (w). M.R. 26
February 1810 by James Warner.

BRIEN, ELISH and Ann S. Miller. M.R. 8 March 1806 by John Chappell.

BRIZENTINE, THOMAS and Polly Driskill, bond 17 September 1807. Thomas
Brizentine (b) and Alexander Driskill (b).

BROCK, WRENNEY and Nancy Rich, bond 6 November 1795. Consent by Nimrod
Rich. Wranney Brock (b) and David Rich (b); Allain Rich (w) and
David Rich (w). M.R. 12 November 1795 by William Flowers lists the
groom as Wrenny Brock.

BROOK, SAMUEL and Sarah Stanley, bond 11 November 1800. Consent by John
Stanley, Sr., father of the bride. Samuel Brook (b) and Benjamin
Jones (b). M.R. 12 November 1800 by Henry Brown lists the groom as
Samuel Brooke.

BROOKS, JAMES and Leanah McKenney. M.R. 31 March 1782 by John W. Holt.

BROOKS, JOHN and Fanny Farthing, daughter of Wm. Farthing, bond 9 May
1808. John Brooks (b) and William Farthing (b). M.R. 11 May 1808
by Obadiah Edge.

BROOKS, THOMAS and Jane Brooks *, bond 3 March 1795. Thomas Brooks (b)
and William Brooks (b); David Staples (w). M.R. __ 1795 by Charles
Cobbs.

BROOKS, WILLIAM and Barbary Moore, bond 12 October 1807. Consent by
"Barbery Moore, for my daughter." William Brooks (b) and James L.
Moore (b); James L. Moore (w) and Samuel Moore (w).

BROOKS, ZACHARIAH and Susanna Martin, bond 24 February 1810. Consent by
Mary Martin, mother of the bride. Zachariah Brooks (b) and Samuel
Martin (b); William Martin (w) and Samuel Martin (w) and William
Brooks (w). M.R. 24 February 1810 by Obadiah Edge.

BROWN, EDWARD and Agnes Parrott*, bond 17 August 1790. Edmund Brown (b)
and John Traylor, Jr. (b); Menoah Lesley (w) and Mary Smithson (w).

BROWN, HENRY and Elizabeth Arnold, daughter of John Arnold, bond 9 De-
cember 1809. Consent Polly Brown, mother of the groom. Henry
Brown (b) and John Arnold (b); Daniel Brown (w) and Lucey C.
Brown (w).

BROWN, HUBBARD and Mary Black, bond 24 January 1791. Hubbard Brown (b)
and John Black (b).

BROWN, JOHN, JR. and Phillis Dudley, bond 19 May 1800. John Brown, Jr.(b)
and Armistead Dudley (b).

BROWN, LEWIS and Judith Bradley, daughter of Mrs. Mary Bradley, bond
15 April 1810. John M. Bradley (b) and Lewis Brown (b).

BROWN, MARRYARTHUR S. and Margaret Lindsey, daughter of James Lindsey,
bond 18 November 1801. MaryArthur S. Brown (b) and James Lindsey (b).
M.R. 19 ____ 1801 by Henry Brown who lists the participants as
MaryArthur Saunders Brown and Margaret Lindsay.

BROWN, PRESTON and Elizabeth Watts, bond 13 October 1802. Consent by
Mary Watts, mother of the bride. Preston Brown (b) and Edward Watts
(b); Edward Watts (w).

BROWN, QUACKEY and Kissiah Walker. M.R. 21 December 1801 by Henry Brown.

BROWN, SAMUEL and Sarah Roberts, bond 5 January 1793. Consent by Johnny
and Sarah Roberts, parents of the bride. Samuel Brown (b) and
Robert'Yancy (b). M.R. 7 January 1793 by Menoah Lesley.

BROWN, WILLIAM and Elizabeth Dale, 22 September 1788. William Brown (b)
and John Dale (b). M.R. no date given but listed after entries of
August 15, 1788 by James Kenney.

BROWN, WILLIAM and Margaret VanNorth, bond 3 March 1792. William Brown (b)
and Jacob Richardson (b). M.R. 9 April 1792 by Joseph Drury.

BRUMFIELD, ELISHA and Cynthia Johns, bond 4 March 1801. Consent by Sarah
Johns, mother of the bride. Elisha Brumfield (b) and Edmund Johns (b);
Edmund Johns (w) and Daniel Johns (w).

BRUMFIELD, JAMES and Mary Seay*, bond 17 June 1795. Consent also by
Joseph Seay, father of the bride. James Broomfield (b) and John
Brooke (b); John Brooke (w). M.R. __ June 1795 by Charles Cobbs
lists the bride as Mary Sea.

BRYAN, JOHN, JR. and Catherine Evans, bond 1 September 1788. Consent by
Rees(?) Evans, father of the bride. John Bryan, Jr. (b) and Samuel
Davison (Davidson) (b); Daniel Evans (w) and Jane Evans (w).

BRYAN, JOHN and Anne Stepp, bond 12 December 1789. John Stepp (b) and
John Bryan (b).

BRYAN, MORRISON and Rhoda Johnson, bond 28 December 1805. Consent by
James Johnson, father of the bride. Morrison Bryan (b) and Rees
Evans (b); Rees Evans (w) and John Rosser (w).

BRYAN, WILLIAM and Betsy Dejarnett, bond 18 April 1806. Consent by
James Dejarnett, father of the bride. William Bryan (b) and
Archer Williamson (b); Archer Williamson (w) and Robert William-
son (w).

BUCKLER, HENRY and Betsy Talbot, bond 23 January 1804. Consent by
Williston Talbot, father of the bride. Henry Buckler (b) and
Pleasant Talbot (b); Betsey Gilbert (w) and Pleasant Talbot (w).
M.R. 23 January 1804 by Edmund Johns.

BUCKNER, JOHN and Patsey Taylor*, bond 5 October 1797. John Buckner (b)
and Benjamin Littlepage (b); Perin Smith (w) and Benjamin Littlepage
(w). M.R. __October 1797 by Charles Cobbs.

BUCKNER, WILLIAM and Patsey Vaughn. M.R. __ February 1795 by Charles
Cobbs.

BULLOCK, JAMES P. and Eliza Slaughter, bond 20 July 1810. Consent by
Charles Slaughter, father of the bride. James P. Bullock (b) and
Glover Davenport (b); Robert Horn Slaughter (w) and Glover Davenport
(w). M.R. 2 July 1810 by Edmund Johns.

BURGESS, JAMES of Pittsylvania County, and Mary Carson, bond 26 November
1792. No consent attached but Mary Carson is named as the daughter
of John Carson in the bond. James Burgess (b) and John Carson (b).

BURGESS, SAMUEL (widower of City of Lynchburg) and Susan Page* (widow of
City of Lynchburg), bond 14 August 1793. '"Both of lawful age"'
certified by Robert Alexander. Samuel Burgess (b) and James Haley
(b); David Cook (w) and John H. Goodwin (w).

BURNETT, JAMES and Rachel Tayler*, bond 14 July 1800. James Burnett (b) and John Wright (b); Wm. Lee (w) and John Wright (w). M.R. 24 July 1800 by William Flowers lists the bride as Rachel Taylor. This return is listed three times in original Register.

BURNETT, WILLIAM, and Susannah Wright*, bond 13 January 1800. Wm. Burnett (b) and Ro. Wright (b); Robert Wright (w) and Charles Wright (w). M.R. 23 January 1800 by William Flowers.

BURTON, JESSE and Elizabeth Norvell, bond 9 March 1801. Consent by Will Norvell, brother and guardian of the bride. Jesse Burton (b) and Samuel J. Harrison (b); James Mosley (w) and Samuel J. Harrison (w). M.R. 12 March 1802 by William P. Martin.

BURTON, ROBERT, JR. and Betsy Powell, bond 11 August 1795. Consent by Wiatt Powell, father of the bride, and Eliza Powell. Robert Burton, Jr. (b) and Samuel Martin (b); James Martin (w) and Samuel Martin (w).

BUTLER, EDWARD and Nancy Harris, bond 17 December 1810. Consent by William Harris, father of the bride. Edward Butler (b) and Benjamin Harris (b). John Harris (w) and Benjamin Harris (w).

BUTLER, JONATHAN and Elizabeth Harris, bond 14 September 1801. Jonathan Butler (b) and William Harris (b). M.R. 3 September 1801 by Henry Brown lists the groom as John Butler.

BUTLER, THOMAS (batchelor) and Sarah Timberlake (spinster), bond 2 October 1783. Thomas Butler (b) and Richard Timberlake (b).

BUTTERWORTH, BENJAMIN and Rachel Moorman, bond 30 August 1786. Consent by Zaachas Moorman, father of the bride. Benjamin Butterworth (b) and Charles Gilbert (b).

BUTTERWORTH, ISAAC and Elizabeth Walker, bond 5 April 1792. Consent by Buckley Walker, father of the bride. Isaac Butterworth (b) and Stephen Butterworth (b). M.R. 12 ___ 1792 by Menoah Lesley.

BUTTERWORTH, JOSEPH and Doshia Tally (Talley)*, bond 24 January 1804. Joseph Butterworth (b) and William Eids (b); Wm. Eids (w). M.R. 2 February 1804 by Henry Brown.

BYBEE, BENJAMIN and Elizabeth Edds, bond 18 August 1805. Consent by Sally Edds, mother of the bride. Benjamin Bybee (b) and Radford Cannefax (b); Joseph Bybee (w) and Radford Connefax (w).

BYRD (BIRD), GEORGE and Polly Finch, bond 13 July 1803. Consent by George Finch, father of the bride. George Bird (b) and William Mitchell (b); Temple Perkins (w) and William Mitchell (w). M.R. 24 July 1803 by Henry Brown lists the groom as George Bird.

BYRD (BIRD), GEORGE and Elizabeth Daniel, daughter of Richard Daniel, bond 10 November 1806. George Byrd (b) and Richard Daniel, Sr. (b). M.R. 10 November 1806 by Edmund Johns.

C

CABELL, FREDERICK and Alice Winston, bond 9 February 1801. Consent by
Edmund Winston, father of the bride. Frederick Cabell (b) and
Wilson Davenport (b); Wilson Davenport (w).

CABELL, JOHN and Elizabeth Jones. M.R. 19 July 1787 by Charles Clay.

CABELL, JOSEPH and Ann E. Duvall (Duval), bond 15 October 1804. Joseph
Cabell (b) and Ro. Alexander (b); Joseph Cabell (w).

CABELL, W. GEORGE and Sarah Winston, bond 19 July 1792. Consent by
Edmund Winston, father of the bride. George Cabell (b) and
Edmund Winston (b); George D. Winston (w) and Edmund Winston (w).

CABELL, WILLIAM L. and Elizabeth L. Payne, daughter of Philip Payne, bond
15 June 1808. William Cabell (b) and Philip Payne (b). M.R. 16 June
1808 by Matthew Easter.

CAFFERY, CHARLES and Nancy Davison, bond 5 August 1800. Consent by James
Davison, father of the bride. Charles Caffery (b) and John Davison (b).
Jno. Davison (w). M.R. 6 August 1800 by William Flowers lists the
bride as Nancy Davidson. This return is entered twice in the original
Register under the same date.

CALDWELL, ALEXANDER (batchelor) and Anne Shearer (widow), bond __ 1786.
Alexander Caldwell (b) and John Thomas Owl (Howel) (b).

CALDWELL, JOHN and Patsy Fields*, bond 17 November 1802. Consent also by
Marget Fields, mother of the bride. Samuel Caldwell (b) and John
Caldwell (b); Samuel Caldwell (w) and Marget Fields (w). M.R.
__ November 1802 by Edmund Johns.

CALDWELL, OLIVER and Isabella Cook*, bond 3 April 1783. Oliver Caldwell (b)
and George Steel (b); George Steel (w).

CALDWELL, SAMUEL and Mary Field, bond 3 January 1793. Consent by Andrew
Field, father of the bride. Sam Caldwell (b) and John Campbell (b);
Samuel Galbraith (w). M. R. 15 ____ 1793 by William Mahon.

CALLAHAN (CALLIHAN), DAVID and Elizabeth Carty, bond 3 November 1788.
Consent by Patrick Carty, father of the bride, and consent by Peter
Funk for his apprentice David Callahan. David Callahan (Callihan)
(b) and Martin Mason (b). M.R. no date given but listed after
15 August 1788 entries, by James Kenney.

CALLAHAN, JOHN and Elizabeth Laine, bond 19 October 1792. Consent by
Elander Laine, father of the bride. John Callahan (b) and James
Hurt (b); Henry Dillon (w) and Jas. Barnes (w).

CALLAWAY, CALEB and Betsy Callaway, bond 19 October 1784. Consent by
John Callaway, father of the bride. Ro. Alexander (b) and Caleb
Callaway (b).

CALLAWAY, FRANCIS and Polly Crews, bond 2 December 1799. Consent by
Josiah Crews, father of the bride. Francis Callaway (b) and William
Crews (b); Wm. Crews (w).

CALLAWAY, WILLIAM and Doshia Callaway*, bond 7 January 1796. William
Callaway (b) and Benjamin Haden (b).

CAMPBELL, JAMES and Jane Means*, bond 27 April 1784. James Campbell (b)
and John Campbell (b); Elizabeth Beird (w), Ratchel Robinson (w)
and James Robinson (w).

CAMPBELL, SAMUEL and Nancy Fleming, bond 13 November 1797. Consent by
Daniel Marshall, husband of the bride's sister. Samuel Campbell (b)
and Samuel Fleming (b); John Marshall (w) and John Brooke (w).

CAMPBELL, WILLIAM and Janet Petticrew (Petecrew)*, bond 11 April 1796.
William Campbell (b) and John W. Reynolds (b); Joseph Torrence (w).
M.R. 19 April 1796 by James Mitchell lists the bride as Jenny
Petticrew.

CAMPBELL, WILLIAM and Luraney Ledbetter, bond 4 January 1799. Consent
by Joseph Ledbetter, father of the bride. William Campbell (b) and
Joseph Ledbetter (b); Joseph Ledbetter (w) and Nancey Ledbetter (w).

CANDLER, JOHN and Phebe Boaz, bond 13 December 1802. John Candler (b) and
James Boaz (b).

CANDLER, JOHN, JR. and Dorothy Stovall, bond 24 July 1799. Consent by
Elizabeth Stovall, mother of the bride. John Candler (b) and Jacob
Stemmons (b); Ja. Thurman (w). M.R. 26 July 1799 by Abner Early
lists the bride as Doritha Stoval, the groom as John Candler.

CANDLER, JOHN, SR. and Penelope Guttery (Guttry), bond 27 July 1801. John
Candler (b) and Henry Candler (b).

CANNIFAX, CHESLEY and Martha Wilson (Willson), bond 31 January 1809.
Consent by John Willson, father of the bride. Chesley Cannifax (b)
and John Willson,,Jr. (b); John Willson (w) and Alexander H. Willson
(w). M.R. 2 February 1809 lists the groom as Chesley Carnifix;
William Flowers, Jr. officiating.

CANNIFAX, EDWARD and Isabella Davidson, bond 17 May 1791. Consent by
Alexander and Lizebeth Davidson. Edward Cannifax (b) and John Dickey
(b); John Dickey (w) and Margret Davidson (w).

CANNIFAX, RADFORD and Anne Edds, bond 16 May 1796. Consent by Salley and
Joseph Edds, parents of the bride. Radford Cannifax (b) and Thomas
Edds (b); Isaac Butterworth (w), Thomas Edds (w) and James Brown (w).
M.R. ___ 1796 by James Kenny.

CANNIFAX, WILLIAM and Nancy Holesapple, bond 8 May 1809. Consent by Philip
Holesapple, father of the bride. William Cannifax (b) and Edward
Cannifax (b); Edward Cannifax (w), John Cannifax (w) and John Holes-
apple (w). M.R. 3 May 1809 by Samuel Davidson gives the groom as
William Canifix.

CARDWELL, ROBERT and Elizabeth Copelin (Coplin), bond 9 November 1807.
Consent by Mary Coplin, mother of the bride, and by Robert Cardwell,
Sr., father of the groom. Robert Cardwell (b) and William Martin
(b); James L. Moore (w) and William Martin (w).

CARDWELL, WILLIAM and Sarah Wood, bond 18 April 1806. Consent by Nancy
and William Moore, parents of the bride. William Moore (b) and
William Cardwell (b).

CARROLL, ETHELDREAD of Sussex County and Toby Butler*, bond 21 March 1796.
Etheldread Carroll (b) and William Harris (b); James Bailey (w) and
William Harris (w). M.R. 28 March 1796 by Menoah Lesley lists the
bride as Tabby Butler.

CARSON, JOHN and Jane Douglass, bond 2 May 1782. Consent by Robert
Douglass, father of the bride. John Carson (b) and John Willson (b).
M.R. 6 May 1782 by John W. Holt.

CARSON, JOHN and Elizabeth Wilson (Willson), bond 20 September 1790. Consent by Nancy Willson. John Carson (b) and William Carson (b).
M.R. 23 September 1790 by William Flowers.

CARSON, JOHN and Elizabeth Askew, bond 10 August 1807. Consent by Anthony
Askew, father of the bride. John Carson (b) and Joshua Douglas (b);
Joshua Douglas (w). M.R. 10 August 1807 by Edmund Johns.

CARSON, THOMAS and Mary Dinwiddie, daughter of James Dinwiddie, bond
1 August 1793. Thomas Carson (b) and James Dinwiddie (b); Joseph
Dinwiddie (w). M.R. 22 August 1793 by William Mahon.

CARSON, WILLIAM, JR. and Calah Glass, bond 30 January 1792. Consent by
Vinson Glass. William Carson, Jr. (b) and William Carson, Sr. (b);
Benjamin Tanner (w) and Ruben Simmons (w). M.R. __ February 1792 by
Charles Cobbs gives the bride as Ceilia Glass.

CARTER, JOHN and Polly Elder*, bond 27 December 1803. Consent by Martha
Elder also. Yancie Bailey (b) and John Carter (b); James Baughan (w)
and Yancie Bailey (w). M.R. ___1803 by Edmund Johns.

CARTER, JOHN D. and Martha White King, bond 10 December 1798. Consent by
Sackville King, father of the bride. John D. Carter (b) and John H.
Brewer (b); John Brewer (w) and John Wiatt (w).

CARTER, PLEDGE and Elisabeth Wooldridge, bond 25 October 1802. Consent not
signed. Pledge Carter (b) and William Wooldridge (b); James Robertson,
Jr. (w) and William Wooldridge (w). M.R. 27 October 1802 by Philip
Mathews gives the bride as Sally Wooldridge.

CARVER, CORNELIUS (batchelor) and Sally Goodman (spinster), bond 14 July
1788. Consent by Bartlette Goodman, father of the bride. Cornelius
Carver (b) and John Goodman (b).

CARWILES, JACOB and Martha Scott*, bond 26 February 1802. Consent also by Elizabeth Scott who states the bride is of "lawful age." Jacob Carwiles (b) and Freeman Moore (b); John Carwiles (w) and Freeman Moore (w).

CARWILES, WILLIAM and Mary Daniel, bond 2 December 1800. Consent by Peter Daniel, father of the bride. William Carwiles (b) and Robert Daniel (b). M.R. 4 December 1800 by Henry Brown.

CHAPEL, JESSE and Martha Finch, bond 7 November 1791. Jesse Chapel (b) and Blagdon Finch (b). M.R. __ November 1791 by Charles Cobbs lists the groom as Jesse Chaple.

CHAPMAN, BENJAMIN of Prince Edward County and Catharine Akers, bond 20 March 1786. Benjamin Chapman (b) and Peter Akers (b).

CHENAULT, WILLIAM and Elisabeth Stevens*, bond 3 January 1810. William Chenault (b) and Jacob Shouls (b); Anderson Crowley (w) and Jacob Shouls (w).

CHEWNING, HARDEN and Elizabeth Nigby*, bond 28 January 1793. Harden Chewning (b) and Thomas Tucker (b); Thomas Fox (w) and Jesse Jennings (w). M.R. 30 __ 1793 by Menoah Lesley.

CHICK, ANDERSON of Pittsylvania County and Lucy Brown*, bond 9 October 1792. Anderson Chick (b) and John Brown (b); James Brown (w) and John Brown (w). M.R. 11 October 1792 by James Kenney lists the groom as Anderson Cheek.

CHILDRESS, FLEMING and Nancy Pugh*, bond 29 November 1805. Fleming Childres (b) and John Faris (b); John Faris (w) and Frank Faris (w).

CHILDRESS, VAULTON and Polly Ann Taylor, bond 19 December 1804. Consent by William Taylor. Vaulton Childress (b) and Peter T. Taylor (b); John Reads (w) and Peter T. Taylor (w).

CHRISTY, ELIJAH and Polly Showls, daughter of Jacob Showls, bond 5 June 1809. Elijah Christy (b) and Jacob Showls (b). M.R. 6 June 1809 by James Warner.

CLARK, BENNETT and Patty Bullock, bond 31 March 1789. Consent by Robert Clark. Bennett Clark (b) and Josias Bullock (b); D. Bullock (w). M. R. 31 March 1789 by James Kenney.

CLARK, DAVID and Mary Clark, bond 24 October 1794. Consent by John Clark, father of the bride. David Clark (b) Ro. Alexander (b); Samuel Fisher (w) and Micajah Clark (w).

CLARK, JAMES and Martha Clark, bond 25 December 1810. Consent by John Clark, father of the bride. James Clark (b) and Richard Clark (b); Richard Clark (w) and Thomas Clark (w).

CLARK, JOHN and Elizabeth Owl (Howle), bond 11 October 1791. Consent by
John Thomas Howle, father of the bride. John Clark (b) and Thomas
Moore (b).

CLARK, PAULETT and Mary Ann Irvine (Irvin), bond 11 October 1798. Consent
by John Irvin, father of the bride. William Hunter (b) and Paulett
Clark (b); William Hunter (w). M.R. 20 October 1798 by Archibald
McRoberts.

CLARK, ROBERT and Nancy Moorman, bond 20 August 1791. Robert Clark (b)
and Thos. Clark (b). M.R. 23 August 1791 by Menoah Lesley.

CLARK, ROBERT AND Susanna Lee, bond 4 June 1804. Consent by John Lee,
father of the bride. Robert Clark (b) and Burwell Lee (b); Stephen
Lee (w) and Burwell Lee (w).

CLARK, THOMAS and Milly Moorman, bond 22 December 1787. Consent by Andrew
Moorman, father of the bride. Jesse Moorman (b) and Thomas Clark (b);
James Clark (w). M.R. gives no date but is listed after entries for
15 August 1788, by James Kenney. Marriage Register Vol. I, 1782- has
the date listed as 1782.

CLARK, WILLIAM and Elizabeth Jones, bond 2 March 1803. William Clark (b)
and Publius Jones (b).

CLARKSON, JAMES F. and Elizabeth Moorman, bond 24 October 1804. The
consent is signed Jesse Moremen, the father of the bride. James F.
Clarkson (b) and Achilles Moorman (b); Lucy Moormen (w) and Achilles
Moormen (w). M. R. ____ 1804 by Edmund Johns.

CLAY, MARSTON and Sally Deering, bond 29 December 1809. Consent James
Deering, father of the bride. Marston Clay (b) and C.S.Adams (b);
John Guy (w) and C. S. Adams (w).

CLAYTON, WILLIAM and Susannah G. Arnold, daughter of John Arnold, bond
18 December 1810. John Arnold (b) and William Clayton (b).

CLAYWELL, SOLOMON and Rachel Webber (Weber)*, bond 2 December 1805.
Solomon Claywell (b) and Henry Webber (b); Henry Weber (w) and
Thomas Coxe(?) (w).

CLEMENT, BENJAMIN and Polly Candler, daughter of William Candler, bond
14 November 1803. Benjamin Clement (b) and William Candler (b).
M.R. 15 November 1803 by Henry Brown lists the bride's name as Mary
Candler. The words "or Mary" have been written in pencil on the
outside of the bond, apparently at a later date.

CLEMENT, JOHN and Jane Butterworth, bond 8 January 1789. Benjamin Butterworth (b) and John Clement (b); D. Bullock (w). M.R. no date given
but listed after returns dated 15 August 1788, by James Kenney.

CLEMENT, WILLIAM and Mary DePriest*, bond 24 June 1794. William Clement
(b) and Thos. Gregg (b); Thos. Gregg (w) and Jas. Newel (w) and
Thos. Gregg (w).

CLEMMONS, GASPER and Polly Clemmons, bond 2 December 1800. Consent by
John Colewell, father of the bride. Gasper Clemmons (b) and James
Douglass (b); James Douglass (w) and Sam Caldwell (w). M.R. 16 ___
1800 by William Flowers. This return is listed three times under
this date in the original Register. In each listing the bride's
name is given as Polly Caldwell. In the first listing the groom's
name is given as Gasper Clemens; in the second as Gasper Clemmons;
in the third as Gasper Clemons. In the Marriage Register Vol. I,
1782- the bride's name is given as Polly Caldwell.

CLIFTON, JONATHAN and Usley Wood, bond 16 June 1795. Consent by John
Wood, father of the bride. Jonathan Clifton (b) and Henry Walthall
(b); Henry Walthall (w) and Robert Watkins (w).

CLOPTON, ABNER W. and Sally B. Warwick, bond 23 September 1803. Consent
by James Warwick, father of the bride. A.W. Clopton (b) and W.H.
Brewer (b); W. H. Brewer (w) and Henry Ward (w).

COBBS, CALEB and Mina Ann Wills, bond 6 July 1792 [sic]. Consent by
Euclid Wills, father of the bride. Caleb Cobbs (b) and John
Wills (b); Betsey Wills (w) and John Wills (w). M.R. ___ July 1791
by Charles Cobbs.

COBBS, CHARLES and Martha Bailey, bond 4 December 1783. Consent by
Elizabeth Bailey, mother of the bride. Charles Cobbs (b) and
Thomas Cobbs (b); Josiah Hundley (w).

COBBS, JAMES and Frances Walker, bond 16 December 1800. Consent by
_____ Walker, sister of the bride. James Cobbs (b) and Thomas
Cobbs (b). M.R. 18 December 1800 by William Flowers. This entry
is made three times in the original Register under this date. In
the first entry the bride is Frances Walker; in the second entry
she is Francis Walker; and in the third entry she is Fanny Walker.

COBBS, JAMES H. and Polly Douglas, bond 12 October 1801. Consent by
James Douglas, father of the bride. James H. Cobbs (b) and John
Douglas (b); John Scruggs (w) and John Douglas (w).

COBBS, JOHN and Christina Wynne, bond 29 March 1797. Consent by Leviney
Wynne; also by Jesse Cobbs, father of the groom. John Cobbs (b)
and John Winton (b); William Stith (w), John Dill (w), John Winton
(w), Thomas Gallagher (w), Edward Douglas (w) and Thomas Cobbs (w).
M.R. ___ 1797 by Charles Cobbs lists the bride as Christeana Wynne.

COBBS, JOHN B. and Jane Dixon, bond 8 October 1810. Consent by John
Dickson, father of the bride. John B. Cobbs (b) and George Dixon
(b); George Dixon (w) and James Dixon (w). M.R. 8 October 1810 by
Edmund Johns gives the bride's name as Jane Dickson.

COBBS, THOMAS and Betty Wills, bond 3 December 1788. Consent by Euclid
Wills, father of the bride. Thomas Cobbs (b) and Josias Bullock (b).

COBBS, THOMAS (widower) and Susannah Adams (widow)*, bond 10 September
1808. Thomas Cobbs (b) and John Adams (b); John Adams (w) and
And. Moorman (w). M.R. 10 September 1808 by Edmund Johns.

COBBS, THOMAS, JR. and Mildred Lucas*, bond 15 August 1808. Thomas
Cobbs (b) and John Faris (b); J. Hurt (w).

COBBS, TILGHMAN and Hannah Marshall, bond 3 October 1803. John Marshall
(b) and Tilghman A. Cobbs (b).

COCK, JOHN and Mary Tweedy*, bond 20 August 1796. John Cock (b) and
Robert Tweedy (b); Joseph Tweedy (w) and Robert Tweedy (w).
M.R. __ 1796 by Charles Cobbs lists the groom as John Cocke.

COCK, THOMAS and Eline(?) Hightower, bond 4 November 1789. Thomas Cock
(b) and George Hightower (b). M.R. 6 November 1789 by James Hurt
lists the bride's name as Eleanor Hightower. Her first name on the
bond is difficult to decipher. The Marriage Register Vol. I, 1782-
gives the bride's name as Eliza Hightower.

COCK, THOMAS JR., and Polly Kent, bond 8 October 1798. Consent by
Thomas Cock, Sr., father of the groom and guardian of the bride.
Thomas Cock, Jr. (b) and Thomas Cock, Sr. (b); Dennis Kelley (w)
and Wm. Cock (w).

COCKE, DRURY W. and Susannah Cox*, bond 22 March 1808. Drury W. Cocke
(b) and Thomas North (b); Thomas North (w) and Abraham North (w).
M.R. 22 March 1808 by William P. Martin.

COHARN, JAMES and Mary Hopkins*, bond 7 October 1784. James Coharn (b)
and Christopher Griffith (b); Mary Ratliffe (w) and Thomas Carson(?)
(w).

COHARN, THOMAS and Obedience Blankinship, bond 26 July 1788. Consent by
Hudson Blankinship, father of the bride. Thomas Coharn (b) and
Jesse Blankinship (b); Jesse Blankinship (w) and Silvanus Massie (w).
M.R. no date given but listed following 15 August 1788 entries, by
James Kenney.

COLBERT, LEMUEL and Phebe Blankinship*, bond 23 November 1790. Consent
certified by John Ward. Lemuel Colbert (b) and John Nash (Red Head)
(b); Benjamin Terrell (w) and James Maloney (w). M.R. 24 November
1790 by James Kenney.

COLE, SAMUEL of Botetourt County and Catharine Bryan, bond 10 October 1789.
Consent by John Bryan, Sr., father of the bride. Samuel Cole (b) and
John Gibson (b); John Gibson (w) and Robert Bryan (w). M.R. 13 October
1789 by James Kenney.

COLEMAN, SPILSBY and Betsy Baugh, bond 9 July 1801. Consent by Bartlet
Baugh, father of the bride. Spilsby Coleman (b) and George Rust (b);
George Rust (w) and Berry Coleman (w).

COLLINS, DAVID and Anne Lee, bond 24 January 1786. David Collins (b) and James Lee (b). M.R. 26 January 1786 by James Kenney.

COLLINS, JOHN and Lockey Jones, bond 31 January 1800. John Collins (b) and Publius Jones (b). M.R. 13 February 1800 by John Chappell.

COLLINS, PETER and Susannah Dillon, bond 8 October 1798. Consent by Henry Dillon. Peter Collins (b) and John Dillon (b).

CONDREY, CALEB and Lucy J. Frances, bond 19 March 1793. Caleb Condrey (b) and William Condrey (b). M.R. 21 March 1793 by Menoah Lesley lists the bride and groom as Caleb Condray and Lucy Jones Frances.

CONDREY, WILLIAM and Susannah Fox, bond 31 July 1805. William Condrey (b) and Richard Fox (b).

CONNIFAR, BENJAMIN and Nancy Paty, bond 6 November 1788. Consent by Larry Paty, father of the bride. Benjamin Connifar (b) and Thomas Vest (b); John Bradly (w).

COOK, BENJAMIN and Sally Fuqua, bond 23 December 1783. Moses Fuqua (b) and Benjamin Cook (b).

COOPER, JOSEPH and Sally Jackson, bond 11 November 1807. Consent by Isaac Jackson, father of the bride. Joseph Cooper (b) and John Evans (b); John Evans (w) and Emry Hughes (w).

COPELING, THOMAS and Anney Hood, bond 23 October 1802. Consent by James Hood. Thomas Copeling (b) and John Hood (b).

COX, ABSALAM of Amherst County and Judith Walker Moore, bond 1 October 1798. Absalom Cox (b) and William Moore (b).

COX, CHARLES and Elizabeth Reese, bond 29 August 1791. Charles Cox (b) and Herod Reese (b). M.R. __ August 1791 by Charles Cobbs lists the bride as Elizabeth Reece.

COX, JAMES and Elizabeth Faris, bond 10 December 1800. Consent by William Faris, father of the bride, and by John Cox, father of the groom. James Cox (b) and John Faris (b); John Faris (w) and Jesse Faris (w).

COX, LITTLEBURY and Mascilda Riddy, bond 20 October 1796. Consent by John Hix, guardian of Miss Riddy. Littlebury Cox (b) and William Hix (b); Tom Hazlewood (w) and William Hix (w).

CRALLE, LINDSAY and Nancy Rosser, bond 30 December 1805. Consent by William Rosser. Lindsay Cralle (b) and John Jones (b); Larken Foster (w) and John Jones (w).

CRAWLEY, BEVERLY and Peggy Porter, bond 14 October 1796. Consent by Margaret Wabber(?). Beverly Crawley (b) and John Morcheson (b); Charles Crawley (w) and John Morcheson (w). M.R. __ October 1796 by Menoah Lesley.

CRAWLEY, CHARLES and Mary Eleanor Pugh. M.R. 18 December 1790 by Menoah
Lesley.

CRAWLEY, CHARLES and Mary Elener Hughes, bond 16 December 1799. Consent
given by Robert Hughes for Charles Crawley "to marry Elener Hughes."
Charles Crawley (b) and John Morrison (b).

CREWS, GIDEON and Elizabeth Oglesby, bond 11 May 1807. Consent by Marey
Oglesby, mother of the bride. Gideon Crews (b) and Samuel Davidson (b);
Samuel Davidson (w). M.R. 20 May 1807 by William Flowers, Jr.

CREWS, JAMES and Judith Bybee, daughter of Edward Bybee, bond 14 January
1807. James Crews (b) and Edward Bybee (b). M.R. 15 January 1807
by James Warner.

CREWS, JOSEPH and Polly M. Elder, bond 18 June 1792. Consent by Joseph
Crews. Joseph Crews (b) and William Matthews (b); John Hawks (w).
M.R. __ July 1792 by Charles Cobbs.

CREWS, LITTLEBERRY and Rachel Davidson*, bond 14 July 1800. Littleberry
Crews (b) and John Dickey (b); Wrenny Crews (w) and John Dickey (w).
M.R. 28 July 1800 by Joshua Worley.

CREWS, NICHOLAS and Drussilla Patterson, bond 4 November 1783. Nicholas
Crews (b) and Benjamin B. Hawkins (b).

CREWS, WILLIAM and Elizabeth Crews, bond 10 February 1801. Consent by
Josiah Crews, father of the bride. William Crews (b) and Josiah
Crews (b); Josiah Crews, Jr. (w) and John Crews (w).

CRIDER, HENRY and Pamelia Lee, bond 14 October 1805. Consent by John Lee,
father of the bride. Henry Crider (b) and Burwell Lee (b); John Lee,
Jr. (w) and Burwell Lee (w).

CROPFF, HENRY and Barbara Jenkins, daughter of Robert Jenkins, bond
12 October 1807. Robert Jenkins (b) and Henry Cropff (b).

CROWLEY (CRAWLEY), JAMES and Nancy Mitchell, bond 13 March 1794. Consent
by James Mitchell, father of the bride. James Crowley (b) and Adams
Mitchell (b); James Thompson (w) M.R. 14 March 1794 by Menoah Lesley
lists the groom as James Crawley. Marriage Register Vol. I, 1782 -
lists him as Crawley.

CRUMP, THOMAS and Pemalia Thorp, bond 26 February 1787. Consent by Iran
Thorp, mother of the bride. Thomas Crump (b) and Caleb Tate (b).
M.R. 11(?) March 1787 by Charles Clay.

CULVER (COLVER), JOSEPH and Nancy Childress, bond 1 October 1789. Consent
by Samuel Childress, father of the bride. Joseph Culver (b) and
Jesse Harvey (b); Clark Campbell (w). M.R. 9 October 1789 by James
Kenney lists the bride as Nancy Childras.

CUMBEE, CHARLES and Nancy Leeson*, bond 20 January 1807. Charles Cumbee (b)
and William H. Walker (b); George Reading (w).

CUMBEE, PETER and Nancy Farthing, bond 25 November 1799. Peter Cumbee (b) and William Farthing (b).

CUMBEE, EMANUEL and Molly Farthing, bond 27 December 1800. Emanuel Cumby (b) and William Farthing (b).

CURL, ARCHIBALD and Jane Irvine. M.R. 3 October 1791 by Menoah Lesley.

CURLE, JOSEPH and Sarah Stratton, bond 20 October 1794. Consent by Joseph Stratton, father of the bride. Joseph Curle (b) and George Fox (b); George Fox (w) and Solomon Thorp (w). M.R. 4 November 1794 by Menoah Lesley.

CYRUS, SOLOMON and Frances Wooldridge*, bond 13 September 1809. Sampson Moore, Jr. makes affidavit that she is of age. Solomon Cyrus (b) and Sampson Moore, Jr. (b). M.R. 13 September 1809 by Obadiah Edge lists the bride as Francis Wooldridge.

D

DABNEY, JOHN and Milly Haden, bond 11 November 1793. Consent by John Haden, Sr., father of the bride. John Dabney (b) and Turner Haden (b); Nathan Harris (w) and Chas. Smith (w).

DAMERON, JOHN and Sarah Moore, bond 24 December 1804. Consent by William Moore. John Dameron (b) and John Moore (b).

DANIEL, ALEXANDER and Nancy Carwiles*, bond 28 March 1805. Alexander Daniel (b) and Peter Daniel (b). M.R. 28 March 1805 by Henry Brown lists bride as Nancy Carwile.

DANIEL, JAMES and Susannah Tanner, bond 25 September 1809. Consent by Benjamin Tanner, father of the bride. James Daniel (b) and Vincent J. Tanner (b). M.R. 30 September 1809 by Obadiah Edge lists the bride as Susanna Taner.

DANIEL, JOSIAH and Pricilla Trent, bond 12 November 1798. Consent by Henry Trent, father of the bride. Josiah Daniel (b) and William Hinton (b); William Hinton (w) and Thomas Daniel (w).

DANIEL, PETER, JR. and Mary Issenberry, bond 14 October 1805. Consent by Jacob Issenberry, father of the bride. Peter Daniel, Jr. (b) and Peter Daniel, Sr. (b).

DANIEL, ROBERT and Sarah Reynolds, bond 16 February 1804. Consent by John Reynolds, Jr. Robert Daniel (b) and John Reynolds, Jr. (b). M.R. 16 February 1804 by Henry Brown.

DANIEL, THOMAS and Polly Jones, daughter of Thomas Jones, bond 14 December 1801. Thomas Daniel (b) and Thomas Jones (b). M.R. 24 December 1801 by Henry Brown.

DANIEL, WILLIAM (batchelor) and Edith Suttenfield (widow)*, bond 11 January 1792. William Daniel (b) and Peter Daniel (b). M.R. 10 January 1792 by Menoah Lesley.

DANIEL, WILLIAM and Sally Trent, bond 9 March 1807. Consent by
Zachariah Trent, father of the bride. William Daniel (b) and John
Daniel (b); John Daniel (w) and Elijah Trent (w).

DAUN (DAWN), WILLIAM and Fanny Finch, bond 3 November 1792. William
Daun (b) and Blagdon Finch (b). M.R. 11 November 1792 by Menoah
Lesley lists the groom as William Dawn.

DAVENPORT, GLOVER and Ann P. Slaughter, bond 20 July 1801. Consent by
Charles Slaughter. Glover Davenport (b) and Robert Cobb (b);
John Poindexter (w) and Robert Cobb (w).

DAVIDSON (DAVISSON), ABNER and Martha Spicer, bond 1 February 1806.
Consent by Isack G.(?) Spiser and Latus G.(?) Spiser, parents of
the bride. Abner Davidson (Davisson) (b) and James Davidson
(Davison) (b); Joseph Davison (w) and James Davison (w). M.R.
6 February 1806 by William Flowers, Jr., lists the groom as Davidson.

DAVIDSON, ALEXANDER and Agnes Crews, bond 10 October 1803. Consent by
Isaac Crews, father of the bride. Alexander Davidson (b) and
Wrenny Crews (b); Wrenney Crews (w) and Littleberry Crews (w).
M.R. 20 October 1803 by William Flowers.

DAVIDSON, GEORGE and Nancy Taylor, bond 9 June 1806. Consent by James
Taylor, father of the bride. George Davidson (b) and Joseph Davidson (b); David Davidson (w) and Joseph Davidson (w). M.R. 10 June
1806 by William Flowers, Jr.

DAVIDSON, JOHN and Mary Ratcliff*, bond 23 February 1801:1805. John
Davidson (b) and Samuel Davidson (b); Samuel Davidson (w), William
Brown (w) and John Irvine (w). M.R. 5 March 1801 by William
Flowers.

DAVIDSON, JOHN and Frances Woodson, bond 30 January 1808. Consent by
John Woodson, Jr., father of the bride. John Davidson (b) and
Anderson Woodson (b). M.R. 4 February 1808 by William Flowers.

DAVIDSON, JOHN and Polly Caffey*, bond 13 June 1803. John Davidson (b)
and Charles Caffery (b); John Thomas (w) and Charles Caffery (w).
M.R. 17 June 1803 by William Flowers lists the bride as Polly
Caffery.

DAVIDSON, SAMUEL and Frances Oglesby*, bond 18 October 1802. Samuel
Davidson (b) and Joseph Davidson (b); Joseph Davidson (w) and James
Davidson (w). M.R. 29 October 1802 by William Flowers.

DAVIDSON, SAMUEL and Elender Lea, bond 14 December 1807. Consent by
Gideon Lea, father of the bride. Samuel Davidson (b) and Charles
Coffey (b); Charles Coffey (w). M.R. 14 December 1807 by Edmund
Johns.

DAVIS, ASARIAH and Betsy Finch, bond 3 April 1807. Consent by John
Finch. Asariah Davis (b) and Morrison Bryan (b); John Akers (w)
and Morrison Bryan (w).

DAVIS, BENJAMIN and Nancy Massacree*, bond 1 June 1805. Benjamin Davis (b) and Samuel Caldwell (b); Samuel Caldwell (w) and John Thomson (w). M.R. 1 June 1805 by LittleJohn Baldwin lists the bride as Nancy Massacre.

DAVIS, JAMES and Nancy Gibbs, bond 13 November 1792. Consent by Matthew Womack. James Davis (b) and Adam Driskill (b); Adam Driskill (w) and David Womack (w).

DAVIS, JOHN and Anne Evans, bond 20 May 1786. Consent by Thos. R. Evans, father of the bride. John Davis (b) and Thomas Moore (b); Daniel Evans (w). M.R. __ May 1786 by James Kenney.

DAVIS, JOHN and Morning Birford*, bond 23 March 1802. John Davis (b) and Jacob Rohr (b); Jacob Rohr (w).

DAVIS, THOMAS and Betty Birmingham, bond 9 September 1799. Thomas Davis (b) and Bernard Finch (b). M.R. 15 ___ 1799 by William P. Martin.

DAVISON, BENJAMIN and Rebeckah Numan, bond 30 November 1791. Consent by Nimrod Numan. Benjamin Davison (b) and John Davison (b); John Davison (w) and Samuel Davison (w). M.R. 8 December 1791 by Menoah Lesley lists the groom as Benjamin Davidson and the bride as Zebeckah Numan.

DAVISON, JOHN and Jane Bryan, bond 16 November 1785. Consent by John Bryan, Sr., father of the bride. John Davison (b) and Joseph Davison (b); John Cole (w) and David Barnett (w). M.R. 4 December 1785 by James Kenney lists the groom as John Dawson.

DAVISON, JOSEPH (batchelor) and Elizabeth Snow (spinster), bond 7 December 1786. Joseph Davison (b) and Thomas Davison (b); __?__ Finch (w).

DAWSEY, JOHN and Sally Donald. M.R. ___ 1786 by John W. Holt.

DEARING, JAMES and Elizabeth Adams, bond 3 April 1783. James Dearing (b) and James Adams (b).

DEJARNETT, JOHN and Judith Moorman, bond 22 August 1805. Consent by Juda Moorman, parent of the bride. John Dejarnett (b) and Archer Williamson (b); Archer Williamson (w) and Robert Williamson (w).

DEJARNETT, WALKER and Nancy Gilliam, bond 10 October 1808. Consent by Elizabeth Gilliam, mother of the bride. Walker Dejarnett (b) and John Twedy (b); William Gilliam (w) and John Twedy (w). M.R. 11 October 1808 by Edmund Johns.

DENTON, JAMES and Patsy Crews, bond 27 April 1804. Consent by Isaac Crews. James Denton (b) and James Crews (b); Jas. Crews (w). M.R. 29 April 1804 by Obadiah Edge.

DEROSSETT, SAMUEL and Polly Solloman*, bond 26 September 1788. Samuel Derosset (b) and Michael Prewitt (b) (?).

DEWS, RICHARD and Sally Black, bond 13 October 1804. Consent by Thos. Black, father of the bride. Reuben G. Dews (b) and Thomas Black, Jr. (b); John Black (w).

DIBRELL, CHARLES and Lucy Patteson* (Patterson), bond 14 September 1801. Consent by Lander Patteson and Little Berry Patteson, sisters of the bride, who is of age. Charles Dibrell (b) and Thos. Jones (b); M.R. 24 September 1801 by Charles Macky lists the bride as Lucy Patterson.

DICKEY, JAMES and Margaret Wilson (Willson), bond ___ 1803. James Dickey (b) and John Wilson (b). M.R. 20 January 1803 by William Flowers.

DICKEY, JOHN and Susanna Davidson, bond 23 February 1789. Consent by Alex and Elizabeth Davidson, parents of the bride. John Dickey (b) and Thos. Carson (b); Thos. Carson (w) and Gabrell Davidson (w). M.R. 26 February 1789 by William Flowers.

DICKEY, SAMUEL and Sarah Bradley, bond 14 April 1806. Consent by William Bradley, father of the bride. Samuel Dickey (b) and Stephen Bradley (b). M.R. 26 April 1806 by William Flowers, Jr.

DICKINSON, AUSTIN and Indah Going free Negroes bond 2 March 1805. Consent by William Heath who certifies that Miss Going consents and is of age. Austin Dickinson (b) and William Heath (b).

DIENER, JACOB and Sally Gunnele, bond 25 January 1785. Jacob Diener (b) and Moses Fuqua (b).

DIESON (DEISON), CHARLES and Sally M. Tate, bond 21 November 1810. Consent by Edmund Tate, father of the bride. Charles Deison (b) and Thos. W. Cocke (b); Thos. W. Cocke (w) and Harriet Tate (w).

DILL, JOHN and Ninea Wynn*, bond 18 March 1797. John Dill (b) and Nathan Tanner (b). M.R. ___ 1797 by Charles Cobbs, lists the bride as Lavina Wynne.

DILLARD, BENJAMIN and Ann Lynch, bond 5 December 1782. Benj. Dillard (b) and Henry Brown (b).

DILLARD, JAMES and Lucy Moorman, daughter of Henry Moorman, bond 4 September 1809. James Dillard (b) and Henry Moorman (b). M.R. 7 September 1809 by S. K. Jennings.

DIMNEY, EDWARD and Luckey Jackson, bond 5 December 1801. Consent by Isaac Jackson, father of the bride. Edward Dimney (b) and William Jackson (b); Reuben Crawford (w).

DINWIDDIE, JOSEPH and Polly Bass, bond 15 September 1798. Consent by
Thos. Walthall, grandfather of the bride. Joseph Dinwiddie (b)
and Thomas Dixon (b); Thomas Dixon (w). M.R. 25 September 1798
by William Flowers. This consent reads: "This is to certify that
I have a granddaughter Polly Bass that I have from a small infant
taken the charge of her from about Fore or Five Days Old and has
lived with me ever since her mother died in a short time after she
was Born and we have kept her and She is now in her Sixteenth year of
her age and her father and mother are dead and he (we?) has left her
no estate Worth Mentioning and as Joseph Dinwiddie and She is agreed
to joyn together in marig I do desire you wod grant them a licens to
be married. I am so old and infirm that I am not able to Ride to your
hous. Do not fail you will not be in the Least Danger in so doing and
will oblige
Thomas Walthall
and Polly Bass"

DINWIDDIE, WILLIAM and Mary Hunter, bond 6 February 1783. Consent by
Ann Wilson, mother of the bride. William Dinwiddie (b) and James
Dixon (b).

DITTO, PETER and Lucy Bowles*, bond 8 February 1802. Peter Ditto (b)
and Samuel Schoolfield (b); Samuel Schoolfield (w).

DIXON, JOHN and Polly McIver, bond 2 July 1810. Consent by James McIver,
Jr., father of the bride. John Dixon (b) and James McIver (b);
James McIver (w) and Joseph McReynolds (w). M.R. 5 July 1810 by
Obadiah Edge gives the groom as John Dickson.

DIXON, THOMAS and Rachel Wilson, daughter of John Wilson, bond 10 August
1807. Thomas Dixon (b) and John Wilson (b). M.R. 31 August 1807
by Drury Lacy.

DIXON, WILLIAM E. and Mary Helm, daughter of John Helm, bond 3 March 1806.
William E. Dixon (b) and John Dinwiddie (b); John Dinwiddie (w) and
James Helm (w).

DODD, THOMAS and Susanna Creasey, orphan of Joseph Kennerley, bond
13 March 1809. Thomas Dodd (b) and Joseph Kennerley (b).

DOSS, HARTWELL M. and Patsey Elam, bond 29 April 1809. Consent by
Susanna Elam, mother of the bride. Hartwell M. Doss (b) and Charles
Arrington (b); Charles Arrington (w) and John Arrington (w). M.R.
29 April 1809 by Edmund Johns.

DOUGHERTY, JARETT and Elizabeth Russell, bond 14 March 1792. Jarrett
Dougherty (b) and James Russell (b). M.R. 16 March 1792 by Menoah
Lesley lists the groom as Jerard Dougherty.

DOUGHERTY, WILLIAM and Letice Goggin, bond 28 March 1786. Consent by
Stephen Goggin. William Dougherty (b) and Richard Goggin (b).

DOUGLAS, EDWARD and Mary Anne Jude, bond 7 January 1795. Consent by
George Jude, father of the bride, and by James Douglas, father
of the groom. Edward Douglas (b) and Albin Rawlins (b); Charles
Howel (w), Sam'l Jordan (w), Betsy Jordan (w) and Albin Rawlins (w).
M.R. __ February 1795 by John Chappell.

DRINKARD, DUNCY and Elizabeth Rector, bond 2 August 1792. Duncy Drinkard
(b) and Thomas Dunn (b).

DRINKWATER, EMANUEL and Elizabeth Turner, bond 10 November 1791. Consent
by Robert Turner, father of the bride. Emanuel Drinkwater (b) and
Edmund Talbot (b).

DRINKWATER, JOHN and Katy Wills. M.R. 15 April 1782 by John W. Holt.

DRINKWATER, SAMUEL and Nancy Turner, bond 16 August 1788. Consent by
Robert Turner, father of the bride. Samuel Drinkwater (b) and John
Marshall (b); John Black (w) and John Marshall (w). M.R. 15 August
1788 by William Dodson.

DRISKILL, ADAM and Sarah Bailey (Baley), bond 14 July 1794. Consent by
William Baley and Marah Baley, parents of the bride. Adam Driskill
(b) and Daniel Driskill (b); Thomas Baley (w) and Poley Baley (w).
M.R. __ July 1794 by Charles Cobbs.

DRISKILL, ALEX. (batchelor) and Susanna Cobbs (spinster), bond 22 August
1786. Consent by Thomas Cobbs. Alexander Driskill (b) and John
Cobb (b).

DRISKILL, DAVID and Elizabeth Holt, bond 28 August 1804. Consent by
Robert Holt, father of the bride. David Driskill (b) and Daniel
Driskill (b).

DRISKILL, RICHARD and Elizabeth Graham, bond 24 May 1794. Consent by
William Graham. Richard Driskill (b) and James Stuart (b); Marshall
Driskill (w), James Stuart (w) and Adam Driskill (w). M.R. __ May
1794 by Charles Cobbs.

DRISKILL, RICHARD and Polly Hubbard Young, daughter of William Young,
bond 3 October 1801. Richard Driskill (b) and William Young (b).

DRISKILL, WILLIAM and Milly Whayne*, "of lawful age," bond 23 November
1796. William Driskill (b) and James Stuart (b); James Stuart (w).
M.R. __ November 1796 by Charles Cobbs, lists the bride as Milley
Wayne.

DUDGEON, ALEXANDER and Elizabeth Farthing, bond 11 January 1793. Consent
by William Farthing, father of the bride. Alexander Dudgeon (b)
and William Farthing (b).

DUDGEON, JAMES and Nancy Marshall, bond 9 January 1784. Consent by
William Marshall. James Dudgeon (b) and Daniel Marshall (b).

DUDGEON, WILLIAM and Martha Farthing, bond 3 April 1794. Consent by
William Farthing, father of the bride. William Dudgeon (b) and
Thomas Farthing (b). M.R. __ April 1794 by Charles Cobbs.

DUDLEY, ABNER and Lucy Barber, bond 26 November 1795. Consent by
Charles Barber. Abner Dudley (b) and Armistead Dudley (b);
John Ward (w) and Armistead Dudley (w). M.R. ____ 1796 by
James Kenny.

DUDLEY, ABSOLOM and Elizabeth Joyner (Joiner), daughter of Peter Joyner,
bond 24 February 1806. Absolom Dudley (b) and Peter Joyner (b).

DUNN, RICHARD and Sarah Gibson. M.R. 16 September 1782 by John W. Holt.

DUNNAVANT, SHADRICK and Frances Gibbs, bond 24 November 1806. Consent
by Edward Gibbs, father of the bride. Shadrick Dunnavant (b) and
Peter Gibbs (b); Peter Gibbs (w) and Shadwick Dunnavant (w). M.R.
24 November 1806 by Edmund Johns lists the groom as Shadrick
Dunnavent, and the bride as Francis Gibbs.

DUPUY, WILLIAM and Elizabeth Fuqua, daughter of Moses Fuqua, bond
21 January 1796. William Dupuy (b) and Moses Fuqua (b). M.R.
__ January 1796 by Charles Cobbs lists the groom as William Dupee.

DUVALL, JOHN and Doshy Gregory, bond 10 November 1805. Consent by John
Gregory, Sr., father of the bride. John Duvall (b) and John
Gregory, Jr. (b).

DUVALL, MARCEN and Susannah Cannifax, bond 2 December 1799. Consent by
John Cannifax and Anne Cannifax, parents of the bride. Marcen
Duvall (b) and Radford Cannifax (b). M.R. 14 December 1799 by
Abner Early lists the groom as Mareen Duvall.

DYER, JOHN and Milly Butterworth*, bond 29 August 1807. John Dyer (b)
and Zach Moorman (b). M.R. 29 August 1807 by William P. Martin
lists the bride as Miley Butler.

E

EARLY, JOSHUA, JR. and Patsey Strange, bond 31 October 1791. Joshua
Early, Jr. ·(b) and Robert Strange (b). M. R. __ November 1791 by
Charles Cobbs.

EARLY, NED and Patty Jones*, bond 14 September 1807. Ned Early (b) and
James Moorman (b).

EAST, JOSEPH and Polly Bell*, bond 2 April 1803. Joseph East (b) and
Radford Connefax (b); Radford Connefax (w) and Isaac East (w).
M.R. 12 May 1803 by Henry Brown lists the bride as Mary Bell.

EAST, SHADRICK and Mary Hundley*, bond 8 September 1784. Shadrick East
(b) and John Boughton (b).

EAST, THOMAS and Mildred Timberlake, bond 19 October 1795. Consent by Charles Timberlake, father of the bride. Thomas East (b) and Publius Jones (b); Publius Jones (w). M.R.__ October 1795 by Charles Cobbs.

EASTER, MATTHEW and Mary Brown*, bond 10 May 1804. Matthew Easter (b) and Richard P. Haden (b); Richard Haden (w) and Lucy Haden (w). M.R. 10 May 1804 by Obadiah Edge lists the groom as Matthew Esther.

ECHOLS, MOSES and Elizabeth Hix*, bond 9 February 1807. Moses Echols (b) and William Hix (b); William Hix (w) and Sibbeller Hix (w).

EDDS (EADDS), JESSE and Elizabeth Brown, daughter of John Brown, bond 20 February 1799. Jesse Edds (b) and John Brown (b).

EDDS, JOHN and Elizabeth Lynch, daughter of Elijah Lynch, bond 5 October 1802. John Edds (b) and Elijah Lynch (b) M.R. 7 October 1802 by Henry Brown.

EIDSON, BARNABAS and Pamalia Patterson, bond 31 August 1792. Consent by Nicholas Crews, father of the bride. Barnabas Eidson (b) and Goodrich Moore (b); William Moore (w) and David Crews (w). M.R. 15 September 1792 by Menoah Lesley lists the bride as Pamalia Patteson.

EIDSON, JAMES and Mary Moorman, bond 7 October 1790. James Eidson (b) and William Moorman (b). M.R. 21 October 1790 by Menoah Lesley.

EIDSON, JOHN and Nancy Clark, bond 12 November 1791. Consent by Thos.(?) Clark. John Eidson (b) and Ro. Alexander (b). M.R. 15 November 1791 by Menoah Lesley.

ELAM, LUALLEN and Nancy Eanes, bond 15 February 1806. Consent by Henry Walthall, guardian of the bride. Luallen Elam (b) and Morris Roberts (b); Morris Roberts (w) and Mack Roberts (w).

ELDER, EPHRAIM (batchelor) of Brunswick County and Patsy Matthews (spinster), bond 9 July 1787. Ephraim Elder (b) and William Matthews (b).

ELDER, JAMES and Polly Mason, bond 9 September 1789. Consent by John Mason, father of the bride. Jesse Mason (b); Jesse Mason (w).

ELGIN, JOHN (batchelor) and Elizabeth Bumpass (spinster), bond 1 February 1787. John Elgin (b) and William Bumpass (b).

ELLETT (ELLIOT), ROBERT and Mary Wilson, bond 4 February 1793. Consent by John Willson. Robert Ellett (Elliot) (b) and Robinson Cheatham (b); Peter Cheatham (w) and Robertson Cheatham (w).

ELLIOTT, WILLIAM and Milly Pribble, daughter of John Pribble, bond 9 December 1799. William Elliott (b) and John Pribble (b), M.R. 13 December 1799 by Abner Early.

ELLIS, DAVID and Lucy Hackett*, free Negroes, bond 12 February 1798. David
Ellis (b) and Morris Freeman (b); Glover Baker (w) and James Ferrall (w).

ELMORE, ANDREW and Mary M. Wolf*, of New London, bond 12 January 1801.
Andrew Elmore (b) and James Boaz (b).

ENGLAND, ISAAC and Mary Burley, bond 20 February 1789. Consent by W.
Garsy Burley, father of the bride. Isaac England (b) and Champion
Wilson (b); Isaac England (w) and Champion Wilson (w).

ENGLAND, JOSEPH and Nancy Burley*, bond 3 January 1788. Joseph England
(b) and William Williamson (b). M.R. 24 January 1788 by Charles
Clay lists the bride as Nancy Burnley.

EPPERSON, LITTLEBERRY and Polly Callaway, bond 23 December 1807. Consent
by Joseph Callaway, father of the bride. Littleberry Epperson (b)
and John Monroe (b). M.R. 23 December 1807 by Edmund Johns.

EPPERSON, RICHARD and Rebecca Haden, bond 10 September 1798. Consent by
Anthony Haden, father of the bride. Richard Epperson (b) and David
Spencer (b); David Spencer (w).

EPPERSON, WILLIAM and Mary Barlow, bond 2 January 1792. Consent by
Thomas Barlow, father of the bride. William Epperson (b) and
Henry Ridgeway (b). M.R. ___ January 1792 by Charles Cobbs.

EVANS, ANTHONY and Mary Boyer (Bowyer), bond 20 October 1792. Consent
by Adam Boyer, father of the bride. Anthony Evans (b) and Lewis
Speece (b); Robert Snoddy (w) and Lewis Speece (w). Marriage
Register Vol. I, 1782- gives the bride's name as Bayer.

EVANS, GEORGE and Polly Bryan, bond 12 October 1808. Consent by Andrew
M. Bryan, father of the bride. George Evans (b) and James Bryan (b);
Thomas Bryan (w) and James Bryan (w). M.R. 12 October 1808 by
Edmund Johns.

EVANS, JOHN and Keziah Bailey, bond 2 October 1788. John Evans (b) and
Edward Woodman (b). M.R. not dated in original Register but entered
after the 15 August 1788 entries, by James Kenney.

EVANS, JOHN and Susanna Tuppence, daughter of James Tuppence, bond 18
October 1806. John Evans (b) and James Tuppence (b).

EVANS, WILLIAM and Jane Mackey*, bond 29 November 1808. William Evans (b)
and William Powar (b); Helen Powar (w) and William Powar (w).

EVE, GEORGE and Patsey Jones, daughter of Thomas Jones, bond 11 January
1806. George Eve (b) and Thomas Jones (b).

F

FARIS, CLAIBORNE, and Martha Ratekin, bond 8 August 1805. Consent by
Rachel Ratekin, mother of the bride. Claiborne Faris (b) and Archer
Williamson (b); Archer Williamson (w). M.R. ___ August 1805 by Edmund
Johns.

FARIS, JOHN and Mary Key, bond 14 November 1789. Consent by Jacob Key, also by William Faris. John Faris (b) and Daniel Jones (b).

FARIS, JOHN and Agatha Seay, bond 2 December 1790. Consent by Francis Callaway, father of the bride. John Faris (b) and Francis Callaway (b).

FARIS, JOHN and Sabra Hix, bond 23 November 1801. Consent by John Hix. John Faris (b) and John Hix (b); John Hix, Jr. (w) and Elizabeth Page Dence(?) (w).

FARIS, WILLIAM AMOSS and Elizabeth Key, bond 3 April 1793. Consent by William Faris, and also by Jacob Key, father of the bride. William A. Faris (b) and Charles Timberlake (b). M.R. __ June 1793 by John Chappell who gives the groom's name as William Amos Faris.

FARMER, JAMES and Elizabeth Arthur, bond 2 February 1792. Consent by Wm. Arther. James Farmer (b) and John A. Anthony (b); Wm. Wheat (w). M.R. 9 February 1792 by James Kenney.

FERGUSON, JOSEPH and Elizabeth Narples, bond ___ 1792. Consent by George Narples, father of the bride, and by Andrew Ferguson, father of the groom. Consents dated August 1792. Joseph Ferguson (b) and William Weber (b); Bernard Finch (w), Arter Litchford (w), Christian Weisenberg (w) and David Harlin (w).

FERRELL, WILLIAM and Mary Bangham, bond 7 June 1792. William Ferrell (b) and John Bangham (b).

FIELD, DANIEL and Rachel Hunter, bond 11 April 1808. Consent by John Hunter, father of the bride. Daniel Field (b) and Andrew Stanton (b); John Hunter (w). M.R. 11 April 1808 by Edmund Johns.

FIELDS, DAVID and Rocksianny Twopence, colour, bond 30 November 1807. Consent by Patsey Mosbey, mother of the bride. Joseph Cooper (b) and David Fields (b); Joseph Cooper (w).

FINCH, BARNET (BERNARD) and Sally Webber (Weber), bond 30 July 1804. Consent by John Weber. Barnet (Barnit) Finch (b) and Martin Weber (b). M.R. 1 August 1804 by Henry Brown lists the groom as Bernard Finch.

FINCH, BLAGDON, JR. and Jane Daun, bond 13 June 1798. Consent by Margit Daun. Blagdon Finch, Jr. (b) and Nelson Brooks (b); Nelson Brooks (w) and Thomas Brooks (w). M.R. __ June 1798 by Charles Cobbs.

FINCH, JOHN and Mary Weber, bond 9 March 1796. Consent by John Weber. John Finch (b) and John Weber, Jr. (b); John Weber, Jr. (w). M.R. 30 March 1796 lists the bride as Nancy Webber, by Menoah Lesley.

FITCH, SAMUEL and Jane McIver, daughter of James McIvar, bond 27 February 1804. Samuel Fitch (b) and James McIvar (b). M.R. 1 March 1804 by William Flowers.

FLEMING, DAVID and Elizabeth Franklin, daughter of Thomas Franklin, bond 14 January 1805. David Fleming (b) and Thomas Franklin (b). M.R. 14 January 1805 by William P. Martin.

FLEMING, JOHN and Mary Campbell. M.R. 14 July 1800 by Arch McRoberts.

FLEMING, JOHN and Janet Franklin, bond 15 March 1804. John Fleming (b) and Thomas Franklin (b). M.R. 15 March 1804 by William P. Martin lists the bride as Jane Franklin.

FLOWERS, SAMUEL and Milly Thomas, bond 9 July 1804. Consent by James Thomas. Samuel Flowers (b) and William Thomas (b); William Thomas (w). M.R. 22 July 1804 by James Denton.

FORE, PETER and Tabitha Harvey, daughter of William Harvey, bond 18 January 1809. Peter Fore (b) and William Harvey (b).

FORSEE, DANIEL and Naomi Flowers, daughter of Valentine Flowers, bond 28 May 1805 [sic]. Daniel Forsee (b) and Valentine Flowers (b). M.R. 13 May 1805 by William Flowers, Jr. lists the groom as Daniel Foshee.

FOSDICK, GEORGE and Mary Strong, bond 5 August 1809. Consent by Keturah Weber, mother of the bride. George Fosdick (b) and Peter Weber (b); Peter Weber (w) and John Strong (w). M.R. 6 August 1809 by James Warner.

FOSHER, JOHN and Elizabeth Landis, bond 17 December 1804. Consent by Henry Landis, father of the bride. John Fosher (b) and James Hicks (b); James Hicks (w) and Lewis Speece (w).

FOWLER, CHRISTOPHER and Conway Oglesby*, bond 12 November 1803. Christopher Fowler (b) and William Fowler (b); William Fowler (w).

FOWLER, JOHN and Vinetta Webb, bond 9 December 1810. Consent by Jesse Webb, father of the bride. John Fowler (b) and George Eve, Jr. (b); George Eve (w) and George Martin (w). M.R. 13 December 1810 by S.K.Jennings lists the bride's first name as Vinestra.

FOX, GEORGE and Susanna Oglesby, bond 27 September 1808 [sic]. Consent by David Oglesby, father of the bride. George Fox (b) and Gregory Blossom (þ); Gregory Blossom (w) and Lodowick McDaniel (w). M.R. 27 September 1809 by William P. Martin lists the bride as Susanna Oglesvie.

FOX, JAMES and Sarah Nigley*, both of "lawful age," bond 10 August 1795. Consent certified by George and Richard Fox. James Fox (b) and Harden Chewning (b); Richard Fox (w), George Fox (w) and Harden Chewning (w). M.R. 15 August 1796 by Menoah Lesley.

FOX, RICHARD and Patience Condrey, daughter of William Condrey, bond 16 August 1796. Richard Fox (b) and William Condrey (b). M.R. 19 August 1796 by Menoah Lesley.

FOX, THOMAS and Martha Harris, bond 14 January 1805. Consent by William
Harris, father of the bride. Thomas Fox (b) and Jonathan Butler (b);
Betsey Butler (w) and Jonathan Butler (w). M.R. 17 January 1805 by
Henry Brown.

FOX, THOMAS and Martha Cock, bond 10 October 1808. Consent by George Cock,
father of the bride. Thomas Fox (b) and William Cock (b); Thomas
Fox (w) and William Cock (w).

FRANKLIN, HENRY and Sally Davis, bond 4 June 1788. Henry Franklin (b)
and John Davis (b).

FRANKLIN, JOHN and Anne Dinwiddie, bond 14 December 180_?_. Consent by
Frances Dinwiddie, mother of the bride. [Anne's name also signed].
John Franklin (b) and Thomas Franklin (b); Pruden Moore (w) and John
Dinwiddie (w). M.R. 17 December 1801 by Henry Brown.

FRANKLIN, JOHN and Sarah Clark, M.R. ___ 1783 by John Anthony.

FRANKLIN, PETER and Sally Farthing, bond 10 May 1802. Peter Franklin (b)
and William Farthing (b).

FRANKLIN, ROBERT and Mary Perrow, daughter of Daniel B. Perrow, bond
8 December 1800. Robert Franklin (b) and Daniel B. Perrow (b).
M.R. 22 December 1800 by Henry Brown.

FRANKLIN, THOMAS and Leticia Evans, bond 3 March 1796. Consent by Riece
Evans, father of the bride. Thomas Franklin (b) and W. Alexander (b);
Daniel Evans (w) and John Bryan (w). M.R. ___ 1796 by William Mahon.

FRASHIER, DANIEL and Rhoda Angel* ("of age"), bond 1 March 1803. Daniel
Frazier (b) and Pendleton Hendrick (b); Pendleton Hendrick (w) and
Thomas Frazor (w). M.R. 3 March 1803 by Henry Brown lists the bride
and groom as Daniel Frazier and Rhoda Angell.

FRASHIER, ELIJAH and Lucy Ray*, ("of age"), bond 5 June 1802. Elijah
Frashier (b) and Pendleton Hendrick (b); Radford Connefax (w) and
Pendleton Hendrick (w). M.R. 10 June 1802 by Henry Brown lists the
bride as Lucy Wray.

FRASHIER, THOMAS and Elizabeth Storer, daughter of Edward Storer, bond
25 August 1802. Thomas Frashier (b) and Edward Storer (b). M.R.
25 August 1802 by Henry Brown lists the bride as Elizabeth Story.

FRASHIER, WILLIAM and Polly Angel (Angill)*, ("of age"), bond 28 August
1805. William Frazier (b) and John Frashier (b).

FRAZER, HENRY and Polly L. King, bond 17 ___ 1810. Consent by Shelley
Lee, guardian of Polly King. Henry Frazer (b) and Marstone Clay (b);
Marstone Clay (w) and Sally Clay (w).

FRAZIER, JOSEPH and Rebekah (Rebecca) Turner*, bond 26 December 1797.
Consent names the groom as Joel Frashure. John Frazier (b) and
Alexander Driskill (b); Alexander Driskill (w). M.R. ___December
1797 by Charles Cobbs.

FRAZIER, MICAJAH and Sarah Edds, bond 10 October 1808. Consent by
Thos. Edds, father of the bride. Micajah Frazier (b) and John
Edds (b); Jesse Edds (w) and John Edds (w). M.R. 27 October 1808
lists the bride as Sarah Ediss, by Matthew Easter.

FREEMAN, MORRIS and Mary Napier (Nappier*) free Negroes bond 30 January 1796. Morris Freeman (b) and Harry Major (b); Harrey Magior (w).
M.R. 2 February 1796 by Jeremiah Hatcher.

Attached to this Freeman-Napier bond is the following:
"I Christopher Johnson being appointed Executor to the Will of
Charles Moorman of Louisa County deceased do hereby certify that
his deed of emancipation to Negro man named Horn now aged about
thirty five years was mislaid at the time of recording the others,
but he was one mentioned in his __?__ Will, and on application
being made to the General Assembly his freedom was confirmed in
1789, agreeable to the intention and request of A. C. Moorman
as directed in his Will given under my hand this 24 day of 1.[1st]
month 1796.

Mr. Morris Freeman is his name in full. C.J."

FRETWELL, LEONARD and Nancy Timberlick, bond 20 October 1810. Consent
by Charles and Nancy Timberlick, parents of the bride. Leonard
Fretwell (b) and Charles Walker (b); Charles Walker (w). M.R.
10 November 1810 by Samuel Davidson lists the groom as Linwood
Fretwell.

G

GALBREATH, SAMUEL and Mary Robinson (Robertson), bond 5 February 1795.
Samuel Galbreath (b) and James Robertson (b).

GALLION, MITCHELL and Levicy Talbot, bond 26 March 1801. Consent by
Williston Talbot, father of the bride. Mitchell Gallion (b) and
Pleasant Talbot (b); John Talbot (w) and Pleasant Talbot (w).
M.R. 26 March 1801 by Henry Brown.

GARDENER (GARDNER), NATHANIEL (batchelor) and Elizabeth Dotson (spinster),
bond 21 August 1787. Consent by Nacy(?) Chilton, mother of the
bride. Nathaniel Gardner (b) and Timothy Barnard (Barnette) (b);
Nacy(?) Chilton (w).

GARDNER, JOHN and Betsy Finch, bond 11 March 1794. Consent by Bernett
Finch, father of the bride. John Gardner (b) and Bernard Hendricks
(b); Bernard Hendricks (w) and Thomas Gregg (w). M.R. 12 March 1794
by Menoah Lesley.

GARRETT (GARROTT), JOSIAH and Elizabeth Williams, bond 30 January 1809. Consent by Anderson Williams, father of the bride. Josiah Garrott (b) and Elijah Garrott (b); John Taylor (w) and Elijah Garrott (w). M.R. 2 February 1809 by Samuel Davidson.

GASH, MICHAEL and Elizabeth Elliott (Ellett)*, bond 18 March 1798. Michael Gash (b) and William Johnson (b); Wm. Johnson (w).

GAUSNEY (GOSNEY), BENJAMIN and Elizabeth Haden, bond 26 December 1786. Consent by Anthony Haden, father of the bride. Benjamin Gosney (b) and Josiah Bullock (b).

GEORGE, BAILEY of Charlotte County and Nancy Crews, bond 24 March 1795. Consent by Josiah and Elizabeth Crews, parents of the bride. Bailey George (b) and William Crews (b); Wm. Crews (w).

GIBBS, PETER and Rebekah Ratekin, bond 20 February 1809. Consent by Rachel Ratekin, mother of the bride. Peter Gibbs (b) and Laurence Ratekin (b); Laurence Ratekin (w). M.R. 20 February 1809 by Edmund Johns.

GIBSON, JOHN and Isabella Robinson, bond 3 January 1793. John Gibson (b) and James Robinson (b). M.R. 8 January 1793 by William Mahon.

GIBSON, ROBERT and Mary Evans. M.R. 18 October 1782 by John W. Holt.

GILBERT, BENJAMIN (batchelor) and Mary Hudson (spinster), bond 10 October 1785. Benjamin Gilbert (b) and Charles Gilbert (b).

GILBERT, BENJAMIN JR. and Milley McKenzie (McKinzie), bond 20 October 1783. Benjamin Gilbert (b) and John Patrick, Jr. (b).

GILBERT, CHARLES and Jenny Haden, bond 7 September 1786. Charles Gilbert (b) and Anthony Haden (b).

GILBERT, JOHN and Patty Scruggs, bond 25 December 1796. John Gilbert (b) and Drury Scruggs (b). M.R. ___ 1796 by Charles Cobbs.

GILBERT, MICHAEL and Anne Allegre, bond 19 June 1786. Consent by Matthew Allegre, father of the bride. Michael Gilbert (b) and James Carver(b). M.R. 25 June 1786 by James Kenney lists the bride and groom as Micajah Gilbert and Ann Aligre.

GILBERT, SAMUEL and Fanny Rosser, bond 22 June 1789. Consent by Jonathan Rosser, father of the bride. Samuel Gilbert (b) and William Rosser (b). M.R. no date given but entered in original Register after entries for 31 March 1789, by James Kenney.

GILCHRIST, CHARLES and Nancy Callaway, bond 2 February 1808. Consent by Joseph Callaway, father of the bride. Charles Gilchrist (b) and John Moore (b); John Moore (w). M.R. 2 February 1808 by Edmund Johns.

GILES, PERRIN and Elizabeth Wright*, daughter of Robert Wright, Sr.,
bond 23 April 1800. Perrin Giles (b) and Robert Wright, Sr. (b);
Anny Wright (w) and Robert Wright (w). M.R. This return entered
three times in the original Register under date of 27 April 1800,
by William Flowers.

GILES, PERRIN and Sarah Dickey, bond 10 November 1806. Consent by
Edward Dickey, father of the bride. Perrin Giles (b) and John
Dickey (b); John Dickey (w).

GILLESPIE, CHARLES and Elizabeth Carson, bond 18 November 1794. Consent
by William Carson, Sr., father of the bride. Charles Gilespie (b)
and Thomas Gregg (b); Peter Lang (w). M.R. 21 November 1794 by
Menoah Lesley lists the groom as Charles Gillispie.

GILLIAM, JAMES and Sally McKinney, bond 30 July 1800. Consent by John
McKine, father of the bride. James Gilliam (b) and John Hubbard (b).

GILLIAM, PATTESON and Elizabeth Walrond, bond 23 February 1805. Consent
by Benjamin Walrond, father of the bride. Patteson Gilliam (b) and
John Walrond (b); John Walrond (w).

GLASS, CHARLES (batchelor) and Nancy Listern (spinster), bond 16 April
1785. Consent by Catharine Listern, mother of the bride. Charles
Glass (b) and Reubin Simmons (b).

GLASS, JAMES and Dorothea Jones, bond 25 November 1803. Consent by
Thomas Jones, father of the bride. James Glass (b) and Thomas J.
Cock (b); John Hunter (w) and Thomas J. Cock (w). M.R. __ November
1803 by Edmund Johns.

GLASS, JOHN and Betsy Webb, bond 21 December 1807. John Glass (b) and
Edmund Webb (b).

GLASS, VINCENT and Susanna Listin, bond 6 January 1790. Consent by
Charles Simmons and Caty Listin. Vincent Glass, Jr. (b) and Nathan
Tanner (b). M.R. 7 January 1790 by William Flowers.

GLASS, VINCENT and Nancy Rosser (Roser)*, bond 28 November 1796. Vincent
Glass, Sr. (b) and Vincent Glass, Jr. (b); Vincent Glass, Jr. (w).
M.R. __ November 1796 by Charles Cobbs lists Vincent Glass, Sr. and
Nancy Roser as the bride and groom.

GLASS, VINCENT and Elizabeth Grishaw, bond 26 October 1809. Consent by
Isaac Grishaw, father of the bride. Vincent Glass (b) and William
Moore (b); Nathaniel Tanner (w) and William Moore (w). M.R. 26 Oc-
tober 1809 by Obadiah Edge.

GLASS, WILLIAM and Lavina Rosser, bond 21 December 1796. Consent by
Nancy Glass. William Glass (b) and Vincent Glass, Jr. (b);
William Rosser (w) and Vincent Glass, Jr. (w). M.R. __ 1796 by
Charles Cobbs.

GLAZEBROOK, JULIUS of Charlotte County and Mary Kevil*, bond 23 December 1790. John Brown (b) and Julius Glazebrook (b); John Brown (w). M.R. 23 December 1790 by Menoah Lesley.

GOAD, THOMAS of Bedford County and Juley Toler, bond 19 January 1793. Thos. Leftwick certifies the bride is of age and has neither parents nor guardian. Edmund Toler (b) and Thomas Goad (b).

GODSEE, HENRY and Margaret Davidson (Davison)*, bond 29 September 1810. Henry Godsee (b) and Charles Caffery (b); Charles Godfry (w) and John Davison (w). M.R. 1 October 1810 by Samuel Davidson lists the bride and groom as Marget Davidson and Henry Godsy.

GOGGIN, ROBERT and Sally Irvine, bond 6 February 1794. Consent by David Irvine, father of the bride. Robert Goggin (b) and Robert Irvine (b); Robert Irvine (w).

GOGINS, RICHARD and Nancy Irvine. M.R. 2 October 1791 by Menoah Lesley.

GOLDING, JACOB and Rachel Martin, bond 30 July 1810. Thomas Martin, father of the bride, certifies she is of age and can consent for self, but he also consents. Jacob Golding (b) and James Martin (b); Janie Martin (w). M.R. 31 July 1810 by Obadiah Edge lists the groom as Jacob Galding.

GOOCH, THOMAS, JR. and Tabitha Arthur*, bond 2 April 1789. Thomas Gooch (b) and Thomas Gooch, Jr. (b). M.R. no date given but is listed in the original Register after entries for 31 March 1789, by James Kenny.

GOODE, ROBERT and Martha W. Scott, bond 14 September 1801. Consent by William Scott, father of the bride. Robert Goode (b) and George Cabell (b); George Cabell (w) and Gabriel Scott (w).

GOODMAN, GIBSON and Elizabeth Crawley, bond 1 June 1786. Consent by John Crawley. Gibson Goodman (b) and William Peck (b); John Goodman (w). M.R. __ June 1786 by James Kenney.

GOODMAN, JOHN and Elizabeth Howeth*, bond 26 October 1791. John Goodman (b) and Ambrose Ambrose (b); Ambrose Ambrose (w). M.R. 29 October 1791 by James Kenney lists the bride as Elizabeth Howette.

GOOLSBY, ARTHUR and Polly C. Anthony, bond 2 January 1794. Consent by John Anthony, father of the bride. Arthur Goolsby (b) and Benjamin Haden (b); W.B. Anthony (w) and William Arthur (w). M.R. 3 January 1794 by Joseph Drury lists the bride as Mary Crenshaw Anthony.

GORDON, JOHN and Virlinchige Wooldridge, bond 28 January 1807. Consent by Buhard Wooldridge, father of the bride. John Gordon (b) and William Wooldridge (b); William Wooldridge, Sr. (w) and William Wooldridge, Jr. (w).

GORDON, JOHN M. and Agnes W. Scott, bond 13 December 1804. Consent by
Samuel Scott. John Gordon (b) and Samuel Telford (b); James Mosely
(w) and Wm. Harrison (w). M.R. 15 December 1805 by William P.
Martin.

GOSNELL, BENJAMIN and Elizabeth Barlow, bond 8 July 1789. Thomas Barlow
(b) and Benjamin Gosnell (b). M.R. 9 July 1789 by James Hurt, lists
the groom as Benjamin Gosnall.

GOSNELL, WILLIAM and Jane Barlow, bond 1 March 1788. Consent by Thos.
Barlow, father of the bride. William Gosnell (b) and Benjamin
Gosnell (b).

GREEN, WILLIAM and Judith Ann Gordon, bond 2 February 1792. Giles
Gordon (b) and William Green (b). M.R. 6 February 1792 by Bennett
Maxey.

GREENWOOD, BARTLETT (batchelor) and Nancy Sublett (spinster)*, bond
11 October 1785. Bartlette Greenwood (b) and Thomas Rodgers (b);
Sam Rogers (w). M.R. 11 October 1785 by John Anthony. This
minister's return seems to have been written in the record at a
much later date, since it's written between the lines, and with
different ink.

GREGORY, JOHN, JR. and Nancy Dobson, bond 29 November 1806. Consent by
William Dobson, father of the bride. John Gregory, Jr. (b) and
Anthony Christian (b); William Lamb (w) and Anthony Christian (w).
M.R. 30 November 1806 by James Warner.

GREGORY, PETER and Polly Dobson*, bond 29 November 1806. Consent also
by William Dobson, father of the bride. Peter Gregory (b) and
Anthony Christian (b); Wm. Lamb (w) and Anthony Christian (w).
M.R. 30 November 1806 by James Warner.

GREGORY, RICHARD and Margaret Lindsay, bond 26 December 1798. Richard
Gregory (b) and Robert Lindsay (b).

GRESHAM, WILLIAM and Jemima Finch, daughter of Blagdon Finch, bond 30
January 1797. William Gresham (b) and Blagdon Finch (b). M.R.
__ February 1797 by Charles Cobbs.

GRIFFITH, WILLIAM and Susannah Wooton, bond 8 July 1793. William
Griffith (b) and John Philips (b). M.R. 10 July 1793 by Menoah
Lesley.

GRISHAM, ISAAC and Mary Copeland (Coplen)*, bond 24 October 1808. Isaac
Grisham (b) and Robert Cardwell (b); Robert Cardwell (w) and Thomas
Coplen (Copeland) (w). M.R. 29 October 1808 by Matthew Easter lists
the groom as Isaac Gresham.

GUTHREY, WILLIAM and Rachel Jones, bond 4 August 1808. William Guthrey
(b) and Thomas Jones (b). M.R. 17 August 1808 by John Chappell.

GUY, JOHN and Milly Dearing (Deering), bond ___ 1803. Consent by James
Deering, father of the bride, is dated 10 November 1803. John Guy
(b) and Jonathan White (b). M.R. 13 November 1803 by Henry Brown
lists the bride as Milly Deering.

H

HAAS, FREDERICK and Lucy Teass, bond 25 April 1808. Frederick Haas (b)
and John Teass (b). M.R. 28 April 1808 by James Mitchell lists the
groom as Frederick Hass.

HACKETT, ISAAC and Lucy Napier, bond 4 January 1792. Consent by Charles
Napier, father of the bride. Isaac Hackett (b) and Humphrey Bobson
(b); Humphrey Bobson (w).

HACKETT, JOSEPH and Winney Roberts   free Negroes   bond 4 December 1785.
Consent by John Lynch. Joseph Hackett (b) and Frank Freeman (b);
John Coplin(?) (w) and Mich Moorman (w).

HADEN, JAMES C. and Nancy Johns, bond 5 December 1809. Consent by Edmund
Johns, father of the bride. James C. Haden (b) and Edmund Brown (b);
William T. Johns (w) and Edmund Brown (w). M.R. 5 December 1809 by
Edmund Johns.

HADEN, JOHN and Rachel Reynolds, bond 12 January 1793 [1798?]. Consent
by Isaac Reynolds, father of the bride, who names the groom as John
Hayden. Samuel Terrell (b) and John Haden (b). M.R. 17 January 1793
by Menoah Lesley.

HAINES, JOHN and Judith Mitchell, bond 23 February 1798. Consent by Richard
Vaughn, guardian and grandfather of the bride. John Haines (b) and
Edmund Johns (b); John Heynes (w). M.R. __ February 1798 by Charles
Cobbs lists the groom as John Hains.

HALE, WILLIAM and Sarah Quarles, bond 7 April 1791:1795. Consent by Sarah
Quarles, mother of the bride. William Hale (b) and John Dabney (b);
John Dabney (w) and Lucy Quarles (w).

HALL, JOHN and Elizabeth Perry, bond 18 October 1806. Consent by John
Perry and John Hall. John Hall (b) and Pleasant Cannady (Canady)
(b); John Wright (w) and Pleasant Cannady (w).

HALL, THOMAS and Betsy McCoy, bond 10 March 1806. Consent by Daniel
McCoy, father of the bride. Thomas Hall (b) and John Arnold (b);
John Arnold (w).

HALL, WILLIAM (batchelor) and Elizabeth Campbell (spinster), bond 1 March
1787. Consent by Archibald Campbell, father of the bride. William
Hall (b) and Charles Hall (b); Wm. Campbell (w) and Samuel Campbell
(w). M.R. 5 March 1787 by Archibald McRoberts.

HAMBLETON, BENJAMIN and Elizabeth Trent, bond 22 November 1800. Consent
by Elijah Trent, father of the bride. Henry Trent (b) and Benjamin
Hambleton (b); Henry Trent (w) and John Trent (w). M.R. 27 November
1800 by Henry Brown.

HAMERSLY, RICHARD and Lucy Hamlet, bond 11 May 1807. James Hamlet (b) and Richard Hamersley (b).

HAMILTON (HAMBLETON), JAMES and Keziah McCoun (?)*, bond 5 June 1802. Consent by Kiziah McCoun. Benjamin Moore (b) and James Hamilton (b); John Morgan (w) and Benjamin Moore (w).

HAMMERSLEY, WILLIAM and Susanna Jones (listed in error as Johns on bond), bond 2 December 1800. Thomas Jones (b) and William Hammersley (b). M.R. 22 December 1800 by John Chappell lists the bride as Susannah Jones.

HAMMOCK (HAMMOND), LEWIS and Betsy Harvey, daughter of William Harvey, bond 4 December 1797. Lewis Hammond (b) and William Harvey (b). M.R. 20 December 1797 by Obadiah Edge.

HANKS, ABRAHAM and Lucy Jennings. M.R. 2 April 1799 by John Chappell.

HANKS, THOMAS and Nancy Brooks. M.R. __ October 1792 by Charles Cobbs.

HANNAH, JAMES and Martha Bailey, bond 20 February 1808. Consent by Savage Bailey, father of the bride. James Hannah (b) and John Reynolds (b); Robert Strong (w) and John Reynolds (w).

HARAWAY, EPPA and Mary Herndon, daughter of Edmund Herndon, bond 24 February 1809. Eppa Haraway (b) and Edmund Herndon (b).

HARDAWAY, DRURY and Martha Hall, bond 19 December 1799. Consent by Martha Hall, mother of the bride. John Dill (b) and Drury Hardaway (b); John Dill (w).

HARDWICK, WILLIAM and Patsey Mann. M.R. 31 January 1810 by Obadiah Edge. Bond in files dated January 31, 1811 - so not included.

HARGROVE, WILLIAM and Patty Watkins, bond 4 March 1808. Consent by Mosey Watkins, father of the bride. William Hargrove (b) and Archer Williamson (b); Reece Watkins (w) and Archer Williamson (w). M.R. 6 March 1808 by Obadiah Edge lists the bride and groom as William Hartgrove and Patsey Watkins.

HARRIS, CHARLES and Mary Calihan, bond 2 September 1784. Charles Harris (b) and Robert Adams (w).

HARRIS, JOHN and Elizabeth Pryor. M.R. 19 ___ 1800 by William Flowers. This minister's return is entered three times in the original Register. One entry spells the bride's name as Elizabeth Prior.

HARRIS, JOHN and Sally Mann, bond 17 October 1801. Consent by Nancy Thopson. Joel Mann (b) and John Harris (b); Joel Mann (w), Love Stratham (w), and Mathew Thopson (w). M.R. 6 November 1801, by William Flowers.

HARRIS, NATHAN and Elizabeth Burley, bond 26 December 1791. Consent by
Gracie(?) Burley, mother of the bride. Nathan Harris (b) and Isaac
England (b); Titus England (w).

HARRIS, WILLIAM and Jane Butterworth. M.R. 23___ 1782 by John W. Holt.

HARRIS, WILLIAM and Rosanna Hutchings, bond 28 December 1790. Consent by
Drury Hutchings, father of the bride. William Harris (b) and Bernard
Cheatham (b); Bearnet Cheatham (w).

HARRISON, JOSEPH and Mary Ann Gregory, bond 23 November 1791. Consent by
John and Nelley Gregory. James Turnley, Jr. (b) and Joseph Harrison
(b); James Turnley, Jr. (w). M.R. 25 ___ 1791 by William Dameron.

HARRISON, SAMUEL J. and Sally Burton, bond 31 January 1801. Consent by
Alexander Burton, brother of the bride. Samuel J. Harrison (b) and
William Burton, Jr. (b); W. Harrison (w) and Will Burton, Jr. (w).
M.R. 4 February 1801 by William P. Martin.

HARRISON, SAMUEL JORDAN and Ann S. Scott, bond 12 March 1798. Consent by
William Scott, father of the bride. Samuel Jordan Harrison (b) and
John F. Powell (b); Samuel Scott (w) and John F. Powell (w).

HARVEY, ISHAM and Elizabeth Fore, daughter of John Fore, bond 12 March 1810.
Isham Harvey (b) and John Fore (b). M.R. 15 March 1810 by Obadiah
Edge lists the groom as Sim Harvey.

HARVEY, JESSE and Sally Johnson, bond 2 July 1789. Jesse Harvey (b) and
John Johnson (b). M.R. not dated but listed after 31 March 1789
entries in the original Register, by James Kenney.

HARVEY, RICHARD and Peggy Field, bond 12 September 1803. Consent by
Margaret Field, mother of the bride. Richard Harvey (b) and Benjamin
Hunter (b); Betsy Field (w) and Ben Hunter (w).

HARVEY, THOMAS, JR. of Charlotte County and Ann Wilson*, bond 25 April 1792.
Consent also by Mary Wilson, mother of the bride. Thomas Harvey, Jr.
(b) and Thomas Wilson (b); Thomas Wilson (w). M.R. 26 April 1792 by
William Mahon.

HARVIE, JACK D. and Clarisa Reid, bond 25 December 1807. Consent by John
Reid, father of the bride. Jack D. Harvie (b) and Theodore Reid (b);
William W. Williamson (w) and Theodore Reid (w).

HATCHER, HENRY and Judith Baber, bond 12 December 1793. Consent by William
Anderson who says, "... Mr. Hatcher has applyed to me for a few lines
to you. I can only say that she [Judith Baber] has lived in my house
for some time past and has been to herself for two years and there is
no objection to the match. Therefore will thank you to issue the
license..." George Baber (b) and Henry Hatcher (b). M.R. 19 December
1793 by Joseph Drury lists the bride as Judith Beaver.

HAWKINS, LITTLEBERRY and Jane Shearer, bond 18 June 1794. Consent by James Shearer, father of the bride. Littleberry Hawkins (b) and Richard W. Hix (b); Samuel Fleming (w) and Richard Taylor (w). M.R. 5 July 1794 by Menoah Lesley.

HAWKINS, WILLIAM and Nancy Suttenfield (Sutinfield), bond 29 December 1791. Consent by James Shearer, step-father of the bride. William Hawkins (b) and Richard Hix (b); Samuel Fleming (w) and Joseph Hawkins (w). M.R. 1 January 1792 by Menoah Lesley.

HAYS, JOHN and Nancy Russell, bond 10 February 1806. Consent by James Russell, father of the bride. John Hays (b) and Gerrard Dougherty (b); Gerard Daugherty (w) and William Russell (w).

HAYTH, WILLIAM and Polly Moorman, daughter of Achillis Moorman, bond 21 October 1800. William Hayth (b) and Achillis Moorman (b). M.R. 23 October 1800 by Henry Brown.

HAZELWOOD, BENJAMIN and Sarah Cox, bond 20 September 1790. Consent by John Cox, father of the bride. Benjamin Hazelwood (b) and Publius Jones (b); Publius Jones (w).

HAZLEWOOD, RICHARD and Sally East*, "of age," bond 30 January 1796. Richard Hazlewood (b), Thomas East (b) and Ezekiel East (b); Ezekiel East (w) and Thos. East (w). M.R. ___ 1796 by James Kenny.

HAZLEWOOD, THOMAS and Martha Hix, bond 23 May 1792. Consent by T. (or F.) Hix. Thomas Hazlewood (b) and William Hix (b); Wm. Hix (w).

HAZLEWOOD, WILLIAM and Molly Cox, bond 31 January 1786. John Cox (b) and William Hazlewood (b).

HELM, JAMES and Sarah Watkins, daughter of Moses Watkins, bond 11 September 1797. James Helm (b) and Moses Watkins (b).

HENDERSON, DANIEL and Mary Glass, bond 13 July 1786. Consent by Vincent Glass. Daniel Henderson (b) and Vincent Glass (b).

HENDERSON, SAMUEL and Christiana Jones, bond 20 December 1788. Consent by Ann Jones, mother of the bride. Samuel Henderson (b) and Daniel Jones (b); George Jones (w).

HENDRICK, ROBERT and Lucy Moorman, bond 26 January 1798. Consent by Judith Moorman, mother of the bride. Robert Hendrick (b) and Achilles Moorman (b); Achilles Moorman (w).

HENNES, WILLIAM and Nancy Hendrick, bond 10 November 1806. William Hennes (b) and Bernard Hendrick (b).

HERNDON, DANIEL and Eleanor Harvey, bond 20 November 1801. Consent by Edmund Herndon. Daniel Herndon (b) and Edmund Herndon (b). M.R. 20 ___ 1801 by Henry Brown.

HERNDON, JACOB W. and Mary Pannill, bond 13 October 1807. Consent by
Jerh. Pannill. Samuel Pannill (b) and Jacob W. Herndon (b);
Samuel Pannill (w), Samuel Jonathan (w) and Joshua Nervimon(?) (w).
M.R. 13 October 1807 by Edmund Johns.

HEWSTON, PETER and Mary Suttenfield, bond 6 September 1787. Consent by
Margret Sheras, mother of the bride. Peter Hewston (b) and John
Kennady (b).

HICKS, JAMES and Anny Landers, bond 1 October 1803. Consent by Henry
Landers, father of the bride. James Hicks (b) and John Robertson
(b); John Robertson (w).

HICKS, RICHARD W. and Mildred Hawkins, bond 26 January 1790. Consent by
Robert Hawkins. Richard Hicks (b) and William Hawkins (b); Linch-
field Sharp (w) and William Hawkins (w). M.R. 27 January 1790 by
James Kenney.

HIGHTOWER, GEORGE and Frances Ann Hall, bond 3 February 1796. Consent by
Robert Hall, father of the bride. George Hightower (b) and John
Stith (b); John Stith (w). M.R. ___ February 1796 by Charles Cobbs.

HIGHTOWER, RICHARD and Polly Stith, bond 4 November 1789. Consent by
Richard Stith who says, "Dickey Hightower to take little Poll in
marriage by way of license." Richard Hightower (b) and John Stith (b).
M.R. 5 November 1789 by James Hurt.

HILEY, JAMES and Nancy Mayberry, bond 4 May 1786. Consent by William
Hiley, father of the groom. James Hiley (b) and Sackville King (b);
Sam Paul (w).

HILL, REUBIN and Polly Wooldridge, bond 10 January 1803. Consent by James
Wooldridge, father of the bride. Reubin Hill (b) and Richard Wooldridge
(b); Richard Wooldridge (w), Daniel Wooldridge (w), Mary Wooldridge (w).
M.R. 13 January 1803 by Philip Matthews.

HINES, JAMES and Caroline B. Ramsey*, bond 28 September 1805. James Hines
(b) and Richard Clark (b). Henry Hines, Jr. (w) and Ann E. Ramsey (w).
M.R. 28 September 1804 by William P. Martin lists the bride as Caroline
D. Ramsey.

HINGE, AMBROSE and Jane Chandler, bond 6 August 1789. Consent by Abraham
Chandler, father of the bride. Ambrose Hinge (b) and Simon Wooldridge
(b); Simon Wooldridge (w). M.R. 14 August 1789 by Joshua Worley
lists the bride as Jane Candler.

HINGS, PEYTON and Sally Jones, bond 20 January 1808. Consent by Robert
Frankling. Peyton Hings (b) and Lewis Franklin, Jr. (b); Lewis
Frankling (w). M.R. 21 January 1808 by John Baldwin lists the groom
as Paton Hings.

HINSON, CHARLES and Abigail Steen*, bond 14 August 1792. Charles Hinson
(b) and James Clark (b); Joseph Nichols (w) and Marget Frasher (w).

HINTON, WILLIAM and Jemima Daniel, bond 9 August 1796. Consent by Peter
Daniel, Mary Daniel and Jemiah Daniel. William Hinton (b), and
Peter Daniel (b). M.R. ___ August 1796 by Charles Cobbs.

HIX, JOHN and Mildred Lucas*, bond 22 August 1808. The consent signed
by the bride states "this is to certify that I am about to join
myself in the holy state of matrimony with John Hix in Preference
to any man of my acquaintance. Above all difficulties that may
arise, I will cheerfully surmount them." John Hix (b) and John
Faris (b); James Hurt (w).

HIX (HICKS), RICHARD W. and Elizabeth Blankinship, bond 27 May 1802.
Consent by Hudson H. Blankinship, father of the bride. Richard
Hicks (b) and Archibald Blankenship (b); Robt. W. Johnston (w).
M.R. May 1802 by Henry Brown lists the groom as Richard Hicks.

HOCKADAY, ISAAC and Amelia Irvine, bond 29 March 1796. Consent by David
Irvine, father of the bride. Isaac Hockaday (b) and Robert Irvine (b);
Robt. Irvine (w) and Magdaline Pane (w). M.R. 3 April 1796 by Menoah
Lesley.

HODGES, CHARLES and Lavina Gilbert. M.R. 25 April 1792 by Menoah Lesley.

HOLDER, ELIJAH and Sophia Lamb*, bond 26 June 1809. Elijah Holder (b)
and John Gregory (b); Henry Weber (w) and John Gregory, Jr. (w).
M.R. 27 June 1809 by James Warner.

HOLLADAY, DAVID and Ann Lee, bond 22 May 1810. Consent by John Lee, Sr.,
father of the bride. David Holladay (b) and Stephen Lee (b);
Stephen Lee (w) and Polley Lee (w).

HOLLEY, JAMES and Ann Williamson, bond 19 November 1791. Consent by
Elizabeth and William Williamson. James Holley (b) and Henry Williamson (b); George Guttery (w) and Nathan Williamson (w). M.R. 24 ___
1791 by William Dameron.

HOLLOWAY, ISAAC and Elizabeth Haws*, bond 25 November 1795. Isaac
Holloway (b) and Thomas Smith (b); Henry Candler (w) and Thos.
Smith (w). M.R. 26 November 1796 by Menoah Lesley lists the bride
and groom as Isaac Halloway and Elizabeth Hayes.

HOLT, ASA and Susanna Mason, bond 7 November 1804. Asa Holt (b) and
William Mason (b).

HOLT, LEONARD and Judith (Juda) Mason, bond 28 September 1800. Consent
by William Mason, Sr. Leonard Holt (b) and Daniel Driskill (b);
Joel Mason (w) and James Mason (w).

HOOD, ALEXANDER and Jane Lain, bond 3 November 1807. Consent by Betsey
Lain, mother of the bride. Alexander Hood (b) and John Hood (b);
John Hood (w) and John Laine (w).

HOOD, JOHN and Nancy Lane*, bond 24 December 1800. John Hood (b) and
William Weaver (b); William Hood (w). M.R. 24 ___ 1800 by John
Chappell.

HOOD, JOHN and Lucy Wilson*, bond 1 May 1793. Ely Brien (b) and John
Hood (b); Ely Brien (w). M.R. ___ May 1793 by Charles Cobbs.

HOOD, WILLIAM and Polly Jackson*, bond 3 March 1800. William Hood (b)
and James Hancock (b); James Hancock (w) and John Hood (w).

HOPKINS, WILLIAM and Polly N. Haden, bond 17 September 1806. Consent by
Benjamin Haden, father of the bride. William Hopkins (b) and John
D. Haden (b); John D. Haden (w).

HOPWOOD, JOHN and Fanny Paterson (Patterson), bond 27 July 1801. Consent
by William and Nancy Baber, parents of the bride. John Hopwood (b)
and William Baber (b); Samuel Clemens (w).

HOSKINS, THOMAS and Betsy Marshall, bond 19 July 1790. Thomas Hoskins (b)
and William Marshall (b). M.R. 4 August 1790 by James Hurt.

HOWERTON, GEORGE and Penelope Stovall, bond 20 August 1810. Consent by
John Stovall, father of the bride. George Howerton (b) and William
Hudson (b); William Hudson (w). M.R. 2 August 1810 by Samuel
Davidson.

HUBBARD, JAMES and Mary Mackey, bond 8 April 1799. Consent by Mary
Mackay, mother of the bride. James Hubbard (b) and John Morcheson (b);
Conrad Spence, Jr. (w) and John Morcheson (w).

HUBBARD, JOHN and Hannah Reid, bond 20 December 1785. Consent by William
Read [Reid], father of the bride. John Hubbard (b) and Hanna Reid (b);
Barnett Finch (w). M.R. 22 December 1785 by James Kenney lists the
bride as Hannah Reid. Rather interesting that Miss Reid is one of
the bondsmen.

HUBBARD, JOHN and Mary McKinney, bond 29 June 1799. Consent by John
McKinney, Sr., father of the bride. John Hubbard (b) and Henry
McKinney (b); William McKinney (w) and Henry McKinney (w).

HUBBARD, NATHANIEL and Sarah Hix, daughter of John Hix, bond 5 September
1796. Nathaniel Hubbard (b) and John Hix (b). M.R. ___ September
1796 by Charles Cobbs lists the groom as Nat Hubbard.

HUBBARD, WILLIAM and Polly Reed (Read), daughter of William Reed (Read),
bond 24 May 1807. William Hubbard (b) and William Reed (Read) (b).
M.R. 24 May 1807 by Edmund Johns lists the bride as Polly Black.

HUDSON, JOHN B. and Elizabeth Calloway, bond 10 April 1802. John B.
Hudson (b) and Joseph Calloway (b).

HUDSON, THOMAS and Frances West, daughter of John West, bond 22 May 1801.
Thomas Hudson (b) and John West (b).

HUGHES, DAVID and Elizabeth Frasier, daughter of William Frasier, bond
1 October 1805. David Hughs (b) and William Frasier (b).

HUGHES, EMORY and Sally Frasier (Freisher), bond 30 October 1809. Consent
by William Freisher, father of the bride. Emory Hughes (b) and
William Frasier (b).

HUGHES, JOHN and Elizabeth Fosdick, daughter of William Fosdick, bond
9 September 1805. John Hughes (b) and William Fosdick (b).

HUGHES, LITTLEBERRY and Mary Walker, bond 9 April 1798. William Walker (b)
and Littleberry Hughes (b). M.R. 3 May 1798 by William Flowers.

HUNT, JOHN of Pittsylvania County and Sally Brown, bond 7 May 1802.
Consent by Polly Brown, mother of the bride. John Hunt (b) and
John Ward, Jr. (b); John Ward, Jr. (w).

HUNTER, ALEXANDER (batchelor) and Nancy Jones (spinster), bond 17 November
1784. Consent by Thomas Jones, Sr. Alexander Hunter (b) and Jesse
Jones (b).

HUNTER, BENJAMIN and Betsy Fields, bond 17 February 1804. Consent by
Magret Fields, mother of the bride. Benjamin Hunter (b) and Oliver
McReynolds (b); Oliver McReynolds (w) and John Hunter (w). M.R.
__ February 1804 by Edmund Johns.

HUNTER, JAMES and Rachel Weber, bond 5 January 1797. Consent by Casper
Weber, father of the bride. James Hunter (b) and Casper Weber (b).
M.R. __ January 1797 by James Kenney lists the bride as Rachel
Webber.

HUNTER, JOHN and Mary Early*, bond 4 February 1790. John Hunter (b)
and Robert Wilson (b); James Hunter (w)   M.R. 5 February 1790 by
James Kenney.

HUNTER, JOHN and Sarah Coffey*, bond 1 September 1800. Consent certified
by Benjamin Cox. John Hunter (b) and Benjamin Cox (b).

HUNTER, JOHN, son of Alexander Hunter, and Nancy Hunter, bond 16 October
1806. Consent by John Hunter, father of the bride. John Hunter (b)
and Benjamin Hunter (b); Ben. Hunter (w). M.R. 19 October 1806 by
Obadiah Edge.

HUNTER, PETER and Sarah Nowlen (Nowlin), bond 12 December 1789. Consent
by Jemima Claywell, mother of the bride. Peter Hunter (b) and
William Patrick (b); Mary Mason (w) and Peter Claywell (w). M.R.
17 December 1790 by James Kenney.

HUNTER, THOMAS and Jemima H. Field, bond 11 October 1810. Consent by
Margaret Field, mother of the bride. Thomas Hunter (b) and John
Hunter (b); John Hunter (w) and Benjamin Hunter (w). M.R. 11 October
1810 by Edmund Johns lists the bride as Jemima Fields.

HUNTER, WILLIAM and Louisa Irvin (Irvine), bond 23 June 1798. Consent by John Irvin, father of the bride. William Hunter (b) and Paulett Clark (b); Polley Irvin (w) and Paulett Clark (w).

HURT, GARLAND and Marshall Thurston. M.R. 22 ___ 1789 by James Hurt.

HURT, JOHN M. and Elizabeth Cock, daughter of George Cock, bond 19 March 1805. John Hurt (b) and George Cock (b).

HUSTON, HENRY (batchelor) and Keziah Criddle (Spinster), bond 2 March 1785. Henry Huston (b) and Charles Timberlake (b).

HUTCHESON (HUTCHERSON), JOHN and Polly Lesley, bond 4 August 1796. John Hutcheson (Hutcherson) (b) and Menoah Lesley (b). M.R. 10 August 1796 by Menoah Lesley lists the groom as John Hutchinson.

HUTCHESON (HUTCHERSON), WILLIAM and Hannah Marshall, bond 6 March 1794. Consent by Thomas Marshall, father of the bride. William Hutcheson (Hutcherson) (b) and Griffin Lewis (b).

HUTS, LEONARD and Sally Owen, bond 26 October 1791. Consent by Phillip Owen, father of the bride. Leonard Huts (b) and Joseph Boyer (b). M.R. 29 October 1791 by Joseph Drury, lists the groom as Leonard Hutts.

HUTSON, WILLIAM H. and Betsy Whelton, bond 10 June 1799. Consent by Thomas Whelton. William H. Hutson (b) and Thomas Moorman (b).

HUTTS, JACOB (batchelor) and Anne Goff (spinster)*, bond 29 April 1786. Jacob Hutts (b) and James Turley (b); Samuel Martin (w).

HUTTS, MICHAEL and Susannah Owen, bond 17 December 1792. Consent by Ursley Owin, father of the bride. Michael Hutts (b) and William Hutts (b); John Calloway (w). M.R. 18 December 1792 by Menoah Lesley.

HUTTS, WILLIAM and Anna Cunningham, bond 28 April 1794. William Hutts (b) and William Cunningham (b). M.R. 30 May 1794 by Menoah Lesley lists the bride as Linna Cunningham.

I

IRVINE, JOSEPH and Nancy McDerment (McDearman)*, bond 27 December 1809. James Wilson (b) and Joseph Irvine (b).

IRVINE, WILLIAM and Patsy Burton, bond 4 December 1788. Consent by Jesse Burton, father of the bride. William Irvine (b) and William Hazlett (b); William Hazlett (w) and Alex. Burton (w).

J

JEANIS (JENNINGS), TYRA and Hannah McKinney, bond 17 April 1792. Consent by Jn. McKinney. Tyra Jeanis (b) and Daniel McKinney (b). M.R. 25 ___ 1792 by Menoah Lesley.

JENKINS, CARY and Fanny Brent Trent, bond 10 October 1807. Cary Jenkins (b) and Fanny B. Trent (b). M.R. 10 October 1807 lists the bride and groom as Cary Jinkins and Fany B. Trent, by Edmund Johns.

JENKINS, FRANCIS and Nancy Jackson, bond 23 February 1786. Francis Jenkins (b) and Joseph Jenkins (b). M.R. 23 February 1786 by James Kenney.

JENKINS, JOSEPH and Mary Jenkins. M.R. 1 February 1786 by James Kenney.

JENKINS, OLIVE and Fanny Jenkins, mulattoes, bond 27 April 1792. Olive Jenkins (b) and William Jenkins (b).

JENKINS, WILLIAM and Elizabeth Brown, bond 10 September 1789. Consent by Ri. Brown, father of the bride and Elizabeth Brown. William Jenkins (b) and John Dale (b); John Brown (w) and Abigail King (w). M.R. 11 September 1789 by James Hurt.

JENKINS, WILLIAM R. and Mary Parrum*, bond 6 May 1793. William Rodgers Jenkins (b) and Bernard Hendrick (b); Bernard Hendrick (w) and Charles Worsham (w). M.R. 12 June 1793 by Menoah Lesley lists the bride and groom as Mary Perrum and Wm. Rogers Jenkins.

JENNINGS, STEPHEN and Polly Wallace, bond 31 July 1804. Consent by Sarah Wallace, mother of the bride. Stephen Jennings (b) and William Wallace (b).

JOHNS, EDMUND (batchelor) and Susanna Bullock (spinster), bond 19 July 1787. Edmund Johns (b) and Josias Bullock (b). M.R. 19 July 1787 by James Kenney.

JOHNS, STEPHEN and Sarah DePriest, bond 7 November 1791. Consent by John DePriest, Sr. Stephen Johns (b) and W. Alexander (b).

JOHNS, WILLIAM and Polly Spencer, daughter of Charles Spencer, deceased, bond 11 July 1803. Consent by P. Spencer, guardian of the bride. William Johns (b) and Moses Spencer (b). M.R. __ July 1803 by Edmund Johns.

JOHNSON, CHARLES and Polly Black, bond 25 February 1807. Consent by John Black. Charles Johnson (b) and William Black (b); Smith Kent (w) and Wm. Black (w). M.R. 25 February 1807 by Edmund Johns.

JOHNSON, CHRISTOPHER and Milly Moorman, bond 18 October 1783. Consent by Mecijah Moorman, father of the bride. Christopher Johnson (b) and John Bryan, Jr. (b); John Cochran (w) and John Davison (w).

JOHNSON, DAVID and Polly Perkins (Pirkins)*, bond 29 December 1806. David Johnson (b) and Thomas Martin (b); David Moorman (w) and Thos. Martin (w).

JOHNSON, ISAAC and Martha Cobbs, bond 21 October 1805. Isaac Johnson (b) and John Cobbs (b).

JOHNSON, JAMES and Susanna Moorman, daughter of Andrew Moorman, bond 22 January 1807. James Johnson (b) and John Alexander (b); James Johnson (w).

JOHNSON, JAMES and Rebeckah Jones, bond 18 November 1807. Consent by Benjamin Jones, father of the bride. James Johnson (b) and George Jones (b); George Jones (w).

JOHNSON, JOHN and Susanna Johnson, bond 22 October 1798. Consent by Moorman Johnson, father of the bride. John Johnson (b) and Christopher Johnson (b); John Smithson (w).

JOHNSON, JOHN, JR. and Polly Harvey, bond 2 November 1799. Consent by William Harvey 48, father of the bride. John Johnson, Jr. (b) and Richard Harvey (b); Richard Harvey (w). M.R. 19 November 1799 by Joshua Worley lists the groom as John Johnson.

JOHNSON, JOHN W. and Milly Johnson, bond 31 October 1807. Consent by Moorman Johnson, father of the bride. John W. Johnson (b) and James L. Johnson (b); Micajah Johnson (w) and James Johnson (w).

JOHNSON, MICAJAH M. and Peggy Carson, bond 8 January 1810. Consent by William Carson. Micajah Johnson (b) and Thomas Baugh (b); Thos. Baugh (w).

JOHNSON, PHILIP and Lucy Herndon, bond 23 December 1805. Philip Johnson (b) and Edmund Herndon (b).

JOHNSON, PLEASANT and Eunice Bernard (Barnard), bond 26 September 1803. Consent by Timothy Barnard, father of the bride. Benjamin Bernard (Barnard) (b) and Pleasant Johnson (b); Benjamin Barnard (w) and James Clark (w). M.R. 29 September 1803 by Henry Brown lists the bride as Eunice Bernard.

JOHNSON, ROBERT and Leauraney Blankinship, bond 26 January 1802. Consent by Hudson Blankinship, father of the bride. Robert Johnson (b) and Hudson Blankinship (b).

JOHNSON, SIMEON and Delila Carroll*, bond 15 September 1805. Consent by Joseph Johnson, father of the groom. The bride signs her consent Delilah Carrell. Simeon Johnson (b) and John Johnson (b); Thomas Johnson (w) and John Johnson (w). M.R. 15 September 1804 by William P. Martin.

JOHNSON, WILLIAM and Abigail Adkins, bond 7 November 1782. William Johnson (b) and Pearce (Pierce) Wade (b). M.R. 7 November 1782 by John W. Holt.

JOHNSON, ZACHARIAH and Polly Butterworth, bond 15 August 1810. Consent by Benjamin Butterworth, father of the bride. Elijah Dyer (b) and Zachariah Johnson (b). M.R. 24 August 1810 by Frederick Kabler.

JOHNSTON, CHARLES and Elizabeth Prentis Steptoe, bond 29 December 1806.
Consent by James Steptoe, father of the bride. Charles Johnston
(b) and George Steptoe (b); George Steptoe (w) and Richard Steptoe
(w). M.R. 30 December 1806 by Samuel K. Jennings lists the groom
as Ch. Johnston.

JOHNSTON, LEROI and Polly Megee, bond 15 March 1792. Consent by Rose
Magee, mother of the bride. Leroi Johnston (b) and John Walthall (b);
John Walthall (w). M.R. 16 March 1792 by Bennett Maxey who lists the
bride and groom as Polly McGee and Leroy Johnson.

JONES, DANIEL and Nancy Credell, bond 27 June 1789. Consent by Mildred
Credell. Daniel Jones (b) and John Faris (b). M.R. 30 June 1789
by Joshua Worley.

JONES, GEORGE and Agga Mann*, bond 12 February 1798. Consent certified
by John Thompson states the bride is an orphan and of age. George
Jones (b) and Richard Mann (b); John Thompson (w) and Margaret
Thompson (w). M.R. 7 February 1798 by William Flowers.

JONES, HADEN and Prudence Booth, bond 24 October 1807. Consent illegible.
Haden Jones (b) and William Booth (b). M.R. 24 October 1807 by
Edmund Johns.

JONES, JAMES and Katharine Stith, bond 17 September 1791. Consent by
Richard Stith, father of the bride. James Jones (b) and John
Stith (b); Robert Hale (w). M.R. __ September 1791 by Charles
Cobbs lists the bride as Catharine Stith.

JONES, JAMES and Betsy Black, bond 27 January 1801. Consent by John
Black. James Jones (b) and William Black (b); Polley Black (w)
and William Black (w). M.R. 5 February 1801 by Henry Brown.

JONES, JESSE and Sally Johns, bond 24 November 1784. Consent by William
Johns, father of the bride. Jesse Jones (b) and Alexander Hunter (b).

JONES, JOEL and Sarah Cock, bond 8 October 1798. Consent by John Cock.
Joel Jones (b) and James Jones (b); Wm. Cock (w) and David Jones (w).

JONES, JOEL W. and Sarah Patrick, bond 18 March 1782. Consent by John
Patrick, father of the bride. Joel Jones (b) and Jesse Jones (b).
M.R. 19 March 1782 by John W. Holt lists the bride as Sarah
Fitzpatrick.

JONES, JOHN and Jenny Hightower, bond 15 March 1794. Consent by George
Hightower. John Jones (b) and George Hightower (b). M.R. __ March
1794 by Charles Cobbs.

JONES, JOHN and Nancy Fields, bond 7 November 1803. Consent by Margret
Fields, mother of the bride. John Jones (b) and Nathan Tanner (b);
Nathan Tanner (w) and Richard Harvey (w). M.R. __ November 1803 by
Edmund Johns.

JONES, JOHN S. and Magdaleen Johns, bond 9 November 1804. Consent by Sarah Johns, mother of the bride. John Jones (b) and Charles Martin (b); Charles Martin (w).

JONES, OAKLEY and Susannah Hambleton, bond 30 July 1800. Consent by Mary Jones, mother of the groom. Oakley Jones (b) and James Hambleton (b); Benjamin Oliver (w) and John Garrett (w).

JONES, PUBLIUS of Charlotte County and Rebeckah Moore, bond 4 December 1799. Consent by William Moore, father of the bride. Publius Jones (b) and John Borden (b); Benjamin Moore (w) and John Borden (w).

JONES, RICHARD and Orenda Wade, bond 13 October 1801. Consent by Henry Wade, father of the bride. Richard Jones (b) and John Wade (b). Zackfield Wade (w) and John Wade (w).

JONES, THOMAS and Agnes Guthry, bond 27 November 1809. Consent by James Guthry. Thomas Jones (b) and Henry Guthrie (b); William Guthry (w) and Henry Guthry (w). M.R. 30 November ____ by Frederick Kabler.

JONES, THOMAS and Elizabeth Wood, bond 25 December 1804. Consent by Edm. Wood, father of the bride. Thomas Jones (b) and Jesse Wood (b); Jesse Jones (w) and Richard Smith (w). M.R. __ December 1804 by Edmund Johns.

JONES, WILLIAM and Elizabeth Thorp*, bond 21 September 1790. Griffin Lewis (b) and William Jones (b); Osa Cock (w). M.R. 21 September 1790 by Andrew Hunter.

JONES, WILLIAM and Nancy Hunter, bond 19 December 1804. Consent by Alexander Hunter, father of the bride. William Jones (b) and John Hunter (b); Ben Hunter (w) and John Hunter (w) and Thomas Hunter (w). M.R. __ December 1804 by Edmund Johns.

JORDAN, GERMAN and Rebecca Reid, bond 25 June 1810. Consent by Thomas Reid, father of the bride. German Jordan (b) and Samuel Jordan (b); Sam Jordan (w) and John T. Reade (w).

JORDAN, WILLIAM JR. and Frances Jones, bond 7 October 1803. Consent by Publius Jones, father of the bride. William Jordan (b) and Publius Jones (b).

JOYNER, WILLIAM and Polly Eidson, bond 3 June 1808. Consent by Henry Eidson, father of the bride. William Joyner (b) and William Eidson (b); Joseph Eidson (w) and William Eidson (w). M.R. 4 June 1808 by James Warner lists the bride as Polley Eidson and the groom as William Joiner.

JUDE, GEORGE JR. and Elizabeth Millener*, bond 28 December 1810. George Jude, Jr. (b) and William W. Weaver (b); W. W. Weaver (w) and Samuel Weaver (w).

K

KEASEY, EDWARD and Mary Williamson, bond 7 July 1791. Consent by William Williamson, father of the bride. Edward Keasey (b) and Micajah Goodwin (b); Micajah Goodwin (w).

KEEN, JEREMIAH and Patsy Moorman, bond 12 December 1807. Consent by Achilles Moorman, father of the bride. Jeremiah Keen (b) and David H. Moorman (b). M.R. 12 December 1807 by Edmund Johns.

KEESEE, AVERY and Jenny Walden, bond 10 January 1803. Consent by Patty Walden, mother of the bride. Avery Keesee (b) and Thomas Green (b); Henry Walden (w) and Thomas Green (w).

KELLEY, DENNIS and Mary Strange, bond 26 September 1804. Consent by Elizabeth Strange, mother of the bride. Dennis Kelley (b) and John Alexander (b); Robt. Strange, Jr. (w), Abraham Moorman (w) and Robert Strange (w).

KELLY, NATHANIEL and Elizabeth Mann*, bond 14 August 1798. Consent also by Elenor Thompson who certifies that the bride is an orphan and of age, and lived with Elenor Thompson. Nathaniel Kelly (b) and Richard Mann (b); John Thompson (w) and Richard Mann (w). M.R. 6 September 1798 by William Flowers.

KENNADY, JOHN (batchelor) and Mary Shearer (spinster), bond 23 March 1787. Consent by James Shearer. John Kennady (b) and Thomas Shearer (b).

KENT, ROBERT and Nancy Cock, bond 18 December 1809. Consent by John Cock, father of the bride. Robert Kent (b) and Thomas J. Cock (b); William Cock (w) and Thomas J. Cock (w).

KENT, SMITH and Sally Black, bond 20 January 1806. Consent by John Black, father of the bride. Smith Kent (b) and Robert Kent (b); Robert Kent (w).

KEY, THOMAS and Betsy Key, bond 21 December 1798. Consent by Wm. Key, father of the bride. Thomas Key (b) and William Key (b). M.R. 25 December 1798 by John Chappell.

KIDD, ARNOLD and Patsy Finch, bond 4 December 1804. Consent by John Finch, father of the bride. Arnold Kidd (b) and Thomas Steen (b); Thomas Steen (w).

KING, JAMES and Mary Brown, bond 16 December 1797. James King (b) and John Brown (b).

L

LACKEY, WILLIAM and Elizabeth Straughan Lewis, bond 20 October 1790. William Lackey (Leckie) (b) and Griffin Lewis, Jr. (b). M.R. 21 October 1790 by James Hurt, lists the bride and groom as Elizabeth Strawan Lewis and William Leckey.

LACY, ARCHIBALD and Juriah Clement, bond 12 December 1793. Consent by Adam Clement, father of the bride. Archibald Lacy (b) and Johnson Clement (b); Johnson Clement (w).

LAINE, ALEXANDER and Sally Barnes*, bond 30 May 1792. Alexander Laine (b) and Dawson Gosnall (b); John Laine (w) and Dawson Gosnall (w).

LAINE, JOHN and Salley McReynolds*, bond 14 October 1805. John Laine (Layne) (b) and William Thomas (b); James Patteson (w) and William Thomas (w). M.R. 30 October 1805 by William Flowers, Jr. lists the groom as John Lane.

LAMB, MORRISON and Lydia Dobson, bond 9 November 1807. Consent by William Dobson, father of the bride. Morrison Lamb (b) and Peter Gregory (b); Peter Gregory (w) and William C. Dobson (w). M.R. 12 November 1807 by James Warner lists the groom as Munson (or Manson?) Lamb.

LAMB, PATRICK and Nancy W. Truitt. M.R. 17 October 1810 by James Warriner.

LAMB, ROBERT and Sophia Gregory, bond 30 January 1806. Consent by John Gregory, Sr., father of the bride. Robert Lamb (b) and John Gregory, Jr.(b); John Gregory, Jr. (w) and James Moorman, Sr. (w).

LAMB, WILLIAM and Amelia Reynolds, bond 16 November 1798. Consent by Isaac Reynolds, father of the bride. William Lamb (b) and John Dabney (b); John Dabney (w) and James Chappell (w).

LAMBETH, GEORGE and Susan Anderson*, bond 1 July 1801. George Lambeth (b) and Nathan Williamson (b); Samuel Martin (w) and Nathan Williamson (w). M.R. 4 July 1801 by William P. Martin lists the groom as John Lambeth.

LAMBETH, WASHINGTON and Elizabeth King, bond 10 November 1806. Consent by William King. Washington Lambeth (b) and Henry Meredith (b); John M. Telford (w) and Henry Meredith (w). M.R. 10 November 1806 by William P. Martin.

LANCASTER, JAMES and Elizabeth Lee, bond 13 December 1802. Consent by John Lee, father of the bride. James Lancaster (b) and Burrell Lee (b); Burrell Lee (w) and Stephen Lee (w).

LANDRUM, JOHN and Susannah Williams, bond 9 January 1796. Consent by Matthias Williams, father of the bride. John Landrum (b) and Matthias Williams (b).

LANE, AARON and Nancy Monroe, bond 25 October 1806. Consent by Robert Monroe, father of the bride. Aaron Lane (b) and Robert Monroe (b). M.R. 25 October 1806 by Edmund Johns.

LANE, ARMISTEAD and Sarah Lea, bond 14 May 1803. Consent by Joseph Lea, father of the bride. Armistead Lane (Laine) (b) and Aaron Lane (Laine) (b); William Laine (w).

LANE, DAVID and Patsy Hayth, bond 5 January 1802. Consent by Thomas
Hayth, father of the bride. David Lane (Lain) (b) and William
Hayth (b); William Hayth (w) and Polley Lain (w). M.R. 16 January
1802 by Henry Brown.

LANE, ELIAS and Nancy Foster, bond 24 September 1810. Elias Lane (b)
and William Foster (b).

LANE, JOHN, of Buckingham County, and Mary Loyd*, bond 2 February 1792.
John Lane (b) and Samuel Duval (b); Ann Doss (w). M.R. 3 February
1792 by James Kenney.

LANG, PETER and Elizabeth Spearman, bond 22 December 1794. Consent by
John Spearman, father of the bride. Peter Lang (b) and William
Nowsom (b); Benjamin Gallaway (w), Elizabeth Spearman (w) and
William Nowsom (w).

LASLEY, JOHN and Elizabeth Terrell, bond 18 February 1804. Consent by
Edward Terrell, father of the bride. John Lasley (b) and S. Terrell
(b); Edward Terrell, Jr. (w) and S. Terrell (w). M.R. 23 February
1804 by Henry Brown lists the groom as John Leslie.

LAWTON, THOMAS and Elizabeth Ann B. Ramsey*, bond 7 December 1806.
Consent signed Ann B. Ramsey. Thomas Lawton (b) and James Hines,Jr.
(b); Richard H. Ramsey (w) and J. A. Hines (w). M.R. 30 December
1806 by S. K. Jennings.

LAY, THOMAS and Caty Conely*, bond 1 December 1796. Thomas Lay (b) and
Jeremiah Swain (b); Andrew Gardener (w) and Jeremiah Swain (w).

LEA, GIDEON, JR. and Phebe Fariss*, bond 11 June 1801. Gideon Lea (b)
and John C. Lamb (b); John C. Lamb (w), Margaret Fox (w) and Lucy
Smithson (w). M.R. 18 June 1801 by Henry Brown lists the bride and
groom as Phoeba Fares and Guideon Lea.

LEE, ABNER and Susannah Sweeney. M.R. 7 March 1810 by Obadiah Edge.

LEE, ALEXANDER and Sarah G. Lee, bond 7 March 1795. Consent by John Lee,
father of the bride. Alexander Lee (b) and William Baber (b);
Burril Lee (w) and William Baber (w). M.R. 11 March 1795 by Joseph
Drury.

LEE, GEORGE and Polly Kidd, bond 30 May 1805. Consent by Obedience Kidd,
mother of the bride. George Lee (b) and John Kidd (b); John Kidd (w)
and Henry Love (w).

LEE, LEVI and Elizabeth Mann*, bond 26 December 1791. Levi Lee (b) and
William W. Reynold (b); Wm. Shinall (w) and William W.(M) Reynolds
(w).

LEE, MILLER and Peggy Carson, bond 1 January 1798. Consent by James and
Mary Carson, parents of the bride. Miller Lee (b) and William
Carson (b); William Carson (w). M.R. __ February 1798 by Archibald
McRoberts.

LEE, WILLIAM and Elizabeth Taylor, bond 29 January 1790. Consent by Alexander Caldwell. William Lee (b) and Levi Lee (b) and Valentine Tucker (b).

LEIGH, GEORGE and Willmarthe Howerton, daughter of Grief Howerton, bond 25 October 1798. George Leigh (b) and Grief Howerton (b). M.R. 6 November 1798 by William Flowers lists the bride as Willmorth Howerton.

LEMMOND, WILLIAM and Frankey Moore, bond 10 February 1798. Consent by Sampson Moore. William Lemmond (b) and Vincent Glass (b); Vincent Glass (w). M.R. __ February 1798 by Charles Cobbs lists the groom as William Lammond.

LEONARD, ROBERT (bachelor) and Susanna Walker (widow)*, bond 7 August 1787. Robert Leonard (b) and William Adams (b).

LESTER, JOSHUA and Lucy Dillon, bond 6 January 1803. Consent by Henry Dillon, father of the bride. Joshua Lester (b) and John Dillon (b); John Dillon (w) and Presley Lester (w).

LESTER, MILES (bachelor) and Selah Finch (spinster), bond 19 December 1787. Miles Lester (b) and Barnit Finch (b). M.R. date not recorded but entry made after 15 August 1788 entries, by James Kenney.

LESTER, WILLIAM of Halifax County and Elizabeth Echols (Eckhols)*, bond 30 September 1798. William Lester (b) and Peter Collins (b); John Faris (w) and Peter Collins (w).

LESTER, WILLIAM and Nancy Webb*, bond 5 March 1803; William Lester (b) and Joshua Lester (b); Joshua Lester (w).

LEWALLEN (LEWELLEN), JAMES and Sally Harrison*, bond 26 December 1805. Morrison Bryan (b) and James Lewallen (b); Morrison Bryan (w) and James Bryan (w).

LEWELLEN (LEWALLEN), CHARLES and Mary Akers, bond 14 November 1803. Charles Lewellen (b) and John Akers (b). M.R. 15 November 1803 by Henry Brown lists the groom as Charles Lewallin.

LEWELLIN, GREEN B. and Elizabeth A. Carter*, bond 26 December 1809. Green B. Lewellin (b) and William George (b); William Clement (w) and William George, Jr. (w).

LEWIS, CORBIN and Polly Rawlins, bond 4 October 1801. Consent by Mary Rawlins, mother of the bride. Corbin Lewis (b) and Herod Reese (b); Charles Jones (w).

LEWIS, GRIFFIN, JR. and Elizabeth Walker, bond 5 July 1791. Charles Walker (b) and Griffin Lewis, Jr. (b).

LEWIS, JOHN and Patsey Puckett*, bond 29 December 1790. John Lewis (b) and Nathaniel Puckett (b); Nathaniel Puckett (w).

LEWIS, LEWIS (bachelor) and Elizabeth Evans (spinster), bond 15 December 1783. Lewis Lewis (b) and Sampson Evans (b).

LILEY, JOHN and Elizabeth Smith*, bond 5 May 1790. John Liley (b) and Charles McGray (b); Charles McGray (w) and Denis Knock (w).

LIPSCOMB, JOHN and Nancy Caldwell*, bond 26 February 1807. John Lipscomb (Lipcomb) (b) and Alex Rutledge (b); Oleander Rutledge (w) and Neil Jones (w).

LITCHFORD, ARTHUR and Milly Franklin, bond 10 March 1794. Consent by Lewis Franklin, father of the bride. Arthur Litchford (b) and Thomas Franklin (b). M.R. 13 March 1794 by William Flowers.

LITTLEPAGE, BENJAMIN and Frances Anderson, bond 20 December 1797. Consent by Robert Anderson, father of the bride. Benjamin Littlepage (b) and Perin Smith (b); Perin Smith (w). M.R. __ December 1797 by Charles Cobbs.

LITTLEPAGE, JOHN and Annie Scott, bond 25 May 1785. John Littlepage (b) and John Scott (b).

LIVINGSTON, JAMES and Sally Walker, bond 2 February 1792. Consent by Buckley Walker, father of the bride. James Livingston (b) and Benjamin Walker (b). M.R. 20 February 1792 by Menoah Lesley.

LODGE, ABEL and Lacy Bangham (Baugham ?), bond 10 January 1795. Consent by Humphrey Bangham, father of the bride. Abel Lodge (b) and John Bangham (b); Benjamin Bangham (w) and William Ferrell (w). M.R. 15 January 1795 by William Dameron lists the bride as Tacy Bangham. The Marriage Register Vol. I, 1782- lists the bride as Tacy Baugham.

LOVALL, JOHN and Obedience Mason, daughter of William Mason, bond 8 December 1800. John Lovall (b) and William Mason (b).

LUCAS, JAMES and Milly Key, bond 6 February 1802. Consent by Jacob Key, father of the bride. Thomas Key (b) and James Lucas (b); Thomas Key (w).

LUCAS, WILLIAM and Rebeckah Rust*, bond 21 January 1786. William Lucas (b) and Enos Priest (b); Jeremiah Rust (w) and William Frances (w). M.R. 23 January 1786 by James Kenney.

LUKE, FAITHFUL and Leoney Hardwich, bond 11 May 1786. Consent by S. King, who says, "the bearer James Webb applys to you for marriage license for the marriage of Faithful Luke an old man workman here to Leony Hardwich of twenty four years old in which can render me as security to indemnify you. You will __?__ his order enclosed. I will pay the cash for the license on sight." Colin Robertson (b) and Faithful Luke (b).

LUSTER, JAMES and Mildred Wood, bond 29 December 1795. Consent by John Wood, father of the bride. James Luster (b) and William Roper (b); Thomas Moore (w) and William Roper (w). M.R. 12 January 1796 by Menoah Lesley lists the groom as James Lester.

LUSTER, PARKER and Leannah Hancock*, bond 23 February 1803. Parker Luster (b) and George Rust (b); William Parker (w) and Thomas Moorman (w). M.R. 24 February 1803 by Henry Brown.

LYNCH, ANSELM and Susan Baldwin*, bond 24 November 1799. Anselm Lynch (b) and William Alexander (b); John Brown (w) and William Brown (w). M.R. ___ 1799 by Samuel Mitchell lists the bride as Susannah Baldwin.

LYNCH, EDWARD and Polly Terrell*, bond 4 March 1796. Edward Lynch (b) and Charles Terrell (b); Charles Terrell (w) and Luis Terrell (w).

LYNCH, ELIJAH and Jesiah Walker. M.R. 28 October 1782 by John W. Holt.

Mc

McALLISTER, JAMES and Mary Steel, bond 16 May 1782. Consent by Alexander Steel, father of the bride. James McAllister (b) and John Steel (b). M.R. 22 May 1782 by John W. Holt.

McALLISTER, JOHN and Elizabeth McReynolds, bond 16 January 1784. Consent by James McReynolds, father of the bride. John McAllister (b) and Robert McReynolds (b).

McALLISTER, JOSEPH and Elizabeth Helm, bond 26 January 1807. Consent by John Helm, father of the bride. James Helm (b) and Joseph McAllister (b); William Helm (w) and James Helm (w). M.R. 29 January 1807 by William Flowers, Jr.

McALLISTER, WILLIAM and Elizabeth Smith, bond 12 May 1789. Consent by William McAllister. James Stuart (b) and William McAllister (McAlister) (b); Thomas Smith (w), John Wayne (w) and Joseph Wayne (w). M.R. 14 May 1789 by James Hurt.

McCAMISH, JAMES and Anne Gilbreath, bond 3 February 1785. James McCamish (b) and Alexander Steel (b).

McCARGO, DAVID and Nancy Overstreet, bond 12 December 1796. Consent by Mary Ward, mother of the bride. David McCargo (b) and Henry Wray (b); Henry Ray (w) and Joshua P. Howe (w). M.R. ___ December 1796 by Charles Cobbs.

McCARTY, THOMAS and Mary Brickard*, bond 14 March 1803. Thomas McCarty (b) and Thomas M. Clark (b); George Rust (w). M.R. 14 March 1803 by Henry Brown.

McCAWLEY, EDWARD and Polly Shannon, bond 31 May 1800. James Shannon (b) and Edward McCawley (b).

McCLANAHAN, JAMES and Elisa Walton, bond 18 April 1808. James McClanahan
(b) and Thomas Scott, guardian of the bride (b).

McCLOUD, ROBERT and Elizabeth Hunter, bond 19 March 1799. Consent by
James Hunter, father of the bride. Robert McCloud (b) and George
Hunter (b); George Hunter (w) and Robert Lindsey (w).

McCOWN, THOMAS (bachelor) and Keziah Galden (spinster), bond 20 December
1786. Consent by Lizbath Galding, mother of the bride. James Vest (b)
and Thomas McCown (b); James Vest (w).

McCOY, JOHN and Lavina Fuqua, daughter of Moses Fuqua, bond 24 January
1795. John McCoy (Mackay) (b) and Moses Fuqua (b). M.R.___ 1795
by Charles Cobbs.

McCOY, THOMAS and Catharine Strong, bond 22 February 1791. Jesse Cobbs (b)
and Thomas McCoy (Mack) (b). M.R. __ February 1791 by Charles Cobbs.

McDANIEL, JAMES and Milly Goodman, bond 30 July 1795. Consent by John
Ward "in lieu of parents." James McDaniel (b) and John Goodman (b).
M.R. 30 July 1795 by James Kenney.

McDANIEL, JOHN and Sarah Snow, bond 19 August 1785. John McDaniel (b) and
Walter Mackey (b).

McDEARMAN, THOMAS, JR. and Fanny Mason, bond 29 September 1808. Consent
by Francis Mason, father of the bride. Daniel Tyree (b) and Thomas
McDearman (McDermen) (b).

McGLASSON, BARNET and Sophis Caldwell*, bond 8 December 1800. Barnet
McGlasson (b) and Samuel Martin (b); Thos. Moorman (w) and Samuel
Martin (w). M.R. 8 December 1800 by William P. Martin.

McGRAH, CHARLES and Frankey Lawrence*, bond 7 January 1796. Charles
McGrah (b) and George Rust (b); William Josy (?) (w).

McIVOR, DANIEL and Elizabeth Bass, bond 30 March 1801. Consent by Thomas
Walthall, grandfather of the bride. Daniel McIvor (b) and James
McIvor (b); James McIvor (w).

McKENNEY, GEORGE and Mary Tanner. M.R. __ June 1793 by Charles Cobbs.

McKENNEY, ROBINSON and Mary Suttenfield, bond 6 October 1791. Robinson
McKenney (b) and Thomas Franklin (b).

McKINNEY, DANIEL and Rachel Gilbert, bond 4 January 1788. John Gilbert (b)
and Daniel McKinney (b). M.R. not dated but entered after 15 August
1788 entries, by James Kenney, lists the groom as Daniel McKenney.

McKINNEY, JEREMIAH and Fanny Womack, daughter of Richard Womack, bond
3 December 1803. Jeremiah McKinney (b) and Richard Womack (b).

McKINNEY, JOHN and Hannah B. Hutcherson*, bond 14 October 1793. John McKinney (b) and Daniel McKinney (b); Henry McKinney (w) and Dan'l McKinney (w). M.R. October 1793 by Charles Cobbs lists the bride as Hannah B. Hutchinson.

McKINNEY, PRESLEY and Molly Roberson McKinney, bond 5 June 1797. Consent by Joseph McKinney, father of the bride. Nathan Tanner (b) and Presley McKinney (b); Alexander Hunter (w) and Nathan Tanner (w). M.R. __ June 1797 by Charles Cobbs.

McKINNEY, VINCENT and Elizabeth Staples, bond 27 August 1801. Consent by William Staples, father of the bride. Vincent McKinney (b) and Nathan Tanner (b); Joseph McHenry (w) and Nathan Tanner (w). M.R. 27 August 1801 by Henry Brown lists the bride as Elizabeth Step.

McKINNEY, WILLIAM (bachelor) and Patsy Williamson (spinster), bond 17 November 1783. Consent by Francis Williamson. William McKinney (b) and William Patrick (b); Rob Williamson (w) and David Williamson (w).

McMINNIMY, JOHN C. and Polly Plunkett, daughter of Benjamin Plunkett, bond 11 June 1798. John C. McMinnimy (b) and Benjamin Plunkett (b). M.R. 12 July 1798 by William Flowers lists the groom as John C. McKenney.

McREYNOLDS, ARCH and Sally Talbot, bond 28 July 1796. Consent by Williston Talbot, father of the bride. Arch McReynolds (b) and Pleasant Talbot (b); Pleasant Talbot (w) and Chas. Talbot (w). Marriage Register Vol. I, 1782- lists the bride as Polly Talbot.

McREYNOLDS, BENJAMIN and Elizabeth Wilson, bond 9 March 1798. Consent by Mathew Willson, father of the bride. Benjamin McReynolds (b) and Mathew Willson (b); Mathew Willson (w). M.R. 12 March 1798 by Archibald McRoberts.

McREYNOLDS, JOHN and Jane Campbell, bond 6 December 1788. Consent by James Campbell, father of the bride. John McReynolds (b) and John Steel (b). M.R. 15 December 1788 by William Mahon.

McREYNOLDS, JOSEPH and Catherine McIver, bond 4 January 1803. Consent by James McIver, father of the bride. Joseph McReynolds (b) and Daniel McIver (b); Daniel McIver (w). M.R. 10 January 1803 by Henry Brown.

McREYNOLDS, OLIVER and Elizabeth Steel, bond 4 February 1796. Oliver McReynolds (b) and Alexander Steel (b). M.R. 8 February 1796 by William Mahon lists the bride as Elizabeth Steele.

McREYNOLDS, SAMUEL and Ginnet (Jenny) Campbell, bond 24 January 1794. Consent by Archibald Campbell, father of the bride. Samuel McReynolds (b) and Samuel Campbell (b); Samuel Campbell (w). M.R. 30 January 1794 by William Mahon.

McREYNOLDS, WILLIAM and Martha Wilson, bond __ February 1782. Consent by Mary Willson, mother of the bride. William McReynolds (b) and Thomas Wilson (b).

MADDOX, JOHN G. and Polly H. Hurt, daughter of James Hurt, bond 17 February 1807. Consent by J. Hurt, father of the bride. John G. Maddox
(Madox) (b) and William C. Hurt (b); John Hurt (w) and W. C. Hurt (w).

MAGANN (MAGAN), PLEASANT and Nancy Nichols, bond 27 December 1797. Pleasant
Magann (b) and Joseph Nichols (b).

MAGORS, HENRY and Dinah Henry* Negroes bond 6 December 1792. Henry Magors
(Magers) (b) and Frank Freeman (b); Christ. Johnsone (w) and Gideon
Lea (w). A note attached to the bond states "Diner Henry is a free
woman formerly the property of Charles Moorman, desc'd, though her
name given by her master formerly was only Diner as she has got it
on the record." M.R. 9 September 1792 by Joseph Drury lists the groom
as Henry Majors.

MAHON, DENNIS and Susanna Neal, bond 11 March 1805. Dennis Mahon (Mahone)
(b) and Thomas Neal (b).

MAHONE, BARNET and Susannah Layne (Lain), bond 3 October 1793. Consent by
James Lain, father of the bride. Barnet Mahone (b) and William
Butler (b); George Wright (w) and Wm. Butler (w). M.R. 5 October
1793 by William Flowers lists the bride and groom as Susannah Lane
and Barnett Mahone.

MAHONE, BARNETT and Catherine Askew, bond 11 November 1802. Consent by
Anthony and Jemima Askew. Anthony Askew (b) and Barnett Mahone (b);
Anthony Askew (w) and Pliant Askew (w). M.R. 29 November 1802 by
William Flowers lists the groom as Barnard Mahone.

MAHONE, PLEASANT and Polly Williams, daughter of Matthias Williams, bond
20 February 1802. Pleasant Mahone (b) and Matthias Williams (b).
M.R. 5____ 1802 by William Flowers.

MANN, FIELD and Elizabeth Thompson*, bond 29 December 1792. Consent also
by Elenor Thompson, mother of the bride. Field Mann (b) and John
Thompson (b); John Thompson (w).

MANN, JAMES and Jane Mann*, bond 15 December 1789. The bride signed the
consent Jaine Mann, spinster. John Mann (b) and James Mann (b);
Fergues Mann (w). M.R. 24 December 1789 by William Flowers.

MANN, JOEL and Margaret Thompson*, bond 10 November 1800. Consent by
Elenor Thompson, mother of the bride. Joel Mann (b) and John
Thompson (b); John Thompson (w) and Mary Smith (w). M.R. 11 No-
vember 1800 by Joshua Worley.

MANN, JOEL and Kitty Black, daughter of John Black, bond 29 October 1805.
Joel Mann (b) and John Black (b).

MANN, RICHARD and Elizabeth Smith, bond 4 August 1792. Consent by Elendor
Thompson. Richard (Rich) Mann (b) and Andrew Thompson (b); Charles
Staples (w) and ___?___ Bryan (w). This bond is actually made out with
Richard Mann as the groom and Elenor Thompson as the bride. The
consent signed by Elendor Thompson gives the bride's name as Elizabeth
Smith. The M.R. dated 19 August 1792, by William Mahon gives the
bride's name as Elizabeth Smith.

MANN, THOMAS and Prudence Blankenship, daughter of Hudson Blankenship, bond 30 September 1800. Hudson Blankenship (b) and Thomas Mann (b).

MANN, WILLIAM and Patsy Marshall, bond 7 January 1790. William Mann (b) and William Marshall (b). M.R. 15 January 1790 by James Hurt.

MANN, WILLIAM and Mary Rock, bond 13 November 1794. Consent by Charles Rock, father of the bride. Levi Lee (b) and William Mann (b); Levi Lee (w) and James Mann (w). M.R. 19 ___ 1794 by William Flowers lists the bride as Mary Roch.

MANSON, NATHANIEL I. and Sally Alexander, bond 10 September 1805. Robert Alexander (b) and Nathaniel Manson (b); R. Morris, Jr. (w). The Marriage Register Vol. I, 1782- lists the groom as Nathaniel Mann.

MARKHAM, JOHN and Jenny Edds, bond 15 January 1784. Consent by Joseph Edds, father of the bride. John Markham (b) and John Edds (b).

MARSHALL, DANIEL and Betsy Mann, bond 12 August 1794. Daniel Marshall (b) and Hubbard Brown (b). M.R. __ August 1794 by Charles Cobbs.

MARSHALL, DAVID and Rebeckah Cock, bond 23 December 1787. Consent by George Cock, father of the bride. David Marshall (b) and William Cock (b). M.R. 27 December 1789 by John Paup.

MARSHALL, JOHN and Patience Mann. M.R. 6 July 1789 by James Hurt.

MARSHALL, THOMAS B. and Mary Marshall, bond 1 January 1793. Consent by Thomas Marshall. Thomas B. Marshall (b) and John Hutcherson (b); John Marshall (w) and John Hutcherson (w). M.R. __ January 1793 by Charles Cobbs.

MARSHALL, THOMAS J. and Elizabeth Cobbs, bond 18 October 1802. Thomas Marshall (b) and John Cobbs (b).

MARTIN, ANDREW and Susanna Botomes, bond 3 May 1802. Consent by Mikagah Botomes. Andrew Martin (b) and Abner Bottoms (b); Martin Bottom (w) and Abner Bottoms (w). M.R. 5 May 1802 by Henry Brown lists the bride as Susanna Bottom.

MARTIN, CHARLES and Lockey Johns, bond 7 January 1793. Consent by Jesse Johns, father of the bride. Charles Martin (b) and Jesse Johns, Jr. (b); Jesse Johns, Jr. (w).

MARTIN, DAVID and Locy Pugh, bond 9 November 1807. Consent by Jonath Pugh, father of the bride. David Martin (b) and Thomas Lancaster (b); Michael Lancaster (w) and Thomas Lancaster (w). M.R. 26 November 1807 by William Flowers, Jr.

MARTIN, DAVID, JR. and Jean Dickey, bond 14 December 1801. Consent by Edward and Jean Dickey, parents of the bride. David Martin, Jr. (b) and John Dickey (b); David Pugh (w), John Dickey (w) and Samuel Dickey (w). M.R. 21 December 1801 by William Flowers lists the bride as Jane Dickey.

MARTIN, JAMES and Mary Martin, bond 2 February 1786. Thomas Frank (b) and James Martin (b).

MARTIN, JAMES and Sally Williamson*, bond 12 November 1798. James Martin (b) and James Holley (b); James Holley (w).

MARTIN, JAMES and Ann Dickey, bond 8 November 1802. Consent by Edward and Jean Dickey, parents of the bride. John Dickey (b) and James Martin (b); John Dickey (w) and Samuel Dickey (w). M.R. 18 November 1802 by William Flowers.

MARTIN, JESSE of Henry County, and Ann Armistead, bond 16 November 1808. Consent by Robert Armistead, father of the bride. Jesse Martin (b) and John S. Armistead (b); James Edwards (w) and John S. Armistead (w).

MARTIN, JOHN and Sarah Pugh, daughter of David Pugh, bond 11 January 1796. David Pugh (b) and John Martin (b). M.R. 14 January 1796 by William Flowers.

MARTIN, JOHN and Elizabeth Reynolds, bond 10 April 1802. John Martin (b) and Thomas Martin (b). M.R. 18 April 1802 by Henry Brown lists the bride as Elizabeth Ronalds.

MARTIN, JOSEPH and Ann Martin, bond 12 December 1808. Thomas Martin (b) and Joseph Martin (b).

MARTIN, MATTHEW and Molly Mills*, bond 19 September 1797. Matthew Martin (b) and John Mann (b); Samuel Hunter (w) and John Mann (w).

MARTIN, SAMUEL and Eley Wilson (Willson), bond 28 September 1800. Consent by John Wilson, father of the bride. Samuel Martin (b) and Alexander Hunter (b). M.R. there are three entries in the original Register under the date of 30 September 1800 by William Flowers, one of which lists the bride's name as Ellender Wilson, and one of which lists the bride as Elenor Wilson.

MARTIN, SAMUEL and Sally Cardwell, bond 9 March 1807. Consent by Robert Cardwell, father of the bride. Samuel Martin (b) and Thomas Martin (b); Robert Cardwell, Jr. (w) and Thomas Martin, Jr. (w).

MARTIN, THOMAS and Lydia Lyon*, bond 22 December 1808. Thomas Martin (b) and Charles Arrington (b); John Arrington (w), Adler Arrington (w) and Charles Arrington (w). M.R. 23 December 1808 by Obadiah Edge lists the bride as Lydda Lyon.

MARTIN, WILLIAM and Polly Austin*, bond 31 December 1808. Chapley Walker (b) and William Martin (b); Samuel Martin (w) and Chapley Walker (w). M.R. 1 January 1809 by Obadiah Edge.

MARTIN, WILLIAM and Hannah Pugh, bond 25 October 1809. Consent by Jonathan Pugh, father of the bride. William Martin (b) and Jacob Galding (b); Wm. Moore (w) and Jacob Galding (w). M.R. 26 October 1809 by Samuel Davidson lists the bride as Hannah Pew.

MARTIN, WILLIS and Mary Wood, bond 16 February 1810. Consent by Patsey
Sleep, mother of the bride. Willis Martin (b), John Martin (b) and
William Martin (b); William Martin (w) and Robertson Abraham (w).
M.R. 18 February 1810 by Obadiah Edge lists the groom as Wilis
Martin.

MASON, ADIN and Polly Womack, bond 18 December 1806. Adin Mason (b) and
Alexander Womack (b).

MASON, JAMES and Betsy Holt, bond 18 December 1806. Consent by Robert
Holt, father of the bride. James Mason (b) and Adin Mason (b);
Adin Mason (w) and Alexander Womack (w).

MASON, JOHN (bachelor) and Mary Nowlin (Nowland) (widow)*, bond 12 February 1785. John Mason (b) and Daniel McCoy (b).

MASON, JOHN and Nancy Clark, bond 18 January 1791. Consent by Nathaniel
Rogers, guardian of the bride. John Mason (b) and Samuel Rogers (b).
M.R. __ January 1791 by Charles Cobbs.

MASON, JOHN (widower) and Francis Brooks (widow), bond 26 September 1794.
John Mason (b) and Peter Bass (b). M.R. __ September 1794 lists the
bride as Francis Brooke, by Charles Cobbs.

MASON, JOHN and Mary Whelan, bond 9 February 1807. Consent by Thomas
Whelan. John Mason (b) and Daniel Snow (b); Daniel Snow (w) and
Rebeckah Whelan (w).

MASON, NATHAN and Elizabeth Jennings, bond 8 December 1800. Nathan Mason
(b) and Abraham Hanks (b); Abraham Hanks (w).

MASON, PHILIP and Betsey Holt, daughter of James Holt, bond 10 January 1810.
Philip Mason (b) and James Holt (b).

MASON, WILLIAM and Jenny Ready, bond 22 November 1796. Consent by Nathan
Ready, father of the bride. William Mason (b) and James Elder (b);
John Elder (w) and James Elder (w). M.R. __ November 1796 by
Charles Cobbs.

MASON, WILLIAM and Elizabeth Pillow, bond 20 June 1792. Consent by Joseph
Pillow, father of the bride. William Mason (b) and James McDowell (b);
George Moore (w) and James McDowell (w).

MASON, WILLIAM and Sarah Diener*, bond 22 July 1810. William Mason (b)
and Daniel Driskill (b); Daniel Driskill (w) and Wm. Moore (w).

MATTHEWS, WILLIAM and Susannah Mitchell, bond 9 September 1790. William
Matthews (b) and Ares Vaughan (b). M.R. 21 September 1790 by James
Hurt lists the bridegroom as William Matthis.

MATTHEWS, WILLIAM and Edith Pillow, bond 8 November 1796. Consent by
Joseph Pillow, father of the bride. William Matthews (b) and Parrin
Smith (b); Wm. Mason (w) and Henry Wray (w). M.R. __ November 1796
by Charles Cobbs lists the groom as William Matthis.

MAXEY, JAMES and Nancy Irvine, bond 22 November 1804. Consent by John Irvin, father of the bride. James Maxey (b) and John Irvin, Jr. (b); John Irvine, Jr. (w) and Mathew Irvine (w). M.R. 15 November 1804 by John Chappell.

MAY, JOHN and Rachel Hamers, bond 9 October 1792. Consent by Elizabeth Hamers, mother of the bride. John May (b) and William Shinall (b); William M. Reynolds (w) and William Shinall (w).

MEANS, ROBERT and Isabella Fields, bond 13 October 1800. Consent by Margret Fields. Robert Means (b) and Samuel Caldwell (b); Samuel Caldwell (w) and James Robertson, Jr. (w). M.R. 15 October 1800 by Joshua Worley.

MEGGINSON (MEGENSON), JOSEPH CABELL and Sarah Bolling, bond 4 September 1792. Consent by Archibald Bolling, Sr. Joseph Megginson (b) and Robert Ferguson (b).

MEHORNEY, ANDREW and Betty Harris*, bond 10 October 1793. Andrew Mehorney (b) and William Harris (b); Wm. Harris (w) and Wm. Moor (w).

MICKLE, WILLIAM and Ruth Johnson, bond 2 August 1789. William Mickle (b) and Robert Johnson (b).

MILLER, ELIJAH and Rachel Johnson, bond 6 March 1783. Elijah Miller (b) and John Miller (b).

MILLER, JOHN and Sarah Brown, bond 25 November 1791. Consent by John Brown, father of the bride. John Miller (b) and James Brown (b). M.R. 1 December 1791 by James Kenney.

MINTON, SIMON and Sarah Roach, bond 4 October 1791. Consent by William Roach, father of the bride. Simon Minton (b) and Benjamin Stith (b); Andrew Wade (w).

MITCHELL, ADAM and Rebeccah Bass, bond 3 February 1791. Adam Mitchell (b) and Josiah Bass (b). M.R. no date given but entered in the original Register following entries for February 1791 and listing the bride as Rebeckah Bass, by Charles Cobbs.

MITCHELL, ARCH and Spicy Goodwin, bond 3 March 1791. Consent by Micajah Goodwin, father of the bride. Micajah Goodwin (b) and Arch Mitchell (b) and James Alexander (b); John Mitchell (w), Jeremiah Taylor (w) and Benjamin White (w). M.R. 7 March 1791 by William Dameron lists the groom as Arthur Mitchell.

MITCHELL, SAMUEL and Nancy Lynch, bond 20 November 1786. Consent by John Ward. Samuel Mitchell (b) and John Ward, Jr. (b).

MITCHELL, WILLIAM of Pittsylvania County and Betsy Black, bond 14 January 1800. Consent by Thomas Black, father of the bride. William Mitchell (b) and Thomas Black, Jr. (b); Thomas Black (w) and Sally Black (w).

MITCHEM, WILLIAM and Priscilla Tranam*, bond 7 April 1796. William
Mitchem (b) and John Marcheson (b); Wm. Tranam (w) and John
Marcheson (w).

MITCHUM (MITCHEM), LITTLEBERRY and Rachel Whelan, bond 23 February 1802.
Consent by Thomas Whelan. Littleberry Mitchum (b) and John
Marcheson (b); John Marcheson (w).

MOHER, CHRISTIAN and Frances M. Cobbs, bond 28 December 1810. Consent by
John Cobbs, father of the bride. Christian Moher (b) and Thomas A.
Cobbs (b); Thos. A. Cobbs (w) and Thos. Marshall (w) and Ben Rice (w).
M.R. 28 December 1810 by Edmund Johns lists the groom as Christian
Moore.

MONROE, JOHN and Frances Calloway, bond 21 November 1797. Consent by
Joseph Calloway, father of the bride. John Monroe (b) and Robert
Monroe (b); Robert Monroe (w).

MOORE, AUSTIN and Sally Eidson, bond 23 January 1799. Consent by Henry
Eidson, father of the bride. Austin Moore (b) and Henry Eidson (b);
Bonibas Eidson (w) and Henry Eidson, Jr. (w). M.R. 15 February 1799
by Abner Early.

MOORE, BENJAMIN and Jenny Moore, bond 24 December 1799. Consent by Wm.
Moore, father of the bride. Benjamin Moore (b) and John Borden (b);
Wm. Moore (w), Publius Jones, Jr. (w) and John Borden (w).

MOORE, CHARLES and Sally Duval, bond 30 December 1806. Consent by Lewis
Duval, father of the bride. Charles Moore (b) and Benjamin Duval
(Duvall) (b); Benjamin Duvall (w) and Daniel Duvall (w).

MOORE, FREEMAN and Sally Cobbs*, bond 25 August 1795. Freeman Moore (b)
and Thomas Hanks (b); James Brooks (w) and Thomas Hanks (w). M.R.
___ August 1795 by Charles Cobbs.

MOORE, GEORGE and Patsy Mason, bond 28 February 1791:1795. George Moore
(b) and William Mason (b). M.R. February 1791 by Charles Cobbs.

MOORE, GOODRICH and Nancy Eidson, bond 28 December 1791. Consent by Henry
Eidson, father of the bride. Goodrich Moore (b) and Thomas Tucker (b);
Thos. Moore (w) and William Moore (w). M.R. 29 December 1791 by
Menoah Lesley.

MOORE, JAMES and Priscilla Read, bond 8 October 1792. James Moore (b) and
William Read (b). M.R. 13 October 1792 by Menoah Lesley lists the
bride as Priscilla Reid.

MOORE, JAMES L. and Obedience Elam, bond 11 May 1809. Consent by Susannah
Elam, mother of the bride. James L. Moore (b) and Enoch Watkins (b);
Enoch Watkins (w) and Patsey Doss (w). M.R. 11 May 1809 by Edmund
Johns.

MOORE, JOHN and Mary Elam, daughter of Richard Elam, bond 12 January 1801. John Moore (b) and Richard Elam (b). M.R. 27 January 1801 by Henry Brown.

MOORE, JOSHUA and Milly Eidson, bond 29 January 1805. Consent by Henry Eidson, father of the bride. Joshua Moore (b) and William Eidson (b); William Eidson (w). M.R. 29 January 1805 by Henry Brown.

MOORE, MARK and Patsy Elder*, bond 1 October 1808. Mark Moore (b) and Jacob Carwiles (b); Jacob Carwiles (w). M.R. 11 October 1808 by Edmund Johns.

MOORE, MATTHEW and Elizabeth Moore*, bond 3 November 1796. Matthew Moore (b) and Henry Brown (b); Henry Brown (w). M.R. 10 November 1796 by Menoah Lesley.

MOORE, OLIVE and Sally Gregory, bond 1 August 1792. John Gregory (b) and Olive Moore (b). M.R. 2 August 1792 by James Kenney.

MOORE, PATRICK and Elizabeth Shearer, bond 14 January 1805. Consent by James Shearer, father of the bride. Patrick Moore (b) and James L. Moore (b); James L. Moore (w). M.R. __ January 1805 by Edmund Johns. The bride's name written in pencil on the back of the bond is given as Elizabeth Shaner.

MOORE, PRIDDEN (PREDHEM) and Judy Franklin, daughter of Thomas Franklin, bond 10 June 1799. Pridden Moore (b) and Thomas Franklin (b). M.R. 21 August 1799 by William Flowers lists the bride and groom as Judy B. Franklin and Predum Moore.

MOORE, ROBERT of Caswell County, N.C. and Anney Driskill, bond 4 February 1793. Consent by Daniel Driskill, father of the bride. Robert Moore (b) and Richard Driskill (b); Adam Driskill (w) and Daniel Driskill, Jr. (w). M.R. __ February 1793 by Charles Cobbs lists the bride as Anne Driskill.

MOORE, SAMPSON and Sally Perdue, bond 22 October 1805. Consent by Frances Perdue, mother of the bride. Sampson Moore (b) and Nathan Tanner (b); Nathan Tanner (w).

MOORE, SAMUEL and Elizabeth Moore, bond 29 January 1793. Samuel Moore (b) and John Moore (b). M.R. 31 ____ 1793 by Menoah Lesley.

MOORE, SAMUEL and Sarah Rosser*, bond 21 December 1795. Consent also by Ann Rosser. Samuel Moore (b) and Ambrose Rosser (b); David Staples (w) and Ambrose Rosser (w). M.R. 23 December 1795 by William Flowers.

MOORE, THOMAS and Elizabeth Sandifer, bond 9 August 1799. Consent by Samuel Sandifer, father of the bride. Thomas Moore (b) and Henry Wray (b); Joseph Pillow (w) and Henry Ray (Wray) (w).

MOORE, WILLIAM and Winifred Terrell, bond 2 October 1789. Consent by David Terrell, father of the bride. William Moore (b) and John Richardson (b). M.R. 3 November 1789 by James Kenney lists the bride as Winnifred Terrell.

MOORE, WILLIAM and Nancy Asbury*, bond 20 December 1791. William Moore
(b) and Thomas Franklin (b); Dan McKinney (w), Charles McKinney (w)
and Thomas Franklin (w). M.R. __ December 1791 by Charles Cobbs.

MOORE, WILLIAM and Mary Hamersley, daughter of William Hamersley, bond
9 December 1795. William Moore (b) and William Hamersley (b). M.R.
10 December 1795 lists the bride as Mary Handsley, by John Chappell.

MOORE, WILLIAM and Elizabeth R. Simpson, bond 3 November 1800. William
Moore (b) and John Simpson (b).

MOORE, WILLIAM and Kissiah Reed, daughter of William Reed, bond 19 January
1801. William Moore (b) and William Reed (b). M.R. 22 January 1801
by Henry Brown lists the bride as Keziah Read.

MOORMAN, ABRAHAM and Susannah W. Lewis, bond 17 October 1810. Consent by
Mary Lewis, mother of the bride. Abraham Moorman (b) and Howell
Lewis (b); Howell Lewis (w) and Samuel Jordan (w). M.R. 18 October
1810 by Matthew Easter.

MOORMAN, ACHILLES and Dorkus Jones, daughter of Thomas Jones, bond 12 March
1798. Achilles Moorman (b) and Thomas Jones (b). M.R. 29 __ 1798
by Abner Early lists the bride as Dorcus Jones.

MOORMAN, JAMES and Betsey Moorman, bond 24 December 1796. Consent by
Judith Moorman. James Moorman (b) and Achilles Moorman (b); Achilles
Moorman (w) and William Moorman, Sr. (w).

MOORMAN, JAMES and Jane Robinson, daughter of John Robinson, bond 13 August
1799. James C. Moorman (b) and John Robinson (b). M.R. 15 __ 1799
by Abner Early lists the groom as James C. Moorman.

MOORMAN, JESSE and Elizabeth Buckner Stith, bond 14 February 1785. Consent
by Richard Stith. Jesse Moorman (b) and John Moorman (b).

MOORMAN, JOHN and Rachel Haden, bond 18 February 1795. Consent by John
Haden, father of the bride. John Moorman (b) and John Dabney (b);
John Dabney (w), Anthony Haden (w) and J. M. Haden (w). M.R.
22 February 1795 by Menoah Lesley.

MOORMAN, JOHN and Nancy Robertson [sic], bond 30 December 1802. John
Moorman (b) and John Robinson (b).

MOORMAN, MICAJAH and Susanna Johnson, daughter of Christopher Johnson, bond
22 September 1802. Micajah Moorman (b) and Christopher Johnson (b).

MOORMAN, MICAJAH C. and Esther Alexander, bond _____ 1803. Micajah C.
Moorman (b) and Ro. Alexander (b); Dennis Kelley (w) and John S.
Payne (w).

MOORMAN, PLEASANT and Polly Moorman, bond 13 January 1802. Consent by
Micajah Moorman, grandfather of the bride. Pleasant Moorman (b)
and Christopher Johnson (b); Christopher Johnson (w). M.R. 14
January 1802 by Henry Brown.

MOORMAN, SAMUEL and Judith Clark, bond 29 February 1796. Consent by John
Clark, father of the bride. Samuel Moorman (b) and David Clark (b);
David Clark (w) and Tucker Clark (w). M.R. 2 March 1796 by James
Mitchell.

MOORMAN, THOMAS and Betsy Henry Terrell, bond 23 December 1804. Thomas
Moorman (b) and Dudley Terrell (b). M.R. __ December 1804 by
Edmund Johns.

MOORMAN, THOMAS and Elizabeth C. Clark, bond 9 January 1809. Consent by
Lucy Clark, mother of the bride. Thomas Moorman (b) and Thomas M.
Clark (b); Micajah Clark (w) and Thomas M. Clark (w).

MOORMAN, WILLIAM of Bedford County, and Elizabeth Martin*, bond 22 October
1792. William Moorman (b) and Matthew Martin (b); Matthew Martin
(w). M.R. _____ 1792 by Charles Cobbs.

MOORMAN, WILLIAM and Betsy Rosser, bond 23 January 1797. Consent by John
Strange, grandfather of the bride. William Moorman (b) and
Nathaniel Strange (b); Nathaniel Strange (w). M.R. __ January 1797
by Charles Cobbs.

MOORMAN, WILLIAM and Patsy Moorman, bond 4 August 1806. William Moorman
(b) and Thomas M. Clark (b).

MORGAN, MOORMAN and Amy Hackett*, bond 18 January 1804. Moorman Morgan
(b) and Roger Williams (b); William P. Martin (w). M.R. ____ 1804
by William P. Martin lists the bride as Amy Hatcher.

MORRIS, JOHN and Lucretia Howell, daughter-in-law of John Goodman, bond
10 February 1800. John Morris (b) and John Goodman (b). M.R.
12 February 1800 by Abner Early lists the bride as Lucretia Howett.

MORRIS, RICHARD and Mary Watts, bond 26 November 1808. Consent by Mary
Watts, mother of the bride. Richard Morris (b) and E. Watts (b);
E. Watts (w) and Charlie Scott (w).

MORTON, JOSEPH of Prince Edward County, and Nancy Fuqua, bond 4 December
1790. Consent by Moses Fuqua, father of the bride. Joseph Morton
(b) and William Fuqua (b); Obediah Fuqua (w) and William Fuqua (w).
M.R. 14 December 1790 by Drury Lacy lists the groom as Josiah Morton.

MORTON, RICHARD and Sally Scott, bond 19 August 1790. Richard Morton (b)
and John Scott (b).

MORTON, WILLIAM and Anna Barnett*, bond 27 May 1799. Consent also by
Nancy Barnett. Peter Ditto (b) and William Morton (b); Petter
Ditto (Detto) (w). M.R. 1 June 1799 by William P. Martin lists
the bride as Anne Barrow.

MOSELEY, JAMES and Keziah Turner. M.R. 17 February 1782 by John W. Holt.

MOSELEY, JAMES and Belinda R. Scott, bond 15 May 1804. Consent by Samuel Scott, father of the bride. James Moseley (b) and Samuel J. Harrison (b); John H. Trent (w) and Samuel J. Harrison (w). M.R. 15 May 1804 by William P. Martin.

MOSELEY, JOHN and Mary Anne Perrow, bond 11 March 1799. John Moseley (b) and William Rosser (b).

MOSELEY, JOSEPH and Patty Teppance, bond 10 September 1804. Consent by James Teppance, father of the bride. Joseph Moseley (b) and John Going (b); John Burger (w), Aron Moser (w) and John Going (w).

MOSS, HARRY and Winney Valentine* free Negroes bond 15 June 1806. Harry Moss (b) and Benjamin Armstrong (b).

MOSS, PETER and Fanny Armstrong, daughter of Benjamin Armstrong, bond 27 December 1809. Benjamin Armstrong (b) and Peter Moss (b).

MOSS, RICHARD and Sarah Johns, bond 14 May 1791. Consent by Mallery Johns, Jr., father of the bride. Mallery Johns, Jr., (b) and Richard Moss (b); John Smith (w) and Henry Moss (w). M.R. 15 May 1791 by James Kenney lists Richard Moss, a Negro and Sarah Johns, a mulatto.

MULLENS, JOSHUA and Betsey Turley, bond 7 March 1786. Consent by James Turley, father of the bride. Joshua Mullens (b) and James Mullens (b).

MURRELL, THOMAS and Frances Christian Truitt, bond 3 November 1806. Consent by Wm. Truhit, father of the bride. Thomas Murrell (b) and William Edds (b); Jesse Harvey (w) and Wm. Edds (w). M.R. 30 November 1806 by James Warner.

MURRELL, WILLIAM and Polly Edds, daughter of Thomas Edds, bond 5 April 1799. William Murrell (b) and Thomas Edds (b).

MYLER, THOMAS and Peachey Lane, daughter of John Lane (Laine), bond 29 January 1805. John Lane (Laine)(b) and Thomas Myler (b).

N

NEIGHBOURS, WILLIAM and Anne Bowe*, bond 23 November 1791. William Neighbours (b) and Micajah Davis (b); Jemima Bowe (w) and Drummong Smithson (w). M.R. 24 November 1791 by Menoah Lesley lists the bride as Nancy Bowe.

NEWBERRY, WILLIAM (bachelor) and Jane Taylor (widow of John Taylor), bond 8 August 1785. William Newberry (b) and John Whorley (b); David Collins (w).

NEWSUM, WILLIAM and Margaret Speece, bond 20 May 1782. Conrad Speece (b) and William Newsum (b). M.R. 21 May 1782 by John W. Holt lists the groom as William Newsam.

NOEL (NOELL), GERMAN and Polly Trent, bond 23 March 1804. Consent by
Elijah Trent, father of the bride. German C. Noel (b) and W. N.
Wilson (b); Henry Trent (w) and W. N. Wilson (w). M.R. _____ 1804
by Edmund Johns is entered twice in the Marriage Register, Vol. I
1782-, once listing the groom's name as German C. Noel, and
secondly under the name of German C. Norvell.

NOEL (NOELL) RODERICK and Luraney Trent, bond 13 November 1805. Consent
by Elijah Trent, father of the bride. John Trent (b) and Roderick
Noel (Noell) (b); John Trent (w) and Francis Perdue (w).

NORRIS, JOHN and Frances Moore*, bond 8 January 1791. John Norris (b)
and George Richardson (b); Benjamin Dillard (w) and George Richerson
(w). M.R. 9 January 1791 by James Kenney.

NORTH, JAMES and Katharine Clark, daughter of John Clark, bond 18 February 1807. James North (b) and John Clark (b). M.R. 23 February
1807 by John Chappell.

NORTH, PETER and Elizabeth Franklin, daughter of Robert Franklin, bond
25 January 1802. Peter North (b) and Robert Franklin (b). M.R.
4 February 1802 by William Flowers.

NORTH, THOMAS, JR. and Nancy Cox, bond 6 February 1810 [sic]. Consent by
John Murrell, guardian of the bride. Thomas North, Jr. (b) and
Drury W. Cocke (b); Drury Cocke (w). M.R. 6 December 1810 by
Samuel K. Jennings.

NORTH, THOMAS and Sarah Franklin, bond 9 December 1805. Thomas North (b)
and Lewis Franklin (b). M.R. 19 December 1805 by William Flowers, Jr.

NORTH, WILLIAM and Mary Franklin, bond 25 July 1795. Consent by Elisabeth
and Alexander Steel. William North (b) and Thomas Franklin (b); Thos.
Franklin (w). M.R. 25 July 1795. This appears to be a recent entry,
and no minister is mentioned.

NORVELL, REUBEN and Polly King, bond 4 June 1792. Consent by S. King,
father of the bride. Reuben Norvell (b) and John J. Thuratt (b).

NOWLIN, SAMUEL and Fanny Pannill, bond 8 November 1808. Consent by
Samuel Pannill, brother of the bride. Samuel Nowlin (b) and Booker
Shelton (b). M.R. 9 November 1808 by David Nowlin.

O

OGLESBY, JACOB and Elizabeth Williamson, bond 13 May 1800. Consent by
Caldwell Williamson, guardian of the bride. Jacob Oglesby (b) and
James Holley (b); James Holley (w) and James Stewart (w).

O'KANE, HENRY and Sarah Stevens, bond 8 June 1793. Henry O'Kane (b)
and Thomas Clifton (b). M.R. 8 June 1793 by Menoah Lesley.

O'NEAL, BARTLEY and Sarah (Susannah) Bell, bond 17 March 1797. Consent
by Mary Grayham, mother of the bride. Bartley O'Neal (b) and
Richard Savage (b); Richard Savage (w) and James Turner (w).
M.R. __ March 1797 by Charles Cobbs lists the bride as Susannah
Graham. On the bond and on the consent the bride's name is given
as Bell, but the bond lists her as Sarah Bell, the consent as
Susannah Bell.

ORGAN, JOHN and Betsy Johnson, daughter of John Johnson, bond 14 August
1799. John Organ (b) and John Johnson, Jr. (b); Philip Johnson (w)
and John Johnson, Jr. (w).

OVERSTREET, JAMES and Nancy Winfree, bond 18 March 1790. Consent by
Charles Winfree, father of the bride. James Overstreet (b) and
John Shannon (b); Nancy Winfree (w), John Winfree (w) and Vaul
Winfree (w). M.R. 20 March 1790 by James Hurt lists the bride as
Nancy Winfry.

OWEN, HARRISON and Susanna Hughes*, bond 23 July 1806. Consent also by
Josiah Hughes, father of the bride. Harrison Owen (b) and Martin
Covington (b); Thomas Dobson (w) and Martin Covington (b).

OWEN, ROBERT and Jemima Mason, bond 5 March 1799. Consent by Martin
Mason, father of the bride. Robert Owen (b) and Daniel Snow (b);
Daniel Snow (w). M.R. 7 March 1799 by Abner Early lists the bride
as Jamima Mason.

P

PACE, JOHN and Margaret Irvine, bond 16 December 1794. Consent by David
Irvine, father of the bride. John Pace (b) and Christopher Irvine
(b); Christopher Irvine (w). M.R. 19 December 1794 by Menoah Lesley.

PAGE, JOHN and Elizabeth Bryan*, bond 7 January 1797. John Page (b) and
George St. John (b); Geo. St. John (w). M.R. __ January 1797 by
Charles Cobbs.

PANNILL, MORTON and Polly B. Johns, bond 12 October 1808. Consent by
Edmund Johns, father of the bride. Morton Pannill (b) and James P.
Bullock (b); James P. Bullock (w) and Ann Johns (w). M.R. 17 Oc-
tober 1808 by Edmund Johns.

PANNILL, SAMUEL of Pittsylvania County and Judith Boughton, bond 31 Janu-
ary 1795. Consent by John Boughton, father of the bride. Samuel
Pannill (b) and Elcane Echols (b); John Goldfinch (w) and Elcaner
Echols (w). M.R. __ January 1795 by Charles Cobbs.

PARKER, WILLIAM and Mary Hurt*, bond 21 October 1808. William Parker (b)
and James Hurt (b); Daniel Hurt (w).

PARRISH, WILLIAM and Peggy Wisenbarger, bond 6 September 1792. William
Parrish (b) and Christopher Wisenbarger (b).

PARROTT, JOHN and Hannah Kenney, bond 28 December 1792. John Parrott (b) and James Kenney (b). M.R. 1 January 1793 by James Kenney.

PATE, EDMUND and Margaret Callaway, bond 12 March 1810. John Callaway (b) and Edmund Pate (b). M.R. 4 April 1810 by Joseph Pinnell.

PATRICK, DAVID F. and Sarah B. M. Pannill*, bond 15 March 1802. David Patrick (b) and Samuel Pannill (b); Samuel Pannill (w) and Samuel Armistead (w).

PATRICK, WILLIAM and Nancy Bullock, bond 11 January 1786. Consent by Patterson Bullock, father of the bride. J. Patrick (b) and William Patrick (b); Louis Bullock (w) and David Bullock (w).

PATTEN, VINCENT and Elizabeth Watkins, bond 10 September 1804. Consent by Mary McKinney, mother of the bride. Vincent Patten (b) and Dennis Kelley (b); Benjamin Walker (w) and Dennis Kelley (w). M.R. __ September 1804 by Edmund Johns.

PATTERSON, CHARLES and Jane Eidson, bond 29 December 1800. Consent by Henry Eidson. Charles Patterson (b) and Henry Eidson (b); Henry Eidson (w). M.R. 31 December 1800 by Henry Brown.

PATTERSON, JACOB (JOAB) and Ann Johnson, bond 28 August 1795. Consent by Ashley Johnson, father of the bride. Jacob (Joab) Patterson (b) and William Strong (b); Thomas Johnson (w) and Wm. Strong (w).

PATTERSON, JOHN and Ann Mann, bond 5 April 1789. Consent by Martha Man. John Patterson (b) and Richard Bloxsom (b). M.R. not dated but listed after entries for 31 March 1789, by James Kenney.

PATTERSON, THOMAS BELL (bachelor) and Mary Russell (widow)*, bond 1 July 1784. Thomas B. Patterson (b) and John G. Caffery (b).

PATTESON, DAVID and Salley Oglesby, bond 7 January 1797. Consent by Thos. Oglesby. David Patteson (b) and Tarlton Patteson (b); Patey Oglesby (w) and Tarlton Patteson (w).

PATY, ELIJAH and Avery (Eve) Parrott, bond 23 August 1794. Consent by Ann Parrott, mother of the bride. Elijah Paty (b) and Ben Cannafax (b); Benjamin Cannafax (w) and John Parrott (w). M.R. __ 1794 by James Kenney lists the bride as Ava Parrott.

PAYNE, JOHN S. and Susanna E. Scott, bond 3 June 1808. Consent by William Scott, father of the bride. John S. Payne (b) and Joel Yancey (b); Gabriel I. Scott (w). M.R. 3 June 1808 by William P. Martin lists the bride as Susannah Scott.

PAYNE, JAMMY and Tabitha Holmes*, bond 15 August 1805. Jammy Payne (b) and Robert Price (b); Robert Price (w).

PEMBERTON, JAMES and Elizabeth Wood, bond 16 June 1795. Consent by John Wood, father of the bride. James Pemberton (b) and Robert Watkins (b); Henry Walthall (w) and Robert Watkins (w).

PEMBERTON, JAMES and Hannah Johnson, bond 26 November 1803. Consent by
John Johnson, father of the bride. James Pemberton (b) and Henry
Robertson (b); Henry Robertson (w) and Jesse Harvey (w). M.R. 1 De-
cember 1803 by Henry Brown.

PENN, WILLIAM and Martha Stovall, bond 17 December 1787. William Penn (b)
and Bartholemew Stovall (b). M.R. 25 December 1787 by Charles Clay.

PERDUE, ISHAM and Rebeckah Powell, bond 10 October 1805. Consent by
Johannah Powel, mother of the bride. Isham Perdue (b) and Nathan
Tanner (b); Nathan Tanner (w), John Powel (w) and Sarah Powel (w).

PERKINS, TEMPLE and Susanna Clement, bond 11 November 1799. Consent by
Adam Clement. Temple Perkins (b) and Johnson Clement (b).

PERRIN, WILLIAM and Letty West. M.R. ____ 1783 by John Anthony.

PERROW, STEPHEN and Dolly Cox, daughter of Benjamin Cox, bond 8 July 1805.
Benjamin Cox (b) and Stephen Perrow (b). M.R. __ June 1804 by
William P. Martin.

PETTICREW, MATTHEW and Ann Akers, bond 5 November 1790. Consent by
William Akers, father of the bride. Matthew Petticrew (b) and John
Akers (b); John Akers (w) and D. Bullock (w). M.R. 11 November 1790
by William Mahon.

PHILLIPS, JOHN and Sally Watzon. M.R. 16 February 1809 by Obadiah Edge.

PHILLIPS, JOHN (widower) and Sarah Thompkins (widow)*, bond 26 December
1795. John Phillips (b) and William Griffin (b); Wm. Griffin (w).
M.R. 27 December 1796 by Menoah Lesley.

PHILLIPS, JOHN and Peggy Weber, bond 12 December 1808. Consent by John
Webber, brother of the bride. John Phillips (b) and John Weber (Webbber)
(b); Jas. C. Moorman (w).

PHILLIPS, JOHN and Sally Jude, bond 6 February 1809. Consent by George
Jude, father of the bride. John Phillips (b) and Lewis Jackson (b);
George Jude, Jr. (w) and Lewis Jackson (w). M.R. 16 February 1809
by Obadiah Edge lists the bride and groom as Sarah Jude and John
Philips.

PHILLIPS, WILLIAM and Jemima Walker, bond 3 January 1809. Consent by
Buckley Walker, father of the bride. William Phillips (b) and Benjamin
Walker (b).

PITTS, RITCHIE and Lucy Brown, bond 7 March 1791. Consent by John Brown,
father of the bride. Ritchie Pitts (b) and Anderson Chick (b); James
Brown (w) and Johannah Brown (w). M.R. 10 March 1791 by James
Kenney.

PLUNKETT, JOHN H. and Elizabeth Walker, bond 28 December 1805. Consent by
Wm. Walker and Hannah Sanders gives the bride's name as Elizabeth
Sanders. John H. Plunkett (b) and Charles Walker (b); Charles Walker
(w) and Thomas Walker (w). M.R. 28 December 1805 by William Flowers,Jr.
gives the bride's name as Elizabeth Sanders.

POINDEXTER, JOHN and Judith Chilton, bond 10 October 1803. Consent by
Richard Chilton, father of the bride. John Poindexter (b) and Joseph
Poindexter (b); Rawleigh Chilton (w) and Elizabeth I. Chilton (w).

POINDEXTER, JOSEPH and Frances I. Harrison, bond 19 May 1800. Joseph
Poindexter (b) and John Marshall (b).

POINDEXTER, REUBIN and Sally McIver, daughter of James McIver, bond 1 August
1806. Reubin Poindexter (b) and James McIver (b). M.R. 13 August
1806 by Obadiah Edge.

POINTER, JOHN and Polly Johnson, bond 28 November 1804. Consent by Chas.
Johnson, father of the bride. John Pointer (b) and William S. Bagby
(b). Moorman Johnson (w) and William S. Bagby (w).

PORTER, FRANCIS (bachelor) and Sarah Carson (spinster), bond 3 January 1788.
Consent by James and Mary Carson, parents of the bride. Francis
Porter (b) and Thomas Carson (b). M.R. 8 January 1788 by Joshua
Worley.

PORTER, JOHN and Ann Arthur, bond 4 September 1794. Consent by William
Arthur. John Porter (b) and Robert Haynes (b); Ro. Haynes (w) and
William Arthur (w). M.R. 8 September 1794 by Menoah Lesley.

PORTER, WILLIAM and Betsy Carson, bond 28 August 1798. Consent by James
and Mary Carson, parents of the bride. William Porter (b) and Thomas
Carson (b); Thos. Carson (w). M.R. 30 August 1798 by William Flowers.

POWELL,CORNELIUS and Elizabeth Perrow*, bond 4 August 1801. Cornelius
Powell (b) and Samuel Holloway (b); Samuel Holloway (w) and Bartlett
Wiley (w). M.R. 5 August 1801 by William P. Martin.

POWELL, JOHN and Margaret Cumbee*, bond 4 June 1808. Consent by Margaret
and Thomas Cumbee also. John Powell (b) and Nathan Tanner (b);
Susanner Cumbee (w), Nancy Cumbee (w) and Nathan Tanner (w). M.R.
entry made twice under date of June 5, 1808 by Obadiah Edge.

POWER, WILLIAM and Helen McKey (Mackay)*, bond 11 January 1808. William
Power (Powar) (b) and Alexander Mackay (b); Jane Mackay (w) and Alex
McKay (w).

PRATER, THOMAS and Siller Johns*, bond 9 June 1806. Thomas Prater (b) and
William Moorman (b); William Moorman (w) and Patsy Merriman (w). M.R.
10 June 1806 by James Warner lists the groom as Thomas Prator.

PREVITT, JAMES and Sarah Matthews, bond 9 September 1791. Consent by
Sally Matthews. James Previtt (b) and Joseph Previtt (b); Rob
Previt (w) and Patsy Previt (w).

PRIBBLE, MARTIN and Nancy Evans, bond 11 January 1808. Consent by Thos.
Evans, father of the bride. Martin Pribble (b) and John Willard (b);
William Power (w) and Becky Evans (w). M.R. 14 January 1808 by James
Warner lists the groom as Martin Prible and the bride as Nancy Evins.

PRICE, BOURNE (widower) and Magdalen Irvine (spinster), bond 18 December
1787. Consent by David Irvine, father of the bride. Bourne Price (b)
and James Adams (b); James Adams (w). M.R. 26 December 1787 by
Charles Clay.

PRYOR, WILLIAM and Spicy Taylor, bond 18 August 1809. Consent by Edmond
Taylor, father of the bride. William Pryor (b) and John Taylor (b);
John Taylor (w). M.R. 18 August 1809 by Samuel Davidson.

PUCKETT, CHARLES and Betsey Ann Akin, bond 2 December 1801. Consent by
Joseph Akin, father of the bride. Charles Puckett (b) and Thomas J.
Cook (b); Benjamin Sublett (w), Charles Martin (w) and Thomas J. Cook
(w). M.R. 1 December 1801 by Henry Brown.

PUCKETT, FLEMING and Polly Buckner*, bond 2 October 1797. Fleming Puckett (b)
and Thomas Alexander (b); Thos. Alexander (w). M.R. __ October 1797
by Charles Cobbs.

PUCKETT, ISHAM and Sallie Laine, bond 4 January 1790. Consent by John Laine,
father of the bride. Isham Puckett (b) and Samuel Drinkwater (b);
John Laine (w) and John Spalding (w). M.R. 7 January 1790 by James
Hurt gives the bride's name as Sallie Lane.

PUCKETT, THOMAS and Polly Webb, bond 2 June 1800. Consent by Edmond Webb,
father of the bride. Thomas Puckett (b) and Joshua Foster (b); Daniel
Webb (w).

PUGH, DAVID and Mary Martin, bond 13 October 1794. Consent by David Martin.
David Pugh (b) and John Martin (b); John Martin (w) and James Martin
(w). M.R. 16 October 1794 by William Flowers.

PUGH, JOHN and Mary Watkins, bond 26 December 1789. John Pugh (b) and Robert
Watkins (b). M.R. 31 December 1790 by James Kenney.

PUGH, JOHN and Elizabeth Loyd, bond 8 August 1797. John Pugh (b) and Jacob
Watkins (b).

PUGH, LOT and Tabitha Cheatham, daughter of Robertson Cheatham, bond 7 November 1808. Lot Pugh (b) and Robertson Cheatham (b). M.R. 10 November 1808 by Obadiah Edge.

PURCELL, THOMAS and Lucy Brown, bond 8 January 1810. Consent by Polly Brown,
mother of the bride. Thomas Purcell (b) and Daniel Brown (b); Daniel
Brown (w) and Joshua Brown (w).

Q

QUISENBERRY, JAMES and Mildred Moorman, bond 1 April 1805. Consent by Wm. Moorman, Sr., father of the bride. James Quisenberry (b) and James Moorman, Jr. (b); John Moorman (w) and J. Moorman, Sr. (w). M.R. __ April 1805 by Edmund Johns.

R

RAINE, JOHN (widower) of Cumberland County and Ann Marshall (widow)*, bond 4 January 1786. John Raine (b) and John Black (b); Thomas Dillon (w) and Betsy Boles (w).

RAINE, WILLIAM and Mary Lewis, daughter of Griffin Lewis, Sr., bond 22 December 1794. William Raine (b) and Griffin Lewis, Sr. (b).

RALEY (REALEY), ISAAC and Judith Spencer, bond 22 June 1803. Consent by Judith Spencer, mother of the bride. Isaac Realey (b) and William Johns (b); William Johns (w).

RANDOLPH, BEVERLY free Negro and Nancy Crank free Negro bond 4 April 1795. Consent by John Lynch who states that Nancy's parents (not named) consent. He certifies that though "still in her minority" she was emancipated by said John Lynch. Consent also by John Johnson, Sr. of Bedford County who certifies that Bevly Randolph "is free man by Record set free by the subscriber." Beverly Randolph (b) and William George (b); Thomas Johnson (w).

RANKEEN, ROBERT and Elizabeth Dinwiddie, daughter of James Dinwiddie, bond 28 November 1798. Robert Rankeen (b) and James Dinwiddie (b).

RANSBARGER, PHILIP and Elizabeth Douglass, bond 20 January 1801. John Carson (b) and Philip Ransbarger (b). M.R. 27 January 1801 by Henry Brown.

RATEKIN, JOHN and Susan Spica Greshaw (Grishaw), bond 17 September 1796. John Ratekin (b) and Isaac S. Grishaw (b). M.R. 21 September 1796 by Menoah Lesley lists the bride as Susan Spisa Greshaw.

RATEKIN, JOHN, JR. and Polly Smart, bond 24 January 1806. Consent by E. C. Smart. John Smart (b) and John Ratekin, Jr. (b); John Smart (w) and Edmund Smart (w).

RATEKIN, LAWRENCE and Nancy Moore (More)*, bond 28 March 1810. James Moore (b) and Lawrence Ratekin (b); James More (w).

READ, JOHN T. W. and Elizabeth Alexander, bond 25 December 1808. John T.W. Read (b) and John Alexander (b); Edmund Read (w). M.R. 25 December 1808 by Edmund Johns.

READ, JOSIAH and Mary Carson, bond 9 November 1791. Consent by Elizabeth Carson. Josiah Read (b) and William Carson (b); William Carson (w) and Robert Carson (w). M.R. 10 November 1791 by Menoah Lesley lists the groom as Josiah Reid.

READ, OBADIAH and Peggy Shearer, bond 9 August 1805. Consent by James
Shearer, father of the bride. Obadiah Read (b) and Morrison Bryan (b);
Morrison Bryan (w). M.R. 9 August 1805 by Matthew Easter lists the
groom as Obadiah Reed.

READEN, WILLIAM (bachelor) and Rebecca Thompson (spinster), bond 6 May 1788.
Thos. Moore certifies she is of lawful age, and "living at my house."
William Readen (b) and Robert Readen (b); George Jones (w), James
Moore (w), Thomas Moore (w), and Thomas Moore, Jr. (w).

RECTOR, JOHN and Mary Boteler, bond 8 September 1798. Consent by Will
Boteler, father of the bride. John Rector (b) and Ancil Manley (b);
Ancil Manly (w). M.R. 25 October 1798 by William Flowers lists the
bride as Mary Bottelar.

RECTOR, LEWIS and Sarah Boteler, bond 3 March 1792. Consent by Will Boteler,
father of the bride. Lewis Rector (b) and Thomas Boteler (b); Thomas
Boteler (w).

RECTOR, LEWIS and Elizabeth Martin, bond 14 January 1799. Consent by David
Martin, father of the bride. Josiah Martin (b) and Lewis Rector (b);
John Rittor (w) and Josiah Martin (w). M.R. 17 January 1799 by
William Flowers.

RECTOR, MARTIN and Betsey Burnett, bond 5 January 1789. Martin Rector (b)
and Thomas Dunn (b). M.R. 10 February 1789 by William Flowers.

RECTOR, MARTIN and Sarah Martin, bond 20 December 1804. Consent by David
Martin, father of the bride. Martin Rector (b) and David Martin (b);
David Martin, Jr. (w) and James Martin (w). M.R. 25 December 1804 by
William Flowers lists the groom as Martin Ractor.

REDD (READ), JOHN PAUL and Achsah Jones *, bond 25 February 1802. Consent
also by Mary Jones, mother of the bride, who states the bride is of
lawful age. John Paul Redd (Read) (b) and John Crockett (b); Oakley
Jones (w) and Susanner Jones (w).

REDDING, ROBERT (bachelor) and Mary Harrison Leason (widow), bond 9 April
1787. Joseph Redding (b) and Robert Redding (b); Thomas Walker (w).

REDDING, THOMAS and Elizabeth Stepp, bond 17 October 1794. John Stepp (b)
and Thomas Redding (b). M.R. __ December 1794 by Charles Cobbs lists
the groom as Thomas Reeding.

REED, JOHN and Jane Noell, bond 13 May 1805. Consent by Joice Noell, mother
of the bride. John Reed (b) and William H. Wilson (b); W. H. Wilson
(w) and German C. Noell (w). M.R. __ May 1805 by Edmund Johns lists
the bride as Jane Norvell.

REEDER, THOMAS and Martha Mann*, bond 13 February 1804. Thomas Reeder (b)
and Russell Boaz (b); Abel Lodge (w) and Russell Boaz (w).

REES, HEROD and Frances Cobbs*, bond 5 November 1810. Herod Reese (Rees)
(b) and William W. Weaver (b); W. W. Weaver (w).

REESE, HEROD and Juday Weaver*, bond 25 May 1789. Daniel Jones (b) and
Herod Reese (b); Daniel Jones (w).

REID, NATHAN and Sophia Thorp, bond 7 January 1784. Nathan Reid (b) and
Bourne Price (b); J. A. Steptoe (w) and Jas. Callaway (w).

REID, THOMAS and Nancy Forbes, bond 30 January 1791. Consent by John
Forbes, father of the bride is dated 1791. Thomas Reid (b) and John
Reid (b).

REVILY, ISAAC and Judith Spencer. M.R. __ June 1803 by Edmund Johns.

REYNOLDS, JOHN and Jane (Jeaney) Moore, bond 30 November 1809. Consent by
Samuel Moore, father of the bride. John Reynolds (b) and James
Reynolds (b); James Reynolds (w) and Thomas Bryan (w). M.R. 30 No-
vember 1809 by Edmund Johns.

REYNOLDS, WILLIAM and Martha Willson. M.R. 14 February 1782 by John W.
Holt.

REYNOLDS, WILLIAM and Rebecca Cannifax, bond 9 December 1801. Consent by
William Cannafix (Cannafax), father of the bride. William Reynolds
(b) and John Cannifax (b); Johnney Cannfix (w) and Nansey Canneyfix
(w). M.R. 10 December 1801 by William Flowers lists the bride as
Rebeckah Cannifax.

RICE, JONATHAN and Rebeccah Hix, bond 14 January 1789. Consent by John
Hix. Jonathan Rice (b) and Josiah Jackson (b). M.R. 15 January 1789
by James Hurt lists the bride as Rebeckah Hix.

RICE, SAMUEL and Mary Moore, bond 26 July 1784. Consent by Thomas Moore,
father of the bride. Samuel Rice (b) and Holcombe Robinson (b).

RICH, ALLEN and Mary McReynolds*, bond 9 April 1810. Allen Rich (b) and
William Thomas (b); William Thomas (w). M.R. 10 April 1810 by Samuel
Davidson lists the bride and groom as Poley McRenels and Alen Ritch.

RICH, DAVID and Mary Barker*, bond 7 October 1794. David Rich (b) and
Thomas Oglesby (b); Thomas Oglesby (w) and William Oglesby (w).

RICHARDSON, JACOB and Sarah McDaniel*, bond 5 August 1791. Jacob Richardson (b) and Micajah Goodwin (b); Micajah Goodwin (w).

RICHARDSON, JOHN and Mary Terrell. M.R. 29 October 1782 by John W. Holt.

RICHARDSON, WILLIAM and Sally Landers*, bond 3 October 1788. William
Richardson (b) and William Moore (b). M.R. not dated but entered in
original Register after entries for 15 August 1788, by James Kenney.
The bride is listed as Sally Saunders.

RICHESON (RICHARDSON), MORGAN and Penelope Eidson, bond 7 December 1785. Martin Mason (b) and Morgan Richeson (Richardson) (b).

RIDGEWAY, SAMUEL and Rosanna Epperson, bond 18 February 1800. Consent by Littleberry Epperson, father of the bride. Samuel Ridgeway (b) and Richard Epperson (b); Richard Epperson (w) and Phebe Roark (w).

RIGGS, GEORGE and Rhoda Cunningham, bond 27 September 1785. George Riggs (b) and William Cunningham (b).

ROACH, JOSHUA and Sarah Morris, bond 4 October 1791. Consent by John Hix, guardian of the bride. Joshua Roach (b) and William Hix (b); Wm. Raine (w) and John Raine (w).

ROBERDS (ROBERTS), BENJAMIN and Annaca Martin*, bond 8 August 1789. The bride signed the consent with only her first name, Annaca. Her last name on the bond is almost impossible to figure out, but has been interpreted and is listed in the Marriage Register Vol.I, 1782- as Martin. Benjamin Roberts (b) and Joseph Jenkins (b); Thos. Moorman (w) and John Cannaday (w).

ROBERTS, BENJAMIN (bachelor) and Mary Ferguson (widow)*, bond 20 July 1784. Nathan Franklin (b) and Benjamin Roberts (b); Nathaniel Rogers (w).

ROBERTS, FEANDER free Negro and Oney (Amy) Pippin free Negro bond 10 March 1800. Feander Roberts free Negro (b) and Frank Freeman free Negro (b).

ROBERTS, HARRY (HENRY) and Hannah Napper, bond 10 November 1806. Consent by Milley Napper, mother of the bride. Harry Roberts (b) and John Timberlake (b); Geo. Fosdeck (w) and John Timberlake (w).

ROBERTS, ISHAM and Betsy George*, bond 17 July 1805. Consent also by Milly George, mother of the bride, which names the groom as Isham Roberds. Isham Roberts (Roberds) (b) and James S. Butler (b); William Butler (w), James S. Butler (w) and Latham Stanton (w).

ROBERTS, JOE, free Negro and Polly Clodhopper, free Negro bond 19 March 1802. Consent by Daniel Clodhopper and Polly Clodhopper, parents of the bride. Joe Roberts (b) and Latham Stanton (b); Latham Stanton (w) and William Butler (w).

ROBERTS, MACK and Nancy Ends Rush, bond 3 September 1798. Consent by George Rust, father of the bride. Mack Roberts (b) and William Carson (b); Thomas Parkinson (w), William Carson (w) and Donald Warrand (w). M.R, 6 September 1798 by Abner Early lists the bride as Nancy Rust.

ROBERTS, MORRIS and Betsy Rust, bond 29 June 1799. Consent by George Rust, father of the bride. Morris Roberts (b) and Archer Williamson (b); Donald Warrand (w) and Archer Williamson (w). M.R. 4 July 1799 by Abner Early lists the bride as Betsey H. Rust (D.G.R.)

ROBERTS, WILLIAM and Elizabeth Spencer*, bond 8 December 1794. Consent als
by Judith Spencer, mother of the bride. David Spencer (b) and William
Roberts (b); David Spencer (w) and Menoah Lesley (w). M.R. 13 Decembe
1794 by Menoah Lesley.

ROBERTSON, ARCHIBALD and Elizabeth M. Bolling, bond 8 June 1801. Consent
by Archibald Bolling, father of the bride. John Steele (b) and
Archibald Robinson (b); John Steele (w) and James Matthews (w).

ROBERTSON, ARTHUR and Jenny McGehee, bond 17 October 1801. Consent by Math
McGehee, father of the bride. Lynch A. McGehee (b) and Arthur Roberts
(b); Lynch A. McGehee (w) and John McGehee (w).

ROBERTSON, HENRY and Nancy Johnson, bond 26 November 1803. Consent by John
Robertson, father of the groom. Henry Robertson (b) and James
Pemberton (b); Jesse Harvey (w) and James Pemberton (w). M.R. 1 De-
cember 1803 by Henry Brown.

ROBERTSON, JAMES, JR. and Bridget Davis, bond 5 January 1805. Consent by
John Davis, father of the bride. James Robertson, Jr. (b) and Henry
Franklin (b); Henry Franklin (w) and John Robertson (w). M.R. 9 Janua
1805 by William Flowers, Sr. lists the bride as Biddey E. Davis.

ROBERTSON, JOHN and Nancy Franklin, bond 12 April 1802. Consent by Elizabe
Steel, mother of the bride. John Robertson (b) and Thomas Franklin (b
John Franklin (w) and Thomas Franklin (w). M.R. 23 April 1802 by
Henry Brown.

ROBINSON (ROBERTSON), CHRISTOPHER and Anna Rice, bond 27 May 1803. Consent
by John Rice, father of the bride. Christopher Robinson (Robertson)
(b) and Peter Furgusson (b); Mason Hill (w) and Peter Furguson (w).

ROBINSON, JOHN and Leany Hix, bond 21 January 1792. Consent by Mary Hix,
mother of the bride. John Robinson (b) and Beverly Crawley (b); Wm.
Arthur (w) and Beverly Crawley (w).

ROBINSON (ROBERSON), JOHN and Ellender (Elanor) Russel, bond 19 January 179
Consent by Ann Russel. John Robinson (b) and James Boaz (b).

ROBINSON, JOHN and Rachel Barnett. M.R. 18 July 1782 by John W. Holt.

ROBINSON, LEWIS and Nancy Ledbetter, bond 15 September 1800. Consent by
Joseph Ledbetter, father of the bride. Lewis Robinson (b) and Joseph
Ledbetter (b); Joseph Ledbetter (w) and Lunaney (?) Campbell (w).

ROBINSON, THOMAS and Lucy Moorman, bond 6 August 1806. Consent by Jesse
Moorman, father of the bride, and by Polly Perkins. Thomas Robinson
(b) and James Moorman (b); James Moorman, Sr. (w).

ROBINSON, WILLIAM and Lucy Wily (Wiley), bond 6 May 1786. Consent by John
Wily. John Robinson (b) and William Robinson (b); Charles Smith (w)
and Reubin Smith (w).

RODGERS, SAMUEL and Elizabeth Brent, bond 17 December 1795. Consent by
Nathaniel Rogers, guardian of the bride. Samuel Rodgers (b) and
William Mason (b); William Mason (w) and James Wilson (w). M.R.
__ December 1795 by Charles Cobbs lists the groom as Samuel Rogers.

ROHR, JACOB and Nancy Davis, bond 5 March 1800. Consent by Thomas Davis,
father of the bride. Jacob Rohr (b) and Leonard Bowers (b); Thomas
Scott (w) and Leonard Bowers (w). M.R. __ 1799 by Samuel Mitchell,
lists the groom as Jacob Rhorr.

ROHR (RHOR), PHILLIP and Sally Barnwell, bond 4 November 1799. Consent by
Elizabeth Barnwell, mother of the bride. Philip Rohr (b) and
Leonard Bowers (b); Leonard Bowers (w).

RORK, CHARLES, JR. and Phebe Epperson, daughter of Littleberry Epperson,
bond 20 May 1797. Charles Rork, Jr. (b) and Littleberry Epperson (b).
M.R. __ May 1797 by Charles Cobbs lists the groom as Charles Rorks.

RORK, OWEN and Elizabeth Garvin, bond 27 October 1801. Consent by Susanah
Garvin, mother of the bride. Owen Rork (b) and Bernard Rork (b); John
Dickey (w) and Barnard Rork (w). M.R. 7 November 1801 by William
Flowers.

ROSE, WILLIAM and (Miss) Aphia Scott, bond 18 October 1805:1803. Consent
by Samuel Scott, father of the bride. William Rose, Jr. (b) and
Charles Hoyle, Jr. (b); W. Gordon (w) and Charles Hoyle, Jr. (w).
M.R. 30 October 1804 by William P. Martin lists the bride as Ashia
Scott. The date on the bond reads 1805. On the outside of the bond
written in pencil is the date 1803.

ROSSER, AMBROSE and Sally Finch, daughter of Blagdon Finch, bond 1 October
1800. Ambrose Rosser (b) and Blagdon Finch (b). M.R. 16 October
1800 by Henry Brown.

ROSSER, JOHN and Nancy Wood, daughter of Edmund Wood, bond 8 February 1808.
John Rosser (b) and Edmund Wood (b); M.R. 8 February 1808 by Edmund
Johns.

ROSSER, JOHN and Margaret Franklin. M.R. __ March 1803 by William Flowers.

ROSSER, PLEASANT and Judith Jones*, bond 27 March 1805. Pleasant Rosser (b)
and Pleasant Talbot (b); Josias Jones (w) and Pleasant Talbot (w).
M.R. __ March 1805 by Edmund Johns.

ROSSER, THOMAS and Nancy Tweedy, bond 5 March 1792. Consent by Joseph
Tweedy, father of the bride. Thomas Rosser (b) and Robert Tweedy (b);
Robert Tweedy (w). M.R. 5 March 1792 by Bennett Maxey.

ROSSER, WILLIAM and Elizabeth Wood, bond 17 February 1786. Consent by John
Wood. Edmund Wood (b) and William Rosser (b). M.R. 25 February 1786
by James Kenney.

ROWLAND, ROBERT and Francis Irvine, bond 10 May 1797. Consent by David Irvine, father of the bride. Robert Rowland (b) and Robert Irvine (b); Safiah Irvine (w) and Robt. Irvine (w).

ROWLING, JOHN and Anne Dudley, daughter of Armistead Dudley, bond 12 March 1807. John Rowling (b) and Armistead Dudley (b). M.R. 12 March 1807 by James Warner lists the groom as John Rawling(?).

ROWZE, THOMAS and Elizabeth Richardson, bond 10 January 1789. Consent by Dolly Richardson. William Patrick (b) and Thomas Rowze (b); Geo. Richardson (w) and Wm. Richardson (w). M.R. 13 January 1789 by James Kenney.

RUSSELL, THOMAS and Sarah Asher, bond 23 January 1797. Thomas Russell (b) and John Asher (b). M.R. __ January 1797 by Charles Cobbs.

RUTLEDGE, WILLIAM and Ann Marshall, bond 26 December 1803. William Rutledge (b) and John Marshall (b).

S

SAINT JOHN, GEORGE and Nancy Bryan*, bond 2 March 1793. John Wynne (b) and George Saint John (b).

ST. JOHN, JAMES and Sarah Thompson (Tompson)*, bond 24 July 1794. James St. John (b) and William Patrick (b); Elizabeth Stepp (w). M.R. __ Jul 1794 by Charles Cobbs lists the groom as James S. St. John.

SANDERS, CHRISTOPHER (bachelor) and Jean Lucas (spinster), bond 17 December 1786. Thomas Kitchen (b) and Christopher Sanders (b).

SANDERS, DANIEL J. and Martha Stith, bond 21 October 1793. Daniel Sanders (b) and Benjamin Stith (b).

SAUL, SAMUEL and Hannah Haley, bond 11 December 1784. Consent by William Haley, son of Hannah Haley. Samuel Saul (b) and Fleming Branch (b).

SAUNDERS, JOHN and Betsy Crowley, daughter of James Crowley, bond 2 October 1809. John Saunders (b) and James Crowley (b). M.R. 28 October 1809 by James Warner lists the bride as Betsey Crawley.

SCHOOLFIELD, BENJAMIN and Ann Thurman (Thurmon), bond 3 December 1795. Benjamin Schoolfield (b) and Richard Thurmon (b). M.R. 5 December 1796 by Menoah Lesley, lists the bride as Ann Thurmon.

SCHOOLFIELD, JOHN and Sally Thurmond, bond __ August 1799. John Schoolfield (b) and Benjamin Schoolfield (b). M.R. 1 ____ 1799 by William P. Martin

SCHOOLFIELD, SAMUEL and Judith Fowler, bond 13 August 1802. Consent by John Fowler, father of the bride. Samuel Schoolfield (b) and Samuel Martin (b); Sam Martin (w) and Jno. Fowler, Jr. (w).

SCOTT, JAMES and Polly Clark, daughter of John Clark, bond 12 September 1808. James Scott (b) and John Clark (b). M.R. 15 September 1808 by Samuel Davidson lists the groom as James Scot.

SCOTT, MATTHIS and Betsy Wayne, daughter of John Wayne, bond 18 December 1804. Matthis Scott (b) and John Wayne (b). The groom signs his name Matthias Scott.

SCOTT, THOMAS and Mary Fowler, bond 11 March 1799. Thomas Scott (b) and Sackville King (b). M.R. ___ 1799 by Samuel Mitchell lists the bride as Margaret Fowler.

SCOTT, WILLIAM and Susannah Hubbard Young, bond 5 February 1803. Consent by Will Young. William Scott (b) and Joseph Young (b). M.R. ___ February 1803 by Edmund Johns.

SCRUGGS, LANGHORNE and Sarah Douglass, bond 3 February 1796. Consent by Drury Scruggs, father of Langhorne Scruggs, and also by James Douglas, father of Sarah Douglas. Langhorne Scruggs (b) and James Douglas (b); George Jude (w) and Edward Douglas (w). M.R. ___ 1796 by Charles Cobbs lists the bride as Sarah Douglass.

SEAY, JOSEPH and Agness Ligen*, bond 16 March 1804. Date of bond given as 1803 in Marriage Register Vol. I, 1782- . Joseph Seay (b) and Alexander Driskill (b); Alexander Driskill (w). M.R. ___ March 1804 by Edmund Johns lists the bride and groom as Agnes Ligon and Joseph Lea.

SEAY, WILLIAM and Elizabeth Howerton, bond 31 December 1799. Consent by Grief Howerton. James Lucas (b) and William Seay (b); James Lucas (w).

SHACKLEFORD, JAMES and Nancy Haynes, bond 24 October 1787. Consent by Parmeanas Haynes, parent of the bride. James Shackleford (b) and John Shackleford (b). M.R. 25 October 1787 by James Kenney.

SHANNON, JAMES and Rachel Field, daughter of Andrew Field, bond 9 December 1794. James Shannon (b) and Andrew Field (b). M.R. 11 December 1794 by William Mahon.

SHEARER, ANDREW and Nancy Adams, bond 3 May 1805. Consent by John Adams, father of the bride. Andrew Shearer (b) and Nathan Adams (b); G. Adams (w) and Nathan Adams (w). M.R. ___ May 1805 by Edmund Johns.

SHEARER, JAMES and Mary Martin*, bond 20 July 1789. James Shearer (b) and John Stepp (b); John Stepp (w).

SHEARER, JAMES and Elizabeth Akers, bond 12 January 1801. Consent by William Akers, father of the bride. James Shearer (b) and William Akers (b). M.R. 16 January 1801 by William Kenyon.

SHEARER, THOMAS and Sarah Massee, bond 27 December 1785. Thomas Shearer (b) and James Suttenfield (b). M.R. 2 January 1786 by James Kenney lists the bride as Sarah Massey.

SHEPHERD, THOMAS and Susannah Bailey, daughter of William Bailey, bond
9 September 1799. William Bailey (b) and Thomas Shepherd (b).
M.R. 11 September 1799 by William Flowers lists the groom as Thomas
Shepperd.

SHERER, JAMES and Margit Martin (Martain)*, bond 10 November 1799. James
Sherer (b) and John Akers (b).

SHEUSTER, PHILIP and Mary Eleanor Crawly. M.R. 30___ 1782 by John W. Holt.

SHOWLS (SHOULS), CONRAD and Sarah Arther, bond 13 July 1807. Consent by
William Arther. Conrad Showls (Shouls) (b) and Alexander Mackey (b);
Barnebas Arther (w) and Alexander Mackay (w).

SHUTTLE, JOHN and Elizabeth Callahan, bond 19 February 1798. Stephen
Callahan (b) and John Shuttle (b).

SILCOCK (SILIOCK), AMOS and Sarah Mason, bond 29 October 1789. William
Mason (b) and Amos Silcock (b).

SKIDMORE, WILLIAM and Mary Randall, bond 12 June 1796. Consent by Isaac
Hatcher, guardian of the bride, who certifies she is "of age."
William Skidmore (b) and Henry Terrell (b); Salley Moorman (w) and
Henry Terrell (w). M.R. 12 June 1796 by Menoah Lesley lists the
bride as Mary Randolph.

SLADE, JOHN and Betty Davis*, bond 12 October 1801. John Slade (b) and
David Moore (b); Henry Sneed (w) and David Moore (w). M.R. 12 October 1801 by William P. Martin lists the groom as John Sledd.

SMART, EDMUND and Sally Hayth, daughter of Thomas Hayth, bond 19 January
1808. Edmund Smart (b) and Thomas Hayth (b). M.R. 19 January 1808
by Edmund Johns.

SMART, JOHN and Elizabeth Farris, daughter of Benjamin Farris, bond
10 October 1808. John Smart (b) and Benjamin Farris (b). M.R.
10 October 1808 by Edmund Johns lists the bride as Elizabeth Faris.

SMITH, FRANCIS, JR. and Anney Frazer (Frazier), bond 27 December 1803.
Consent by William Frazer (Frazier), father of the bride. Francis
Smith (b) and Jonathan White (b); Jonathan White (w) and James
Deering (w).

SMITH, JOSEPH (bachelor) and Sarah Thompson (spinster), bond 20 November
1786. Consent by Sarah Thompson, mother of the bride. Joseph Smith
(b) and Tristram Coggeshall (b); Benjamin Beachbord (w) and Tristram
Coggeshall (w).

SMITH, ROBERT and Agnes Moorman, bond 19 January 1801. Consent by Mary
Strange, mother of the bride. Daniel Kelley (b) and Robert Smith (b);
James Glass (w) and Daniel Kelley (w). M.R. 22 January 1801 by
Henry Brown.

SMITH, STEPHEN and (Miss) Polly Wilson (Willson), bond 1 January 1798.
Consent by Nathaniel Rogers, guardian of the bride. Jane Wilson (b)
and Stephen Smith (b); Jane Wilson (w). M.R. __ January 1798 by
Charles Cobbs.

SMITHSON, JOHN M. and Lucy Dabney*, bond 2 April 1801. John Q. Dabney
(b) and John M. Smithson (b); Samuel Smithson (w), John Lasley (w)
and John Q. Dabney (w). M.R. 3 April 1801 by Henry Brown.

SMITHSON, SAMUEL and Mary Terrell, bond 23 February 1802. Consent by
Edward Terrell, father of the bride. Samuel Smithson (b) and William
Terrell (b); William Terrell (w). M.R. 24 February 1802 by Henry
Brown.

SMITHSON, TYRE and Seley Murrell, bond 5 December 1809. Consent by
Thomas Murrell, father of the bride. Tyre Smithson (b) and James C.
Haden (b) and Edmund Brown (b); James C. Haden (w), Simeon Austin (w)
and Edmund Brown (w). M.R. 7 December 1809 by James Warner lists the
groom and bride as Tiry Smithson and Secelia Murrell.

SNEAD, EVAN and Molly Fowler, bond 20 June 1797. Consent by John and Ann
Fowler. William Snead (b) and Evan Snead (b); James Martin (w) and
William Snead (w).

SNEAD, WILLIAM and Sally Martin, bond 1 February 1792. Consent by John
and Ann Fowler, parents of the bride. William Snead (b) and James
Martin (b); Mary Fowler (w) and Samuel Martin (w).

SNODDY, ROBERT and Sophia Shuttle, bond 6 September 1790. Bourne Price
certifies "she's of age" and has no father living, or guardian. Peter
Claywell (b) and Robert Snoddy (b). M.R. 8 September 1790 by Andrew
Hunter lists the bride as Sophia Shartil.

SNOW, DANIEL and Cona Mason, bond 14 November 1797. Martin Mason (b) and
Daniel Snow (b).

SNOW, HENRY and Martha Cheek. M.R. _____ 1783 by John Anthony.

SNOW, VINCENT and Polly Walden, bond 17 December 1803. Consent by Pattsy
Walden, mother of the bride. Vincent Snow (b) and Lewis Walden (b);
Henry Walden (w) and Lewis Walden (w).

SOWELL, PHILIP (bachelor) and Jane Johnson (spinster), bond 29 October 1787.
Consent by Benjamin and Martha Johnson, parents of the bride. John
Snoddy (b) and Philip Sowell (b); Jane Johnson (w) and John Snoddy (w).

SPEECE (SPACE), CONRAD and Rachel Claywell, bond 3 November 1796. Consent
by Margaret Webber. Robert Alexander (b) and Conrad Speece (b); Peter
Claywell (w) and John Morcheson (w). M.R. ____ 1796 by Menoah Lesley.

SPEECE, GEORGE and Sally Fosdick, daughter of William Fosdick, bond
3 August 1810. William Fosdick (b) and George Speece (b). Simeon
Austin (w).

SPEECE (SPACE), PETER and Isabella Tribble, bond 9 March 1801. Peter Speece (b) and John Tribble (b).

SPENCER, BEVERLY and Lotty Gosnay, bond 6 December 1792. Beverly Spencer (b) and William Patterson (b).

SPENCER, DAVID and Elizabeth Epperson, bond 23 December 1795. Consent by Littleberry Epperson, father of the bride. David Spencer (b) and Richard Epperson (b); Polly Forrest (w) and Rudd Epperson (w).

SPENCER, MOSES and Nancy Johns, daughter of James Johns, bond 11 July 1803. Consent by James Johns, father of the bride. Moses Spencer (b) and William Johns (b); James Benagh (w) and William Johns (w). M.R. __ July 1803 by Edmund Johns.

STANLEY, JAMES and Sibby Hix, bond 7 July 1802. Consent by John Hix. James Stanley (b) and Thomas Hazlewood (b); John Hix, Jr. (w) and Thomas Hazelwood (w). M.R. __ July 1802 by Edmund Johns lists the bride as Sibeller Hix. Her name is given as Libby Hix in the Marriage Register Vol. I, 1782-

STANTON, AARON and Lydia Fosdick, bond 8 March 1802. William Fosdick (b) and Aaron Stanton (b).

STAPLES, GARLAND and Franky Elam, bond __ February 1790. Garland Staples (b) and Richard Elam (b). M.R. 9 February 1790 by James Kenney lists the bride as Frances Elam.

STAPLES, ISAAC and Jane Staples. M.R. 29 January 1791 by William Flowers.

STAPLES, JOHN N. (or U.) and Elizabeth Baugh, bond __ December 1800. Consent by Thomas Trent, guardian of the bride. Robert Wright (b) and John Staples (b); Alexander Hunter (w), Sheran Watkins (w) and Robert Wright (w). The M.R. by William Flowers is entered three times under date of 11 December 1800, in one of which the groom is listed as John U. Staples.

STAPLES, SAMUEL and Judith Pendleton, stepdaughter of Robert Wilson, bond 23 December 1806. Samuel Staples (b) and Robert Wilson (b). M.R. 27 December 1806 by William Flowers, Jr.

STAPLES, WILLIAM and Betsy Wilmoth*, bond 16 August 1805. William Staples (b) and Henry Terrell (b); Henry Terrell (w). M.R. 19 August 1805 by Matthew Easter.

STEEL, ALEXANDER and Elizabeth Franklin*, bond 12 April 1794. Consent also by John Steel who offers to go security for his father, Alexander Steel, if necessary. Alexander Steel (b) and Robert Alexander (b). M.R. 14 April 1794 by William Mahon lists the groom as Alexander Steel, Sr.

STEEL (STEELE), ALEXANDER and Sally Akers, bond 26 February 1799. Consent by William Akers, Sr., father of the bride. Alexander Steel (b) and Mathew Peticrew (b); Mathew Peticrew (w). M.R. 28 February 1799 by William Flowers lists the groom as Alexander Steele.

STEEL, ARCH and Judith S. Rice, bond 23 July 1806. Consent by John Rice, father of the bride. Arch Steel (b) and Thomas Smith (b); William Ward (w) and Thomas Smith (w). M.R. 23 July 1806 by William P. Martin lists the groom as Archibald Steel.

STEEN, JOHN and Nancy Wood*, bond 9 June 1797. Charles Henson (b) and John Steen (b); Jesse Jennings (w) and William Jennings (w).

STEEN, WILLIAM and Jane Schoolfield, daughter of David Schoolfield, bond __ August 1799. David Schoolfield (b) and William Steen (b). M.R. 1 September 1799 by William P. Martin.

STEPHENS (STEVENS), THOMAS and Sally Mitchell, bond 15 August 1809. Consent by John Mitchell, father of the bride. Thomas Stephens (b) and Stark Whitington (b); George Baber (w) and Nunnery Bailey (w).

STEPP, JOSEPH and Patsy Woods, bond 26 December 1801. Joseph Stepp (b), Patsy Woods (b) and Nathan Tanner (b). M.R. 26 December 1801 by Henry Brown.

STEPP, SOLOMON and Mourning Wynne, daughter of Jones Wynne, bond 30 December 1794. Solomon Stepp (b) and Jones Wynne (b). M.R. __ January 1795 by Charles Cobbs.

STERN, FRANCIS of Charlotte County and Lucy Rawlins*, bond 21 March 1796. Francis Stern (b) and Herod Reese (b); Herod Reese (w). M.R. 15 February 1797 by John Chappell, lists the bride as Rollens.

STEVENS, JOHN of Halifax County and Cona Armistead, bond 18 November 1806. Consent by Robert Armistead, father of the bride. John Stevens (b) and Francis Armistead (b); Francis Armistead (w) and Thomas Ripley (w).

STEVENS, JOHN and Elizabeth Welch, bond 10 November 1800. John Stevens (b) and Amos Gore (b).

STEWART, HENRY and Polly Armstrong, daughter of Benjamin Armstrong, bond 6 April 1805. Benjamin Armstrong (b) and Henry Stewart (b).

STEWART, JOHN and Anne Gauldin, bond 16 November 1795. William Bosher certifies she is of age. William Bosher (b) and John Stewart (b). M.R. __ November 1795 by Charles Cobbs.

STIMMONS, JACOB and Nancy Stovall, bond 3 May 1787. Consent by Elizabeth Stovall, mother of the bride. Robert Hunter (b) and Jacob Stimmons (b).

STITH, JOHN and Lucy Ann Hardaway*, bond 17 September 1806. Consent also by Joseph Stith for son John "an infant." John Stith (b) and John Stith, Jr. (b); Lucy Stith (w) and John Stith (w). M.R. 17 September 1806 by Edmund Johns.

STITH, JOHN and Susannah Hightower*, bond 22 April 1801. John Stith (b) and Thomas Cock (b); Thos. Cock (w) and Ellenor Cock (w).

STITH, JOSEPH and Nancy Cock, bond 9 September 1782. Consent by George Cock, father of the bride. William Jordan (b) and Joseph Stith (b); William Talbot (w) and Chas. M. Talbot (w). M.R. 8 September 1783 by John W. Holt.

STITH, RICHARD and Betsy Jones, bond 28 December 1798. Consent by Thomas Jones, father of the bride. Richard Stith (b) and Thomas Stith (b); Thomas Stith (w) and Wm. Stith (w).

STITH, THOMAS and Rhoda Jones, bond __ March 1793. Consent by Thomas Jones, father of the bride. Thomas Stith (b) and Robert Alexander (b). M.R. __ March 1793 by Charles Cobbs.

STITH, WILLIAM and Nancy Jones, bond 28 December 1796. Consent by Thomas Jones, father of the bride. William Stith (b) and Thomas Stith (b); Thomas Stith (w) and Daniel Sanders (w). M.R. ____ 1796 by Charles Cobbs.

STOAKES, THOMAS of Lunenburg County and Polly Wade, bond 1 February 1797. Consent by Henry Wade, father of the bride. Thomas Stoakes (b) and Zackfield Wade (b); Pauline Thurston (w). M.R. __ February 1797 by Charles Cobbs lists the groom as Thomas Stokes.

STONE, WILLIAM and Elizabeth Callaway, bond 15 November 1806. Consent by John Calloway who states "Whereas a marriage is intended between Wm. Stone and Elizabeth Callaway (daughter of Caleb Callaway late of this County) who is now gone to Kentucky, and her mother dead and having no guardian, I, as her next friend think there will be no impropriety in your granting them a license, which I hope you will do..." David Callaway (b) and William Stone (b); David Calloway (w).

STORER, ARCHER and Elizabeth Flowers, bond 9 July 1804. Consent by Rolin and Elizabeth Flowers, parents of the bride. Archibald Storer (b) and Henry Candler (b); Henry Candler (w). M.R. 30 August 1804 by William Flowers, Sr. gives the groom's name as Archibald Storey. The groom signs his name Archibald Storer.

STORRY (STORER), PLEASANT and Patty Nichols, bond 3 December 1798. Consent by Joseph Nichols. Pleasant Storrey (Storer) (b) and Pleasant Magann (b); Pleasant Magann (w) and John Merritt (w). M.R. 10 December 1798 by William P. Martin lists the groom as Pleasant Story, and the bride as Patty Nicholes. The groom signs his name Pleasant Storer.

STOVALL, GEORGE and Sarah Oglesby*, bond 9 April 1804. George Stovall (b) and Wrenny Crews (b); James Crews (w) and Wrenny Crews (w). M.R. 9 April 1804 by William P. Martin lists the groom as George Stoveall, and the bride as Sarah Oglesvie.

STOVALL, JOHN and Jenny Patterson, bond 25 November 1782. John Stovall (b) and Tarleton Patterson (b).

STOVALL, TERRITIA and Linda Rilly Bailey (Baley), bond 10 September 1804.
Consent by William Baley, father of the bride. Territia Stovall (b)
and George Stovall (b); George Stovall (w) and Thomas Sheppard (w).
The Marriage Register Vol. I, 1782- lists the groom as Terisha Stovall.

STRANGE, JOHN, SR. and Mary Moorman*, bond 14 July 1800. John Strange (b)
and Thomas W. Clark (b); Thomas W. Clark (w).

STRANGE, NATHANIEL and Elizabeth Moorman, "both of the County of Campbell,
Parish of Russell," bond 19 February 1787. Consent by Chas. Moorman.
Nathaniel Strange (b) and Benjamin Faris (b); Martha Haden (w).

STRATTON, DANIEL and Elizabeth Walker, daughter of William Walker, bond
14 March 1808. Daniel Stratton (b) and William Walker (b). M.R.
19 March 1808 by William Flowers, Jr.

STREET, ANTHONY of Halifax County, and Iriphena Sturman, bond 30 January
1786. Consent by Valentine and Elizabeth Sturman, parents of the bride.
William Sturman (b) and Anthony Street (b).

STRONG, DAVID and Lucretia Irvine, daughter of John Irvine, bond 30 May
1794. John Irvine (b) and David Strong (b). M.R. 5 June 1794 by
William Mahon.

STUART, JAMES and Elizabeth Harrod Majors, bond 6 September 1789. Two
consents are attached to the bond. In different handwriting, one is
signed Philip Magor, and the other is signed Philip Majors. James
Stuart (b) and John Wayne (b); John Wayne (w). M.R. 18 September
1789 by James Hurt. The Marriage Register Vol. I, 1782- lists the
bride as Elizabeth Mayors.

STUART (STEWART), JAMES and Nancy B. Warwick, bond 8 June 1801. Consent
by William Warwick, father of the bride. James Stuart (b) and Wilson
Davenport (b); Wilson Davenport (w) and Rod'k Taliaferro (w).

SUBLETT (SUBLEY), BENJAMIN and Mary Akin, daughter of Joseph Akin, bond
8 November 1797. Benjamin Sublett (b) and Joseph Akin (b). M.R.
9 November 1797 by Joshua Worley. The groom signs his name Benjamin
Subley.

SUBLETT (SUBLEY), SAMUEL and Fanny Taylor, bond 22 August 1799. Consent
by Charles Taylor, father of the bride. Samuel Sublett (b) and
William Taylor (b); John Fore (w) and William Taylor (w). M.R. 29
August 1799 by Joshua Worley. The groom signs his name Samuel Subley.

SUBLETTE (SUBLET), WILLIAM and Sally Akin, bond 20 December 1787. Consent
by Joseph Akin, father of the bride. William Sublett (b) and Alexander
Dudgeon (b). The groom signs his name William Sublet.

SUBLITE (SUBLETT), GEORGE ALLEN and Isabella Akin, bond 14 November 1791.
Consent by Joseph Akin, father of the bride. William Akin (b) and
George Allen Sublite (b). The groom signs his name George Allen
Sublett.

SUBLITT (SUBLET), MATHEW and Frankey Key, bond 18 February 1803. Jacob
Key (b) and Mathew Sublitt (b). M.R. 24 February 1803, by Joshua
Worley lists the bride as Francis Key. The groom signs his name
Mathew Sublet.

SUTTENFIELD, JAMES (bachelor) and Edith Roberts (spinster), bond 25 May
1787. Consent by Aisley (?) Roberts, parent of the bride. James
Suttenfield (b) and Patrick Gibson (b); John Bryan (w) and Patrick
Gibson (w). M.R. 28 May 1787 by James Kenney.

T

TALBOT, MATTHEW and Jane Quarles, bond 25 September 1784. Matthew Talbot
(b) and Charles M. Talbot (b).

TALBOT, WILLISTON and Anna Shearer, bond 20 September 1805. Consent by
Anna Lorry Caldwell, mother of the bride. Williston Talbot, Jr. (b)
and James Shearer (b); James Shearer (w) and Nancy Caldwell (w).
M.R. 20 September 1805 by Edmund Johns.

TALEFERRO (TALIAFERRO), RODERICK and Susannah Price*, bond 30 April 1801.
Roderick Taleferro (b) and Meredith Lambeth (b); M. Lambeth (w) and
Elizabeth Lambeth (w). M.R. 30 April 1801 by William P. Martin lists
the bride as Susan Price; she signs her consent Susan Price. The
groom signs his name Roderick Taliaferro.

TALLEY, CARTER and Patty Gaulden. M.R. 17 December 1788 by James Hurt.

TALLEY, CLABOURN (CLABREN) and Polly Hayth, bond 5 January 1802. Consent
by William Hayth, father of the bride. Clabourn Talley (b) and
William Hayth (b); William Hayth (w) and Benjamin Hayth (w). M.R.
16 January 1802 by Henry Brown. The groom signs his name Clabren
Talley.

TANKERSLEY, GEORGE and Polly Mathis (Mathews)*, bond 1 September 1790.
George Tankersley (b) and William Jones (b); Josiah Bass (w) and William
Mathis (w). M.R. 2 September 1790 by James Hurt lists the groom as
George Tanttersley.

TANNER, BRANCH and Elizabeth Asher, bond 9 November 1801. Consent by John
Asher, father of the bride. Branch Tanner (b) and John Asher (b).

TANNER, JOHN and Leviney Daniel, bond 14 January 1809. Consent by Peter
Daniel, father of the bride. John Tanner (b) and James Daniel (b);
James Daniel (w) and John Daniel (w). M.R. 14 January 1809 by
Edmund Johns.

TATE, CALEB and Nancy Cooper*, bond 16 April 1790. Caleb Tate (b) and
Robert Alexander (b).

TAYLOE, JOHN and Sally Read, bond 28 September 1809. Consent by William
Read, father of the bride. John Tayloe (b) and John Read (b); John
Read (w). M.R. 28 September 1809 by Edmund Johns lists the groom as
John Taylor.

TAYLOR, ARCHIBALD (bachelor) and Rachel Shanault, bond 3 March 1785.
Consent by Benjamin Shanault, father of the bride. Archibald
Taylor (b) and Robert Wright (b).

TAYLOR, GEORGE and Sally Hudson, bond 22 March 1809. George Taylor (b)
and George Hudson (b). M.R. 22 March 1809 by Samuel Davidson lists
the bride as Sary Hutson.

TAYLOR, HEZEKIAH and Polly Oglesby, bond 19 May 1807. Consent by Mary
Oglesby, mother of the bride. Hezekiah Taylor (b) and Samuel Davidson (b); Samuel Davidson (w). M.R. 20 May 1807 by William Flowers,Jr.

TAYLOR, JOHN and Elizabeth Smith*, bond 9 August 1787. Consent also by
Judah Smith, parent of the bride. John Taylor (b) and Josiah
Chambers (b); Josiah Chambers (w). M.R. 9 August 1787 by James
Kenney.

TAYLOR, JOHN and Luckey Williams, daughter of Anderson Williams, bond 14
November 1808. John Taylor (b) and Anderson Williams (b). M. R.
20 November 1808 by Samuel Davidson.

TAYLOR, WILLIAM and Mary Walls (widow)*, bond 5 March 1799. William
Taylor (b) and George Wright (b); William Taylor (w), George Wright
(w) and George Ranig (w). M.R. 9 March 1799 by William P. Martin.

TAYLOR, WILLIAM and Sally Smith*, bond 5 February 1795. William Taylor
(b) and Thomas Oglesby (b); Thomas Oglesby (w) and William Newbury (w).

TAYLOR, WILLIAM and Katherine Angler. M.R. 17 September 1782 by John W.
Holt.

TAYLOR, WILLIAM and Milly Patterson, bond 26 January 1799. Consent by
Nancy Baber, mother of the bride. William Taylor (b) and William Baber
(b); John Lee (w) and William Baber (w). This marriage bond gives the
contracting parties as William Taylor and Nancy Baber, which is
evidently in error since the consent by Nancy Baber states "that William
Taylor intermarrys with my daughter Milly Patterson." Campbell County
General Index to Marriages and Marriage Register Vol. I, 1782-
apparently failed to catch this detail since they list the bride as
Nancy Baber.

TERRELL, DUDLEY and Polly Hutcherson, bond 22 December 1801. Consent by
Mary Hutchen, mother of the bride. James Terrell (b) and Dudley
Terrell (b); James Terrell (w). M.R. 22 December 1801 by Henry Brown.

TERRELL, HENRY and Charity Judkins, bond 27 December 1797. Consent by
William Judkins, father of the bride. Henry Terrell (b) and Joel
Judkins (b); Joel Judkins (w) and David Judkins (w).

TERRELL, JAMES and Penelope Adams, bond 16 June 1798. Consent by L. Adams,
father of the bride. James Terrell (Terrill) (b) and Howard Bennett
(b); Howard Bennett (w). M.R. 16 June 1798 by Abner Early.

TERRELL, JAMES and Letty Bolling*, bond 28 December 1801. James Terrell (b) and Edmund Herndon (b); Edmund Herndon (w). M.R. 31 December 1801 by Henry Brown.

TERRELL, PETER and Nancy Hutcherson, bond 12 December 1799. Consent by Mary Hutcherson. Peter Terrell (b) and James Terrell (b).

TERRELL, SAMUEL and Nancy Reynolds, bond 10 September 1796. Consent by Isaac Reynolds, father of the bride. Samuel Terrell (b) and John M. Smithson (b); E. Raeder (w).

TERRELL, THOMAS MOORMAN and Rebeckah Judkins, bond 1 November 1800. Consent by William Judkins. Thomas M. Terrell (b) and Joel Judkins (b); Joel Judkins (w). M.R. 2 November 1800 by Henry Brown lists the bride as Rachal Judkins.

TERRELL, TIMOTHY and Betsy Black, bond 17 November 1798. Consent by John Black, brother of the bride. Timothy Terrell (b) and Woodson Jordan (b); William Lewis (w) and Woodson Jordan (w).

TERRILL (TERRELL), CHARLES L. and Sally Lynch, bond 6 April 1789. Consent by Charles Lynch, Sr., father of the bride. Charles Terrill (b) and Robert Alexander (b). M.R. by James Kenney, no date given but listed after entries for 31 March 1789. The groom signs his name Charles Terrell.

TERRILL (TERRELL), WILLIAM and Jemima Smithson, bond 23 February 1802. Consent by Drummond Smithson, father of the bride. William Terrill (b) and Samuel Smithson (b); Samuel Smithson (w). M.R. 25 February 1802 by Henry Brown. The groom signs his name William Terrell.

THOMAS, WILLIAM and Martha McReynolds*, bond 10 February 1800. William Thomas (b) and Mathew Willson (b). M.R. by William Flowers is entered three times, twice under date of 19 February 1800 and once under date of 9 February 1800.

THOMKINS, JAMES and Polley Hurt. M.R. 4 September 1789 by James Hurt.

THOMPSON, DAVID and Elizabeth Thompson*, bond 13 November 1797. David Thompson (b) and William Campbell (b). M.R. 14 November 1797 by James Mitchell gives the last names of both bride and groom as Thomson.

THOMPSON, JOHN and Margaret Davison, bond 21 March 1796. Consent by Alexander Davison, father of the bride. John Thompson (b) and Samuel Davison (b). M.R. 24 March 1796 by William Mahon lists the groom as John Thomson.

THOMPSON, JOHN and Heziah Franklin, bond 3 November 1796. Consent by Lewis Franklin, father of the bride. John Thompson (b) and Thomas Franklin (b). M.R. 10 November 1796 by William Flowers.

THOMPSON, MATHEW and Patsey Hurt (Hurd)*, bond 20 December 1796. Mathew Thompson (b) and Samuel Thompson (b).

THOMPSON, MATTHEW and Ellender (Elenor) Evans, bond 13 April 1801. Consent
by Daniel Evans, father of the bride. Matthew Thompson (b) and David
Thompson (b); David Thompson (w) and Aron Terrens (w). M.R. 14 May
1801 by William Flowers.

THOMPSON, WILLIAM and Nancy C. Franklin, bond 14 November 1807. Consent
by Thomas Franklin. William Thompson (b) and John Thompson (b).
M.R. 19 November 1807 by Frederick Kabler.

THORP, JAMES and Lucy Depriest*, bond 27 October 1800. James Thorp (b)
and Austin Depriest (b).

THURMAN, JOHN and Nancy Robins, bond 3 March 1787. Consent by John Thurman,
also by Margrit Robins. John Thurman (b) and William Mathews (b).

THURMAN, RICHARD and Sally Lewellin, bond 2 December 1805. Consent by
Elizabeth Lewellin, mother of the bride. Richard Thurman (b) and
James Lewellin (b).

THURMAN, RICHARD and Sarah Shelson*, bond 14 April 1806. Richard Thurman
(b) and William P. Martin (b); Joseph Bradley (w). M.R. 14 April 1806
by William P. Martin.

TIMBERLAKE, CHRISTOPHER and Mary Farley*, bond 22 March 1809. Consent by
Edward Farley, Sr. Christopher Timberlake (b) and Henry Farley (b).
M.R. 23 March 1809 by Frederick Kabler.

TIMBERLAKE, PHILIP and Elizabeth Johnson, bond 24 July 1790. Consent by
Christopher Johnson, father of the bride. Philip Timberlake (b).
M.R. 9 ___ 1791 by Joseph Drury.

TORRANCE, ANDREW and Winney (Winifred) Rosser, bond 16 January 1789. Consent
by David Rosser, father of the bride. Andrew Torrance (b) and Joseph
Torrance (b). M.R. 19 January 1789 by James Kenney lists the groom as
Andrew Terrence.

TRANAN, ANDERSON and Elizabeth Showls, daughter of Jacob Showls, bond
14 March 1808. Anderson Tranan (b) and Jacob Showls (b). M.R.
17 March 1808 lists the bride as Betsy Showls, and the groom as
Anderson Trunan, by James Warner.

TRAYLOR, JOHN and Lucy Brown, bond 13 October 1782. John Traylor (b) and
Shadrack Brown (b). M.R. 15 October 1782 by John W. Holt.

TRAYLOR, ROBERT and Peggy Jones, bond 4 December 1799. Consent by Thomas
and Caty Jones, parents of the bride. Robert Traylor (b) and David
Jones (b).

TRENOR, JAMES and Elizabeth Goggin, bond 12 April 1786. Consent by Stephen
Goggin, father of the bride. James Trenor (b) and Richard Goggin (b).

TRENT, HENRY and Nancy Reynolds, bond 23 January 1797. Consent by James
Reynolds, father of the bride. Henry Trent (b) and Thomas Russell (b).
M.R. ___ January 1797 by Charles Cobbs.

TRENT, JOHN and Candice Nowell (Noell), bond 23 April 1804. Consent by Joice Noell, mother of the bride. John Trent (b) and German C. Nowell (Noell) (b). M.R. 26 April 1804 by Henry Brown lists the bride as Candice Norvell.

TRENT, OBEDIAH and Nancy Blankenship, bond 9 December 1810. Consent by Hudson Blankenship, father of the bride. Obediah Trent (b) and Zachariah Blankenship (b). M.R. 12 December 1810 by James Warner.

TRENT, WILLIAM and Catharine Weber*, bond 9 December 1805. William Trent (b) and Barnit Finch (b).

TRIGG, WILLIAM and Sarah Anthony, bond 1 December 1804. Consent by Jno. Anthony. William Trigg (b) and John Willard (b).

TROWER, ROBERT and Nancy Anderson, bond 20 April 1791:1795. Robert Trower (b) and Joseph Johnson (b).

TURNER, JAMES and Eliza Wright, bond 3 May 1809. Consent by Silvia Wright, mother of the bride. James Turner (b) and Robert Wright (b). M.R. 3 May 1809 by William P. Martin.

TURNER, JOHN and Frances McHaney, bond 5 December 1788. Consent by Cornelius McHaney, father of the bride. John Turner (b) and Clayburn Puckett (b).

TWEDEY (TWEEDY), ROBERT and Susanna Rosser, bond 27 April 1805. Consent by Ann Rosser, mother of the bride. Robert Twedey (b) and Archer Williamson (b). M.R. __ April 1805 by Edmund Johns, lists the groom as Robert Twedy, and the bride as Susannah Rosser.

TWEEDY, JOHN and Polly Arrington, bond 27 June 1803. Consent by Adler Arrington, father of the bride. John Tweedy (b) and Archer Williamson (b). M.R. 30 June 1803 by Henry Brown lists the groom as John Tweady.

TWEEDY, JOSEPH, JR. and Elizabeth Franklin, bond 19 September 1791. Consent by Elizabeth Franklin, mother of the bride. Joseph Tweedy, Jr. (b) and Robert Franklin (b). M.R. 22 September 1791 by Menoah Lesley.

TYNES, OBEDIAH of Halifax County and Edith Barlow, bond 20 August 1794. Consent by Thomas Barlow. Obediah Tynes (b) and Daniel Dejarnett (b).

TYREE, PLEASANT and Matilda Anderson, bond 30 August 1810. Consent by Sally Anderson, mother of the bride. Pleasant Tyree (b) and John Anderson, Jr. (b).

TYREE, RICHARD and Mildred Douglas, bond 31 December 1805. Consent by Achillis Douglas, father of the bride. Richard Tyree (b) and John Lynch, Jr. (b). M.R. __ January 1806 by William P. Martin. This return is at the top of the page and is almost concealed by the book binding, hence is difficult to determine.

TYREE, RICHMOND and Polly Anderson, daughter of William Anderson, bond
13 January 1806. Richmond Tyree (b) and William Anderson (b).

U

URQUART, WALTER (bachelor) and Molly Farmer (spinster), bond 29 January
1785. Consent by Thomas Farmer, father of the bride. Daniel McCoy
(McKoy) (b) and Walter Urquart (b).

V

VANNERSON, WILLIAM and Elizabeth Thorp, bond 4 December 1789. Consent by
Francis Thorp, father of the bride. Christopher Clark (b) and William
Vannerson (b); Thomas Crump (w), William Harris (w) and J. A. Steptoe (w).

VAUGHN, NICHOLAS and Jennie Watson*, bond 17 May 1804. Thomas Hayth (b)
and Nicholas Vaughn (b); Thomas Hayth (w) and Gion (?) Rust (w).

VENABLE, JACOB and Mary Venable, bond 23 August 1785. Consent by John
Venable, father of the bride. Jacob Venable (b) and Abraham Venable
(b); Elizabeth Moormen (w), Nathaniel Strange (w) and Robert Venable (w).

VERNON, JONATHAN and Suckey (Luckey) Matthews (Mathews), bond 2 October 1809.
Consent by William Matthews, father of the bride and Susanna Matthews.
Jonathan Vernon (b) and Jacob Carwiles (b); Jacob Carwiles (w). M.R.
2 October 1809 by Edmund Johns lists the bride as Suckey Matthews.

VEST, ROBERT PARKER and Betsy Bailey (Baly), bond 27 December 1786. Consent
by Elebath Baly, mother of the bride. Thomas McCune (b) and Robert
P. Vest (b); James Vest (w) and Thomas McCune (w).

VIA, LITTLEBERRY and Mary Stratton, bond 10 August 1789. Consent by Joseph
Stratton, father of the bride. Thomas Tucker (b) and Littleberry
(Littlebery) Via (b); Jack Hames (w). M.R. not dated but listed after
entries for 31 March 1789, by James Kenney who gives the groom's name
as Littleberry Vias.

W

WADE, EDMUND and Mildred E. H. Marshall, bond 11 June 1810. Edmund Wade
(b) and Henry Brown (b).

WADE, JAMES and Jane Henry King, bond 6 May 1803. Consent by Sackville
King, father of the bride. James Wade (b) and John D. Carter (b);
John Carter (w) and James Henry (w).

WADE, ZACKFIELD and Polly Johnson, bond 12 August 1799. Consent by John
Johnson, father of the bride. Zackfield Wade (b) and John Johnson (b);
John Johnson, Jr. (w) and Philip Johnson (w).

WALDEN, CHARLES and Elizabeth Wall, bond 30 November 1782. Charles Walden
(b) and Thomas Leftwich (b).

WALDEN, RICHARD and Levina Pemberton, bond _____ 1807. Richard Walden (b) and Joseph Pemberton (b).

WALKER, CHARLES and Anne Johns, bond 18 July 1785. Consent by Jesse and Sarah Johns, parents of the bride. Charles Walker (b) and Thomas Marshall (b).

WALKER, CHARLES and Frances Roper*, bond 14 February 1810. Charles Walker (b) and William Whitlow (b); William Whitlow (w) and Sarah Walker (w).

WALKER, EDMUND W. and Elizabeth Armistead, bond 22 November 1804. Consent by Robert Armistead. Edmund Walker (b) and Francis Armistead (b); Francis Armistead (w) and John Armistead (w).

WALKER, GEORGE and Elizabeth Woodall, bond 2 September 1808. Consent by Jacob Woodall, father of the bride. George Walker (b) and William Walker (b); Wm. H. Walker (w) and L. Hawse (w).

WALKER, JOHN and Catherine Miller*, bond 13 November 1797. John Walker (b) and Lewis Speece (Space) (b); Anthony Evans (w) and Lewis Speece (Space) (w). M.R. 14 November 1798 by Anderson Weekes.

WALKER, JOHN and Mary Stepp, bond 23 December 1807. Consent by Jinny Stepp, mother of the bride, and by Shapel Walker, parent of the groom. John Walker (b) and Joseph Stepp (b); Joseph Stepp, Jr. (w).

WALKER, JOHN, JR. and Judith Brown, bond 9 February 1807. Consent by Richard Brown, father of the bride. John Walker, Jr. (b) and William Walker (b); Thomas Walker (w) and William Walker (w). M.R. 19 February 1807 by William Flowers, Jr.

WALKER, WILLIAM and Peggy Loving*, bond 21 January 1807. William Walker (b) and George Taylor (b); George Taylor (w). M.R. 22 January 1807 by William Flowers, Jr.

WALKER, WILLIAM and Delilah R. Whitlow, bond 14 September 1798. William Walker (b) and Henry Whitlow (b).

WALKER, WILLIAM and Sarah Holcombe, bond 23 March 1804. Consent by J. Holcombe, father of the bride. William Walker (b) and Edward Moseley (b); Samuel Venable (w) and Edward Moseley (w).

WALKER, WILLIAM and Elizabeth Bass, bond 2 January 1792. Josiah Bass (b) and William Walker (b).

WALSH, JAMES and Catharine Jenkins, bond 27 February 1807. James Walsh (b) and David Alvis (b); David Alvis (w) and James Franklin (w). M.R. 1 March 1807 by William Flowers, Jr.

WARD, ROBERT A. and Elizabeth Terrell, bond 26 December 1807. Consent by Chas. L. Terrell, father of the bride. Robert A. Ward (b) and Anselm Lynch (b); Anselm Lynch (w) and Henry Ward (w).

WARWICK, WILLIAM and Luanna Dawson*, bond 12 November 1804. William
Warwick (b) and Robert Morris (b); Sarah Morris (w), Belinda
Moseley (w) and Robert Morris (w).

WATKINS, AARON and Elizabeth Helm*, bond 23 November 1801. Aaron Watkins
(b) and James Helm (b); James Helm (w). M.R. 26 November 1801 by
William Flowers.

WATKINS, BENJAMIN and Mary Johnson, bond 11 July 1791. Consent by
Benjamin and Martha Johnson, parents of the bride. Moses Watkins (b)
and Benjamin Watkins (b); Moses Watkins (w).

WATKINS, ENOCH and Elizabeth Elam, bond 10 March 1808. Consent by
Susanah Elam, mother of the bride. Enoch Watkins (b) and Walker
Dejarnett (b); Archer Williamson (w) and Walker Dejarnatt (w). M.R.
10 March 1808 by Edmund Johns.

WATKINS, REECE and Rachel Martin, bond 8 March 1802. Consent by David
Martin, Sr., father of the bride. Reece Watkins (b) and David Martin,
Jr. (b); James Helm (w) and David Martin, Jr. (w). M.R. 11 March
1802 by William Flowers.

WATKINS, ROBERT and Hannah Pugh, bond 3 April 1790. Robert Watkins (b)
and Enoch Watkins (b). M.R. 8 April 1790 by James Kenney.

WAYNE, JOSEPH and Mary Drinkwater*, bond 15 April 1790. Joseph Wayne (b)
and John Wayne (b); John Wayne (w). M.R. 15 April 1790 by James Hurt.

WEAKS, ELIJAH and Margaret Thompson, bond 12 April 1802. Consent by
Andrew Thompson, father of the bride. Elijah Weaks (b) and David
Thompson (b). M.R. 29 May 1802 by Anderson Weekes. Second entry
under date of 29 May 1802 lists the groom as Elijah Weeks.

WEATHERFORD, ANDERSON and Nancy Holt, bond 18 January 1806. Consent by
Robert Holt, father of the bride. Anderson Weatherford (b) and
Daniel Driskill (b); Daniel Driskill (w) and Davy Driskill (w).

WEATHERFORD, JOHN and Nancy Bailey, bond 22 December 1806. Consent by
Mary Bailey, mother of the bride. John Weatherford (b) and Adam
Driskill (b).

WEAVER, MATTHEW and Lucy Jude, bond 16 February 1801. Consent by George
Jude, father of the bride. Matthew Weaver (b) and Corbin Lewis (b).
M.R. 19 February 1801 by John Chappell.

WEAVER, WILLIAM W. and Mackey R. B. Jennings, bond 5 November 1810. Consent by Pleasant Jennings, father of the bride. William W. Weaver
(b) and Samuel Weaver (b).

WEAVER, WILSON and Polly Dokeridge*, bond 22 December 1806. Wilson
Weaver (b) and Samuel Wilson (b).

WEBB, GEORGE and Lucy Gaulding, bond 2 November 1789. Consent by Elizabeth Gaulding, mother of the bride. George Webb (b) and Benoni Carter Talley (b). M.R. 3 November 1789 by James Hurt.

WEBB, JESSE and Mary Jones*, bond 7 December 1802. Jesse Webb (b) and Achilles Moorman, Jr. (b). M.R. 9 December 1802 by Henry Brown.

WEBBER (WEBER), JOHN, JR. and Ruth Akers, bond 17 April 1797. Consent by William Akers, Sr., father of the bride. John Webber, Jr. (b) and William Akers, Jr. (b).

WEBBER (WEBER), MARTIN and Hannah Finch, bond 25 July 1804. Consent by Barnit Finch. Martin Webber (Weber) (b) and Barnit Finch (b). M.R. __ July 1804 by Edmund Johns.

WEBBER (WEBER), PETER and Keturah Stone*, bond 20 January 1807. Peter Webber (Weber) (b) and Daniel Snow (b). M.R. 27 January 1807 by Matthew Easter lists the bride as Catharine Strong.

WEBER, ADAM and Elizabeth Phillips, bond 8 October 1804. Adam Weber (b) and John Phillips (b).

WEBER, HENRY and Elizabeth Misa (?) Gregory, daughter of John Gregory, bond 26 March 1801. Henry Weber (b) and John Gregory (b).

WEBER, JOHN and Peggy Porter*, bond 2 October 1794. John Weber (b) and Henry Weber (b). M.R. 3 October 1794 by Menoah Lesley lists the groom as John Webber.

WEBER, WILLIAM and Nancy Walker, bond 5 November 1792. Consent by Buckley Walker, father of the bride, and by Casper Weber, father of the groom. William Weber (b) and Benjamin Walker (b). M.R. 15 November 1792 by Menoah Lesley lists the groom as William Webber.

WEST, BENJAMIN (bachelor) of Pittsylvania County and Rebecca Canifax (spinster), bond 4 October 1787. Benjamin West (b) and John Carnifax (b). M.R. 19 October 1787 by James Kenney.

WEST, JESSE and Polly Willan, daughter of John Willan, bond 11 January 1808. Jesse West (b) and John Willan (b).

WEST, JOHN and Fanny Hughes, daughter of Benjamin Hughes, bond 20 November 1806. John West (b) and Benjamin Hughes (b).

WEST, OBEDIAH and Cora Hogan, bond 5 September 1785. Consent by Emille (?) Hogan, parent of the bride. Obediah West (b) and Enoch Hogan (b).

WEST, REUBEN and Ann Arthur. M.R. 5 March 1783 by John Anthony.

WEST, THOMAS and Betsy Hogan, bond 30 August 1790. Consent by Milley Hogan, mother of the bride. Thomas West (b) and Enoch Hogan (b).

WEST, WILLIAM and Sally Arthur, bond 13 April 1801. Consent by Joseph
Arthur, father of the bride. William West (b) and Ambrose Morris (b).

WHAYNE, BENJAMIN and Ann Tankersley*, bond 11 April 1801. Benjamin Whayne
(b) and William Bosher (b). M.R. 16 ____ 1801 by Henry Brown.

WHITE, ANDERSON and Marjory Pullium, bond 27 February 1786. Anderson
White (b) and Isham Pullium (Pullim) (b).

WHITE, JONATHAN and Nancy Deering, bond 25 December 1801. Consent by
James Deering, father of the bride. Jonathan White (b) and Joseph
Eidson (b).

WHITE, RICHARDSON and Mary Moorman, bond 11 February 1799. Consent by
Mary Mooreman, mother of the bride. Richardson White (b) and Robert
Clark (b).

WHITE, URIAH and Lucy Trent. M.R. 29 October 1807 by Edmund Johns.

WHITLOCK, THOMAS and Susannah Webb. M.R. __ December 1788 by James Hurt.

WHITLOW, ANDREWS and Charlotte Crews, daughter of Josiah Crews, bond
1 December 1806. Andrew S. Whitlow (b) and Josiah Crews, Sr. (b).

WHITLOW, WILLIAM and Sarah Walker, daughter of Charles Walker, bond
29 November 1806. William Whitlow (b) and Charles Walker (b).

WHITTINGTON, JAMES and Elizabeth McGeorge, bond 8 February 1802. Consent
by Lawrence McGeorge, father of the bride. James Whittington (b)
and James Martin (b).

WIATT, THOMAS and Sally Miller, bond 18 May 1793. Consent by John Miller,
father of the bride. Thomas Wiatt (b) and Thomas Higginbotham (b).

WIGGINTON, BENJAMIN and Harriett Baughn Scott, bond 22 December 1806.
Consent by William Scott, father of the bride. Benjamin Wigginton
(b) and Gabriel Scott (b); Gabriel Scott (w). M.R. 22 December 1806
by William P. Martin.

WILBOURN, RICHARD B. and Nancy Matthews, bond 8 November 1810. Richard
B. Wilbourn (b) and Samuel Matthews (b).

WILEY, BARTLETT and Elizabeth Perrow*, bond 5 April 1792. Bartlett
Wiley (Wily) (b) and Samuel Fleming (b); Jesse Harvey (w) and Samuel
Fleming (w). M.R. 5 April 1792 by Menoah Lesley lists the groom as
Bartlett Wily.

WILKERSON, JOSEPH and Nancy McKinney*, bond 10 October 1810. Joseph
Wilkerson (b) and Allen Wade (b); Allen Wade (w) and Parson
Wilkson (Wilkerson) (w). M.R. 14 October 1810 by Frederick Kabler.

WILKERSON, PARSON (bachelor) and Anna Butler (spinster), bond 31 August
1784. Consent by Anna Anderson, mother of the bride. Parson Wilkerson (b) and Robert Alexander (b).

WILKERSON, WILLIAM and Catherine Franklin, bond 27 September 1805. Consent by Edmond Franklin, grandfather of the bride. William Wilkerson (Wilkinson) (b) and Peyton Chanler (b); James Franklin (w) and Paton Chanler (w). M.R. 27 September 1805 by LittleJohn Baldwin.

WILLIAMS, GEORGE and Maria P. Blount, bond 25 January 1806. Consent by Charles Blount, father of the bride. George Williams (b) and Joseph McAllister (b); Thomas Helm (w), Moses Carson (w) and Joseph McAllister (w).

WILLIAMS, JAMES and Polly Burns*, bond 17 December 1805. James Williams (b) and Timothy Terrell (b); S. Terrell (w), Nancy Terrell (w) and Timothy Terrell (w).

WILLIAMS, REUBIN and Elizabeth Botelar, bond 22 June 1801. Reubin Williams (b) and Thomas Botelar (Botler), father of the bride (b). M.R. 25 June 1801 by William Flowers lists the bride as Elizabeth Butler.

WILLIAMS, ROGER and Ester Hackett*, bond 15 January 1804. Roger Williams (b) and William Peters Martin (b); Wm. P. Martin (w), Sarah Nelson (w) and Nathan Weedon (w). M.R. __ January 1804 by William P. Martin who lists the word coloured after the entry and the bride as Eustis Narkete.

WILLIAMS, THOMAS and Elizabeth Woodson, bond 9 December 1805. Consent by Anderson Woodson, father of the bride. Thomas Williams (b) and William Walker (b); John E. Woodson (w) and Wm. Walker (w). M.R. 13 December 1805 by William Flowers, Jr.

WILLIAMS, WILLIAM and Ann Cannafax (Cannafix)*, bond 2 December 1808. William Williams (b) and William Bradley (b); Wm. Bradley (w) and William Cannafix (w). M.R. 3 December 1808 by Samuel Davidson lists the bride as Ann Canifax.

WILLIAMSON, DEBRIX and Patsey Roberds, bond 7 December 1791. Consent by Ressley (?) Roberds, father of the bride. Robert Tweedy (b) and Debrix Williamson (b); Robert Tweedy (w). M.R. 12 December 1791 by Menoah Lesley, lists the bride as Patsey Roberts.

WILLIAMSON, NATHANIEL and Elizabeth Johnson*, bond 11 February 1799. Nathaniel (Nathan) Williamson (b) and John Lacy (b); Wm. Bowell (w). M.R. _____ 1799 by Samuel Mitchell, lists the groom as Nathan Williamson.

WILLSON, PETER and Dicey Campbell*, bond 18 May 1798. Samuel Wilson (b) and Peter Willson (Wilson) (b); Samuel Wilson (w), Joseph Callaway (w) and Joseph Wilson (w). M.R. __ May 1798 by Charles Cobbs.

WILLSON, THOMAS and Elizabeth Gaston*, bond 5 August 1800. Samuel Galbreath (b) and Thomas Willson (Wilson) (b); Samuel Galbreath (w) and Jean Dinwiddie (w). M.R. 7 August 1800 by Obadiah Edge.

WILSON, JOSHUA and Lucy Davis*, free mulattoes, bond 25 October 1804. Joshua Wilson (b) and Thomas Morris (b); Joseph Wilson (w), Samuel Wilson (w) and Thomas Morris (w).

WILSON, MATHEW and Elizabeth Stovall, bond 11 October 1804. Consent by
Bartholomew Stovall, father of the bride. Thomas Stovall (b) and
Mathew Wilson (Willson) (b); Martha Wilson (w).

WILSON, ROBERT and Janey Wilson, bond 6 December 1806. Robert Wilson
(b) and Samuel Wilson (b).

WILSON, THOMAS and Elizabeth Wood, bond 2 August 1792. Thomas Wilson (b)
and John Wood (b).

WILSON (WILLSON), THOMAS and Anne Dinwiddie, daughter of James Dinwiddie,
bond 4 August 1798. Thomas Wilson (b) and James Dinwiddie (b). M.R.
15 August 1798 by Archibald McRoberts.

WINFORD, JOSHUA and Jane Gee, bond 28 February 1786. Consent by John and
Sarah Gee, parents of the bride. Joshua Winford (b) and Samuel
Wilson (b); Job Gee (w) and Benjamin Gee (w).

WITT, ROLAND and Sally Duvall, bond 31 January 1793. Roland Witt (b) and
Skinner Duvall (b). M.R. 31 January 1793 by Joseph Drury.

WOMACK, JOEL and Sally Pruitt, bond 22 November 1800. Consent by Michael
Pruitt. Joel Womack (b) and David Womack (b); Richard Womack (w) and
David Womack (w).

WOOD, EDMUND and Jane Franklin, bond 26 January 1788. Consent by Owen
Franklin, father of the bride. Edmund Wood (b) and William Rosser
(b). M.R. not dated but entered in the original Register after
entries for 15 August 1788, by James Kenney.

WOOD, JOHN and Patsey Mason, bond 17 November 1790. Consent by John Mason.
John Wood (b) and John Mason (b); James Elder (w) and John Mason (w).
M.R. 2 November 1790 by Charles Cobbs.

WOOD, JOHN and Kesiah Franklin, bond 5 April 1793. Consent by Elizabeth
Franklin. John Wood (b) and Robert Franklin (b); Robert Franklin
(w) and Edna Wood (w). M.R. 12 April 1793 by Menoah Lesley.

WOOD, JOSEPH and Sally Finch, bond 18 January 1810. Consent by Barnit
(Bernard) Finch, father of the bride. Barnit Finch, Jr. (b) and
Joseph Wood (b). Barnit Finch (w). M.R. 19 January 1810 by James
Warner.

WOOD, PAUL and Rhoda Moore, bond 4 November 1808. Paul Wood (b) and
Matthew Moore (b). M.R. 4 November 1808 by Edmund Johns.

WOOD, ROBERT and Caty Glass, bond 24 July 1810. Consent by Charles
Glass, father of the bride. Robert Wood (b) and Vincent Glass (b);
Vincent Glass (w) and Joseph Dinwiddie (w). M.R. 26 July 1810 by
Obadiah Edge lists the bride as Cathy Glass.

WOOD, SAMUEL and Jenny Thompson, bond 31 May 1802. Samuel Wood (b) and Andrew Thompson (b). M.R. 8 June 1802 by Anderson Weekes lists the bride as Ginny Thompson, a second entry under the same date lists her as Jenny.

WOODS, ROBERT of Henry County and Frances Strange, bond 11 March 1784. Robert Woods (b) and Nathaniel Strange (b).

WOODS, THOMAS and Priscilla Jennings, bond 15 October 1804. Consent by Francis Perdue, stepfather of the bride. Nathan Tanner (b) and Thomas Woods (b); Jerry Perdue (w). M.R. __ October 1804 by Edmund Johns.

WOODSON, OBADIAH and Mary Martin, bond 2 November 1805. Consent by Josiah Martin, father of the bride. Obadiah Woodson (b) and David Martin (b); John Martin (w) and Daniel Martin (w). M.R. 7 November 1805 by William Flowers, Jr.

WOOLDRIDGE, JOHN (bachelor) and Fleming Creasy (spinster)*, bond 22 September 1783. John Wooldridge (b) and Thomas Franklin (b); Edna and Thomas Franklin (w).

WORLDLY, RANEY and Nancy Worldly, bond 10 February 1787. Raney Worldly (b) and John Worldly (Worley?) (b).

WORLEY, DANIEL and Rachel Copeland, bond 25 June 1787. Daniel Worley (b), Joseph Worley (b) and William Bumpass (b).

WORLEY, MOSES and Rhoda Worley, bond 15 May 1789. Consent by Joseph Worley, father of the bride. Moses Worley (b) and Joseph Worley (b); John Worley (w). M.R. 10 June 1789 by Joshua Worley.

WRAY, JOHN and Agness Pillows*, bond 8 September 1808. John Wray (b) and John Lovell (b); Daniel Driskill (w), David McCargo (w) and John Lovell (w).

WRIGHT, GEORGE and Agnes Doss*, bond 8 March 1802. George Wright (b) and Jacob Golding (b); Jacob Golding (w) and David Elliott (w).

WRIGHT, JOHN and Martha Guttery, bond 13 January 1806. Consent by James Guttery, father of the bride. Henry Candler (b) and John Wright (b) Henry Guttery (w) and John Candler (w).

WRIGHT, ROBERT and Rachel Paxton, bond 3 November 1791. Consent by William and Mary Betts, parents of the bride. Robert Wright (b) and Henry Williamson (b); Henry Williamson (w) and John Paxson (w). M.R. 6 November 1791 by William Dameron.

WRIGHT, ROBERT and Anna Doss*, bond 20 October 1798. Robert Wright (b) and John Rector (b); Charles Wright (w) and John Rector (w). M.R. 27 October 1798 by William Flowers lists the bride as Anne Doss.

WRIGHT, ROBERT and Frances Staples. M.R. 21 __ 1798 by William Flowers.

WRIGHT, ROBERT and Polley Godsey, bond 9 October 1806. Consent by Molley Godsey, mother of the bride. Robert Wright (b) and Archer Williamson (b); Joseph Tweedy, Jr. (w) and Archer Williamson (w). This bond states Robert Wright and Molley Godsey intend to marry - but Molley signs consent for her daughter, Polley, to marry Robert Wright.

WRIGHT, ROBERT and Kezia Gilinwaters*, bond 10 October 1808. Robert Wright (b) and Thomas Jones (b); Thomas Jones (w). M.R. 12 October 1808 by Samuel Davidson lists the bride as Kesniah Gilinwaters.

WYNNE, JOHN and Polly St. John. M.R. __ July 1795 by Charles Cobbs.

Y

YANCEY, JOEL and Betsy Macon, bond 17 October 1809. Consent by Thomas Miller, guardian of the bride, who states Betsy Macon "resides at Mr. John Burton's." Joel Yancey (b) and John Alexander (b); Spottswood Henry (w).

YANCEY, JOEL and Nancy Burton, bond 7 July 1796. Consent by Alex Burton, guardian of the bride. Joel Yancey (b) and Will Norvell (b); Will Burton, Jr. (w) and Jesse Burton (w).

YANCEY, JOELL and Elizabeth Yancy. M.R. 26 October 1809 (1808?) by William P. Martin.

YOUNG, MATTHEW and Elizabeth Bailey, bond 11 December 1809. Consent by Savage Bailey, father of the bride. Matthew Young (b) and John B. Cobbs (b); John B. Cobbs (w) and William Cobbs (w).

YOUNG, WILLIAM H. and Sarah Bailey, bond 16 July 1808. Consent by Elizabeth Bailey, mother of the bride. William H. Young (b) and James M. Bailey (b); Mathew Young (w) and James M. Bailey (w). M.R. 6 July 1808 by Edmund Johns.

SECTION II

QUAKER MARRIAGES OF CAMPBELL COUNTY

1782 - 1810

These records include marriages from the three Meetings in Campbell County: South River, Seneca and Hills Creek.

The marriages herein recorded were taken from photostats of original Quaker records in the Archives Division of the Virginia State Library. See Preface, pp. xi-xii.

The South River Meeting-house when built was in Bedford County, but in 1782 fell into the newly-created Campbell County. Today it is within the corporate limits of the City of Lynchburg.

ABOUT QUAKER MARRIAGES

There are a number of books about the early Quakers which contain excellent commentaries on Quaker marriages. Among these books are those of James Pinkney Bell, Douglas Summers Brown, and Thomas Clarkson, all of which are listed in our Preface. We are indebted to Brown's book[1] for having directed us to Clarkson's, A Portraiture of Quakerism, which is contemporary with the period of the marriages in this compilation. From these three books we have abstracted the following information about Quaker marriages.

These authors point out that the Quakers really "marry themselves" or as they say "take each other in marriage."

Specific steps had to be taken before the man and woman arrived at the point of matrimony. First, consent of the parents or guardians had to be obtained; then the consent of the Meeting. In olden times, an appearance before the men's Meeting and then before the women's (Monthly Meeting) was necessary to "declare their intentions" in writing, after which the Monthly Meeting appointed a Committee to visit them and ascertain whether they were free from any other engagements and had the full consent of their parents or guardians. After a favorable report by this Committee, they could be married as soon as they desired. The Monthly Meeting that accepted this report then appointed another Committee to attend the marriage to see that it was conducted in the proper manner and report to the next Monthly Meeting.[2]

The marriage usually took place at one of the week day meetings for worship. On that day, the participating parties with their friends went to the Meeting-house, where the congregation and the man and woman sat in silence. After a suitable length of time, the two arose, took each other by the hand, and declared publicly that they thus took each other as husband and wife. They were given a certificate of marriage, and the marriage was recorded in the Proceedings of the Monthly Meeting.[3]

Many Quakers were "disowned" for "marrying out", which meant marrying one of another denomination or being married by a "hireling priest," as the ministers of other churches were called. Because these disownments constituted a serious loss to their Meetings, Quakers were later permitted to marry those of other churches provided they were married in a "Friends' Ceremony."[4]

Brown, pp. 152-53.
Bell, p. iv.
Clarkson, v. 2, p. 6.
Bell, p. iv.

QUAKER MARRIAGES

BAILEY, THOMAS and Elizabeth Timberlake were married at South River
Meeting-house 16 June 1803. The following witnesses signed the
marriage certificate: Lydia Johnson, Susanna Ballard, Polly
Timberlake, Hannah Pennock, Mary Butler, Sarah Johnson, Priscilla
Butler, James Stanton, James Martin, John Timberlake, Jonathan
Johnson, Josiah Bailey, John Pennock

BALLARD, BYRUM and Sarah Hutton were married at South River Meeting-
house 20 September 1792. The following witnesses signed the
marriage certificate: Minto P. Perdue, Christopher Anthony, James
Erwin, Mary Embree, Elizabeth Embree, Sarah Turner, Sarah Lewis,
Elizabeth Turner, Newman Rugus, James Mazley, Edward Tend, William
Pidgeon, Evan Lewis, Esther Richards, Elijah Richards, Delia Turner,
Joel Lewis, Sarah Lewis, Hannah Larrew, Mary Anthony, Nathan Hale,
Samuel Oliphant, Jesse Lewis, Polly Haynes, Henry Thurman, Magdalen
Erwin, Susanna Perdue, Mary Erwin, Alice Bond, Rebekah Moorlan,
Rachel Coffee, Thomas Cadwalader, Moses Embree, Ruth Paxon, Benjamin
Paxon, Elizabeth Hamner, Joseph Evoute, Rachel Pidgeon, John Coffee,
Nancy Moorlan, Moses Cadwalader, William Ballard, Jr., Amos Ballard,
Jesse Cadwalader, Mourning Ballard, Elizabeth Ballard, Ruth Cadwalader.

BALLARD, JAMES, son of Barclay and Judith Ballard, of Bedford County and
Betsy Butterworth, of Campbell County, were married at South River
Meeting-house 13 February 1806. The following witnesses signed the
marriage certificate: William Ballard, Benjamin Butterworth, Josiah
Bailey, Jonathan Johnson, William Butler, John Lynch, James S. Butler,
Thomas Burgess, Wm. Davis, Jr., Polly Butterworth, Milley Butterworth,
Nancy Ballard, Susanna Bailey, Mildred Ratcliff, Anna Lynch, Matilda
Roberts, Drucilla Burgess, Sally Lodge, Mildred Tyree, Judith Johnson,
Betsy Douglass, Alice Grewell, Mary Butler, Zalinda Davis, William
Stanton.

BALLARD, WILLIAM and Elizabeth Anthony were married at South River Meeting-
house 24 April 1788. The following witnesses signed the marriage cer-
tificate: Mary Anthony, Molly Anthony, Mary Ballard, Anna Sea, Mary
Johnson, Judith Ballard, Phebe Stanton, Penelope Johnson, Salley Johnso
Robert Hanna, Ashley Johnson, James Candler, Elizabeth Douglas, Betty
Johnson, Jane Gipson, Hepzabih Holloway, Edward Lynch, Christopher
Johnson, Achillis Douglas, William Johnson, William Ballard, John
Lynch, Mary Timberlake, Rachel Ballard, Sarah Tate Anthony, Barclay
Ballard, Moses Cadwalader, Jr., Charles Anthony, John Timberlake,
William Clement, Robert Johnson, Timothy Johnson, Sarah H. Tate,
Christopher Anthony, Jr., Christopher Anthony, William Stanton, John
Candler, Mary Lynch, Matilda Lynch.

BALLARD, WILLIAM, son of Barclay and Judith Ballard of Bedford County, and
Nancy Butterworth, daughter of Benjamin and Rachel Butterworth, of
Campbell County, Virginia, were married at South River Meeting-house
14 November 1805. The following witnesses signed the marriage certificate: Barclay Ballard, Benjamin Butterworth, James Ballard,

William Stanton, James Candler, Joseph P. Swinney, Edward Lynch,
Timothy Grewell, Isaac Pidgeon, Polly Butterworth, Betsy Butterworth,
Polly Ballard, Huldah Stanton, Nancy Johnson, Deborah Douglas, Mildred
Ratcliff.

BLOCKSOM, WILLIAM and Mary Butler were married at South River Meeting-house
21 January 1795. The following witnesses signed the marriage cer-
tificate: Agatha Johnson, Patty Terrell, Mary Johnson, Sarah Johnson
Nancy Davis, Susannah Terrell, Elizabeth Pidgeon, Harrison Ratcliff,
William Johnson, Gideon Blocksom, Jonathan Butler, John W. Johnson,
Charles Smith, Isaac Pidgeon, Thomas M. Clark, Mary Davis, Drucilla
Crew, Sally Butler, Mildred Ratcliff, Nancy Butler, Mary Blocksom,
Richard Blocksom, Sr., James Butler, Nicholas Crew, David Terrell,
Abner Grigg, Wm. Johnson, Richard Blocksom.

BRADFIELD, JOSEPH and Cynthia Cary were married at South River Meeting-house
13 September 1798. The following witnesses signed the marriage cer-
tificate: Martha Baugham, Mary Lynch, Mary Terrell, Sarah Millburn,
Elizabeth Lea, Jesse Williams, Joseph Fisher, Jr., Benjamin Hanna,
Thomas Maddox, John Bradfield, William Butler, Samuel Cary, Rachel
Cary, Sarah Cary, John Cary, John Fisher.

BURGESS, DANIEL, son of Joseph and Deborah Burgess, of the County of Campbell,
and Ruth Milliner, daughter of Beverly and Ann Milliner of Halifax County,
were married at South River Meeting-house 14 November 1805. The following
witnesses signed the marriage certificate: William Stanton, Barclay
Ballard, Stephen Butler, Mary Butler, Enoch Roberts, Isaac Pidgeon,
Polly Burgess, Grace Plummer, Thomas Burgess, John Burgess, Joseph
Burgess, Jr.

BURGESS, JOSEPH C., son of Jonathan and Margaret Burgess, of Campbell County
(Margaret deceased), and Martha Johnson, daughter of Christopher and
Sarah Johnson (both deceased), of Bedford County, were married at South
River Meeting-house 13 April 1808. The following witnesses signed the
marriage certificate: Stephen Butler, Josiah Bailey, Jonathan Burgess,
Charles T. Arthur, Thomas Burgess, Benjamin Johnson, Nicholas Johnson,
Joseph Johnson, Samuel Fisher, Daniel Burgess, John H. Moorman, Caleb
Johnson, Nancy Johnson, Matilda Johnson, Elizabeth Fisher, Mary Burgess,
Betty Burgess, Rhoda Johnson, Agatha Johnson, Susanna Bailey, James
Mallory.

BUTLER, WILLIAM, son of Stephen and Mary Butler, and Nancy Johnson, daughter
of William and Susanna Johnson, both of Campbell County, were married
at South River Meeting-house 15 April 1806. The following witnesses
signed the marriage certificate: Latham Stanton, Stephen Butler, Jr.,
Edward Butler, Jonathan Butler, Harrison Ratcliff, Deborah Butler,
Jepha Johnson, Enoch Roberts, William Johnson, Jr., Mary Butler,
Susannah Johnson, Sarah Lodge, Huldah Stanton, Elizabeth Douglas,
Newby Johnson, Sarah Johnson, Matilda Roberts, Mary Douglas, Zalinda
Davis, Jonathan Johnson, Stephen Butler, William Johnson, Sr., Robert
Johnson, Deborah Douglas, Elizabeth Douglas, Sarah Johnson, Judith
Johnson.

CADWALADER, MAHLON, son of Thomas and Jane Cadwalader, and Elizabeth
Douglas, daughter of Achillis and Elizabeth Douglas, were married at
South River Meeting-house 10 June 1809. The following witnesses
signed the marriage certificate: Achillis Douglas, Thomas Cadwalader,
Joseph Stratton, Jonathan Johnson, John Lynch, Sr., Richard Tyree,
Benjamin Johnson, Reubin Moorman, Isaac Pidgeon, Etchison Grigsby,
Jonah Cadwalader, Joel Lewis, Judith Johnson, Deborah Douglas, Mildred
Tyree, Polly Lynch, Penelope Anthony, Mary Butler, Susanna Johnson,
Elizabeth Cadwalader, Sarah Johnson.

CADWALDER, MOSES, JR. and Mary Ballard of Bedford County were married at
South River Meeting-house 23 May 1792. The following witnesses signed
the marriage certificate: Joseph Teazel, Abigal Moorlan, Rebecca
Moorlan, Elizabeth Teazel, Susan Morlan, Thomas Davis, Henry Hurt,
Joseph Moorland, Christopher Anthony, Ann Moorland, Mevory Anthony,
Annis Davis, Sarah Johnson, Rachel Pidgeon, Rachel Coffee, Sarah
Hutton, Ruth Cadwalader, Judith Ballard, Elizabeth Ballard, William
Pidgeon, Samuel Davis, Moses Cadwalader, Joseph Wright, Philip
Teazle, Aden Moorland, Moses Hurt, Byrum Ballard, Thomas Cadwalader,
Jesse Cadwalader, Polly Haynes.

COGGSHALL, TRISTRAM and Lucy Terrell were married at South River Meeting-
house 21 March 1790. The following witnesses signed the marriage cer-
tificate: Sarah Terrell, William Johnson, Byrum Ballard, Mary Davis,
Samuel Davis, Betty Hendrake, Susanna Johnson, Dosha Moorman, Nancy
Moorman, Achillis Douglas, Mary Betts, Ann Fowler, Elizabeth Douglas,
Betty Johnson, John Paxon, Thomas Bedford, John Candler, Jr., William
Bloxom, Rachel Paxon, Mary Baughan, Anna Terrell, Ruth Pidgeon, Sarah
Tennison, Sarah Johnson, Susanna Davis, Sarah Johnson, William Stanton,
William Davis, Rachel Ballard, Sarah Hutton, James Candler, Henry
Terrell, Robert Hanna, Ashley Johnson, Richard Bloxom, Robert Johnson.

DAVIS, WILLIAM, son of Samuel and Annis Davis, of Bedford County and Zalinda
Lynch [Bell gives this as Zelinda Davis], daughter of John and Mary
Lynch, of Campbell County, were married at South River Meeting-house
13 May 1793. The names of witnesses: William Johnson, Arch Lacy,
William Stanton, Susanna Miller, Vernon Metcalf, Matilda Roberts, Mary
Terrell, Ann Terrell, Sally Lynch, Elizabeth Douglas, Polly Fowler,
Sarah Lodge, Agatha Dicks, Elizabeth Johnson, John Lynch, Samuel Davis,
Enoch Roberts, John Davis, Sr., Achillis Douglas, Thomas Davis, Mary
Timberlake, Gideon Lea, Ashley Johnson, John Baughan, David Johnson,
William Dicks, Ashley Johnson, Jr., Edward Terrell, Newberry Johnson,
Dudley Cave, Penelope Johnson, Susanna Johnson, Millie Johnson,
Rebecca Preston, Joseph Johnson, Sarah Terrell, Mildred Johnson, Anna
Lea, Alice Taylor, Tace Nichols, Micajah Terrell, Jr., Samuel Terrell,
Robert Johnson, Christopher Johnson, Robert Burton, Isaac Parrish,
James Martin, Tace Baugham, Mary Terrell, Mourning Johnson, George
Roberts, Robert Hanna, Catharine Hanna, Gerard Johnson.

FISHER, ELIAS, son of Joseph and Ann Fisher, and Hannah Curle, daughter of
Joseph and Rebecca Curle, all of Campbell County, were married at
South River Meeting-house 24 September 1793. The following witnesses

signed the marriage certificate: Wm. Stanton, Wm. Johnson, Gerard Johnson, Robert Johnson, Robert Hanna, Robert Wright, Catharine Hanna, Abel Lodge, Benjamin Hanna, Thomas Hanna, Jane Tillus, Elizabeth Douglas, Humphrey Baugham, Sally Lynch, Elizabeth Lea, Ann Leer, Sarah Johnson, Phebe Stanton, Martha Baugham, Sarah Lodge, Joseph Curle, Joseph Fisher, Robert Fisher, John Baugham, Samuel Fisher, Samuel Cary, Ann Curle, Tacy Baugham, Cynthia Cary.

FISHER, JOHN, son of Joseph Fisher, and Rachel James, daughter of Thomas James, of County of Campbell, were married at South River Meeting-house 17 October 1799. The following witnesses signed the marriage certificate: William Stanton, Stephen Butler, Phebe Stanton, Mary Butler, Hannah Fisher, Mary Holloway, Joseph Fisher, Elias Fisher, Isaac James.

HALLOWAY, WILLIAM and Sarah Stanley of Bedford County, were married at South River Meeting-house, in Campbell County 19 July 1790. The following witnesses signed the marriage certificate: Micajah Davis, Wm. Stanton, William Ballard, John Lynch, Robeda Hanna, Abijah Richards, Achillis Douglas, David Terrell, Tristram Coggshall, William Snead, Mary Betts, Rachel Coffee, Ruth Pidgeon, Rachel Pidgeon, Sarah Bloxom, Susanna Johnson, Sarah Lewis, Anna Lea, Rachel Ballard, Amos Holloway, Wm. Stanton, Catharine Stanton, Hepzibah Halloway, Jane Johnson, Elizabeth Douglas, Sarah Stanley

HOLLOWAY, ABNER and Betsy Hanley [Bell gives this as Betsy Stanley], of Bedford, were married at South River Meeting-house 14 October 1797. The following witnesses signed the marriage certificate: Elias Fisher, Jesse Williams, Aaron Stanton, Mourning Johnson, Sarah Cary, Nancy Ferrell, William Butler, Elizabeth Curle, Christopher Johnson, Robert Hannah, Richard Bloxsom, Elizabeth Hendricks, Benj. Hanna, John Johnson, Thos. Hanna, John Lynch, Amos Halloway, Hapzibah Holloway, Wm. Stanton, Latham Stanton, Huldah Stanton, Mary Butler, Mary Halloway.

HOLLOWAY, AMOS and Hepzibah Stanton of Campbell County were married at South River Meeting-house 20 October 1785. The following witnesses signed the marriage certificate: William Stanton, William Johnson, Achillis Douglas, John Fowler, Ashley Johnson, William Stanton, Jr., James Johnson, William Ferrell, Matilda Lynch, Mary Lynch, Latitia Wileman, Rachel Ballard, Susanna Johnson, Rachel Moorman, Ann Fowler, Sarah Johnson, Ruth Johnson, Mary Anthony, Ann Lea, Elizabeth Douglas, Judith Feddell.

JAMES, JOHN, son of Thomas and Sarah James, and Martha Baugham, daughter of Humphrey and Elizabeth Baugham were married at South River Meeting-house 18 April 1799. The following witnesses signed the marriage certificate: Thomas Reeder, Pricilla Reeder, Joseph Fisher, Thomas Hanna, Jonathan Carey, James Butler, Lucy Baugham, John Lynch, Stephen Butler, Sarah Lodge, Judith Douglas, Mary Lynch.

JOHNSON, ANSELM, son of Benjamin and Mary Johnson, of Bedford County and
Deborah Douglas, daughter of Achillis and Elizabeth Douglas were
married at South River Meeting-house 10 July 1810. The following
witnesses signed the marriage certificate: Achillis Douglas, Benj.
Johnson, Lemuel Johnson, Samuel Johnson, Samuel Fisher, Nicholas
Johnson, Mahlon Cadwalader, James S. Butler, Etchison Grigsby, James
Cox, Garland Johnson, Stephen Butler, Jr., Nathan Dicks, Wm. Davis, Jr.,
Samuel Davis, William Davis, Harrison Ratcliff, Stephen Butler, John
Lynch, Josiah Bailey, Latham Stanton, Daniel Burress, Isaac Pidgeon,
Edward Lynch, Jonathan Butler, Elias Fisher, Elizabeth Fisher, Mary
Lynch, Mary Butler, Zalinda Davis, Matilda Johnson, Lucy Johnson,
Jonathan Johnson, Nancy Butler.

JOHNSON, CHARLES and Susanna Terrell of Campbell County were married at
Hill Creek Meeting-house 17 March 1796. The following witnesses
signed the marriage certificate: David Terrell, Wm. Johnson, Henry
Terrell, David Terrell, Jr., Samuel Terrell, Charles Moorman, David
Johnson, John Richardson, Richard Bloxom, Nancy Davis, Milly Johnson,
Molly Johnson, Mathew Davis, Letitia Wildman, Mary Davis, Mildred
Ratcliff, Susanna Davis, Druscilla Crew, Agatha Johnson, Rachel
Johnson, Molly Richardson, Mourning Johnson, Betsy Moorman, M. Davis.

JOHNSON, JOHN of Bedford County and Rhoda Moorman of Campbell, were
married at South River Meeting-house 21 October 1789. The following
witnesses signed the marriage certificate: Micajah Moorman, William
Johnson, Joseph Johnson, Andrew Moorman, James Johnson, Samuel John-
son, Thomas Moorman, William Bloxom, Charles Moorman, Thomas Johnson,
Moorman Johnson, Thomas Johnson, Joseph Stratton, Samuel Davis, Richard
Bloxom, Mary Davis, Annis Davis, Agatha Johnson, Susanna Johnson, Betty
Moorman, Dosha Moorman, Sarah Stratton, Milley Johnson, Susanna Johnson,
Nancy Moorman, Rachel Johnson, Prudence Moorman.

JOHNSON, JONATHAN, son of William and Susanna Johnson, and Judith Douglas,
daughter of Achillis and Elizabeth Douglas all of Campbell County, were
married at South River Meeting-house 17 January 1805. The following
witnesses signed the marriage certificate: Achillis Douglas, Wm. Johnson,
Mildred Douglas, Micajah Terrell, Robert Johnson, Nancy Johnson,
Matilda Roberts, Zalinda Davis, Elijah Johnson, Mary Butler, Wm. Butler,
Richard Tyree, Deborah Douglas, Betsy Terrell, Polly Lynch, Wm. Davis,
Jepetha Johnson, Joseph Fisher, William Stanton, Newby Johnson.

JOHNSON, JOSEPH and Agatha Moorman, daughter of Zachariah Moorman, were
married at South River Meeting-house 17 April 1785. The following
witnesses signed the marriage certificate: Christopher Johnson,
John Lynch, William Stanton, Christopher Anthony, Ann Candler, Milley
Johnson, Molly Johnson, James Johnson, William Davis, Elizabeth
Douglas, Judith Ballard, Susanna Miller, John Candler, Samuel Davis,
Mary Timberlake, Rachel Johnson, Mary Johnson, Salley Johnson, Samuel
Johnson, Zachariah Moorman, Rachel Ballard, John Johnson, Rachel
Moorman, Achillis Douglas, Betty Johnson, Ann Lay, Susanna Johnson.

OHNSON, NEWBY, son of William Johnson, and Sarah Douglas, daughter of
Achillis Douglas were married at South River Meeting-house 13 February
1800. The following witnesses signed the marriage certificate: Wm.
Johnson, Sr., Achillis Douglas, Elizabeth Douglas, Charles L. Terrell,
Sarah Lodge, Nancy Johnson, John Lynch, Wm. Stanton, Harrison Ratcliff,
Ann Lynch, Enoch Roberts, Ann Pidgeon, Mildred Ratcliff, Sarah James,
Betsy Lea.

OHNSON, PLEASANT and Nancy Moorman, both of Campbell County, were married
at Seneca Meeting-house 14 January 1801. The following witnesses
signed the marriage certificate: Agatha Johnson, Polly Moorman, Lydia
Moorman, Betsy Moorman, Mary Ferrall, Mildred Ratcliff, Letitia Wildman, Mary Timberlake, Wm. Johnson, Sr., Thomas Moorman, James Johnson,
Daniel Stratton, Ashley Stratton, Micajah Moorman, Charles Johnson,
William Johnson, Jr., Joseph Stratton, Jr.

OHNSON, SAMUEL of County of Campbell, and Susanna Moorman, of said County,
were married at South River Meeting-house 20 January 1788. The follow-
ing witnesses signed the marriage certificate: Rachel Ballard, Judith
Ballard, Rhoda Moorman, Dosha Moorman, Micajah Moorman, John Johnson,
David Terrell, Eleanor Ballard, Elizabeth Douglas, Mary Johnson, Ruth
Johnson, Sarah Johnson, Susanna Miller, Betsy Johnson, Charles Moorman,
James Johnson, William Johnson, Christopher Anthony, Samuel Davis,
Micajah Davis, Mary Anthony, William Ballard, Christopher Johnson,
William Davis, Charles Brooke, Achillis Douglas, Barclay Ballard,
Ashley Johnson.

OHNSON, WILLIAM, son of William Johnson, and Sarah Bloxom, daughter of
Richard Bloxom, all of Campbell County were married at South River
Meeting-house 30 November 1791. Names of witnesses to marriage cer-
tificate: William Bloxom, Benjamin Stanton, William Johnson, Richard
Bloxom, John Johnson, Micajah Moorman, Joseph Johnson, Thomas Johnson,
William Johnson, James Johnson, Charles Moorman, Samuel Johnson, David
Johnson, Christopher Johnson, Henry Terrell, Charles Johnson, Thomas
Moorman, Achillis Moorman, Barclay Ballard, Benjamin Johnson, Henry
Brown, Ashley Johnson, Gerard Johnson, Jr., Mary Davis, Betty Johnson,
Neoma Stratton, Agatha Johnson, Judith Johnson, Betty Moorman, Dosha
Moorman, Rachel Moorman, Nancy Moorman, Africa Moorman, Jean Johnson,
Milley Johnson, Salley Moorman, Mary Herndon, Salley Johnson.

EWIS, EVAN, son of Jehu Lewis and Alice his wife of Bedford County, and
Sarah Tennison, daughter of John and Ann Tennison, of Amherst County,
were married at South River Meeting-house in Campbell County 22 April
1790. The following witnesses signed the marriage certificate:
William Johnson, William Ballard, Ashley Johnson, Robert Johnson,
William Betts, Enoch Roberts, Christopher Gatt, Micajah Boudlas,
Susanna Johnson, Betty Johnson, Sarah Johnson, Rachel Ballard, William
Stanton, John Johnson, Christopher James, Robert Hanna, John Davis,
Henry Tennison, Salley Johnson, Salley Martin, Rachel Paxon, Mary
Baugham, Penelope Johnson, Mary Fowler, Phebe Stanton, Zalinda Lynch,
Mary Betts, Jane Tullas, Jesse Lewis, Ann Lewis, Matilda Roberts,
Margaret Tennison.

LEWIS, JESSE, son of Jehu and Alice Lewis of Bedford County, and Rebecca
Morelan, daughter of Jason and Nancy Morelan, were married at South
River Meeting-house 20 February 1793. The following witnesses signed
the marriage certificate: Amos Ballard, William Ballard, Nathan Hale,
Sarah Ballard, Moses Hurt, William Reardson, Elizabeth Ballard, Edna
Dickenson, Eliza Ballard, Rachel Feazel, Susannah Hanna, Elizabeth
Wright, Mourning Ballard, Ruth Straasberry, Judith Ballard, Jonan
Moorlan, Thomas Johnson, John Davis, Sr., Micajah Davis, Elizabeth
Hamner, Sarah Blackley, Jason Moorlan, Joel Lewis, George Lewis,
Nancy Morelan, Joseph Richardson, Abigal Moorelan, Martha Rhodes,
Betty Richardson, Evan Lewis, Joseph Rhodes, Esther Richards, Ada
Moorlan, Moses Embree, Mary Moorelan, Jr., Aaron Feazle, Barnet Feazle.

LODGE, JOCABAD, son of Jocabad and Catharine Lodge, and Sarah Johnson,
daughter of William and Susannah Johnson of Campbell County, were
married 22 November 1792 at South River Meeting-house. The following
witnesses signed the marriage certificate: William Johnson, William
Stanton, John Davis, Alice Fisher, Gerard Johnson, Robert Johnson,
Achillis Douglas, Polley Fowler, Betsy Fisher, Betty Johnson, Elizabeth
Douglas, Jonathan Johnson, William Johnson, John Preston, John Johnson,
Edward Lynch, Robert Fisher, Ashley Johnson, Mary Tenner, Matilda
Roberts, Rebecca Preston, Ruth Micker, John Headon, James Martin,
Joseph Fisher, Mariah Wright, John Roberson, Robert Hanna, Rachel
Wright, Zalinda Lynch, Nancy Johnson, Sarah Johnson, Mourning Johnson.

McPHERSON, DANIEL, son of Stephen and Mary McPherson, and Mary Bond,
daughter of Edward and Mary Bond, all of Bedford County, were married
at South River Meeting-house 20 June 1793. The following witnesses
signed the marriage certificate: Rebecca Lewis, Nancy Morelan, Jonah
Dobins, William Pennock, Moses Cadwalader, William Pennock, Sr., John
Pennock, Thomas Dobins, Chas. Pidgeon, James Cadwalader, Stephen
Morlan, Phillip Williams, Ruth Paxon, Hannah Lerrow, Sarah Pidgeon,
Ruth Cadwalader, Joel Lewis, Sarah Lewis, Mary Anthony, Chris Anthony,
Benj. Bond, Moses Embree, Allan Bond, Mary Kutzs, Samuel Erwin, Wm.
Pidgeon, Rachel Pidgeon, John Coffee, Abijah Richards, Jane Cadwalader,
Rachel Coffee, Edward Bond, Mary Bond, Samuel Oliphant, Henry Newman,
Hannah Harris, Elizabeth Dobins, Magdala Erwin, Alice Pennock, Jane
Erwin, Mary Harris, Hannah Pidgeon, Sarah Holmes.

MACY, MICAJAH of Bedford County, and Sarah Holloway of Campbell County,
were married at South River Meeting-house 25 September 1794. The
following witnesses signed the marriage certificate: Samuel Cary,
James Johnson, Mary Betts, Achillis Douglas, John Lynch, Elizabeth
Douglas, Cynthy Cary, Salley Snead, Thomas Hanna, Judith Douglas,
Elihu Macy, Amos Holloway, Asa Holloway, Isaac Holloway, Hepzibah
Holloway, William Johnson, Hannah Fisher, Mourning Johnson, Sarah
Fisher, Nancy Johnson, Tacy Baugham, Rachel Wright, Elizabeth Lea,
Hannah Fisher, Jonathan Johnson, William Stanton, Sr., Phebe Stanton,
William Stanton, Jr., John Preston, Joseph Coffin, Robert Hanna,
Catharine Hanna, Rebecca Preston, James Stanton, Daniel James, Mary
Stanton, Mary Holloway, Zacheus Stanton, Abner Holloway, Sarah
Douglas, Mathew Baugham, Harry Major.

MACY, MICAJAH, son of John Macy of Bedford County and Sarah Fisher, daughter of Joseph Fisher of Campbell County, were married at South River Meeting-house 18 April 1799. The following witnesses signed the marriage certificate: Hepsibah Holloway, Nancy Johnson, William Stanton, Benjamin Hanna, John Timberlake, Matilda Roberts, Joseph Fisher, Jr., Humphrey Baugham, Robert Hanna, Mary Lynch, Ann Fisher, William Johnson, Sr.

MILNER, DUDLEY, son of Beverly Milner, and Mary Anderson, daughter of John Anderson, were married at South River Meeting-house 13 December 1800. The following witnesses signed the marriage certificate: Daniel Easley, Nimrod Farguson, Richard Kirby, Joseph Fisher, Jr., William Davis, Jr., Edward Lynch, Robert Hanna, William Johnson, Micajah Terrell, Jonathan Johnson, Anna Anderson, Ruth Milner, Orpha Kirby, Mary Butler, Susanna Davis.

MORELAND, JASON, son of Jason and Ann Moreland, and Martha Tullis, daughter of Richard and Jane Tullis of Bedford County were married at South River Meeting-house in Campbell County 14 May 1796. The following witnesses signed the marriage certificate: Sarah Johnson, Lydia Johnson, Susanna Moorman, Lydia Ballard, Rhoda Johnson, Wm. Stanton, Mary Butler, Thomas Hanna, Ashley Johnson, Barclay Ballard, Benjamin Hanna, Mary Lynch, Betsy Johnson, Milly Johnson, Matilda Roberts, William Davis, Christopher Johnson, Achillas Douglas, Zacheus Stanton, John Lynch, Elijah Johnson, Richard Tullis, William Fowler, Joseph Bradfield, Jonathan Johnson, Samuel Cary, Hannah Fisher, Mary Holloway, Rebecca Preston, Jallis Tullis, John Tullis, Ann Tullis, Betty Hendrick, Sarah Hendrick, Mary Anderson, Hepzibah Holloway, Robert Hanna, Mildred Johnson, Mary Betts, Mourning Johnson.

MORGAN, HUGH and Judith Johnson were married at Seneca Meeting-house, Campbell County, 19 January 1803. The following witnesses signed the marriage certificate: Gerard Johnson, Elias Fisher, Charles Moorman, Charles Johnson, Ashley Johnson, Wm. Johnson, Micajah Moorman, Susanna Moorman, Elizabeth Terrell, Rachel Johnson.

PIDGEON, CHARLES, son of William Pidgeon, and Ann Gregg, daughter of Abner Gregg, all of Campbell County were married at Seneca Meeting-house 15 May 1799. The following witnesses signed the marriage certificate: Ashley Johnson, Benjamin Stratton, Daniel Burgess, Naomi Stratton, Isaac Pidgeon, Susanna Johnson, Abraham Wildman, Thomas Burgess, William Pidgeon, Elizabeth Pidgeon, Dosha Moorman, Mary Bloxom.

PLUMMER, ASA, son of Joseph Plummer of Berkley County, and Grace Burgess, daughter of Joseph Burgess of Campbell County, were married at Seneca Meeting-house 13 January 1796. The following witnesses signed the marriage certificate: M. Randle, Nancy Moorman, Pricilla Butler, Rachel Hatcher, Lettia Wildman, Susanna Johnson, Ann Blocksom, Ann Blocksom, Jr., Mary Blocksom, Mary Moorman, Sarah Moorman, Mary Blocksom, Sr., Wm. Johnson, Abner Grigg, Richard Blocksom, Richard Blocksom, Jr., Benj. Stratton, Gideon Blocksom,

Joseph Burgess, Thomas Burgess, Daniel Burgess, John Burgess,
Druscilla Burgess, James Butler.

ROBARDS, ENOCH of Campbell County (late of Philadelphia) and Matilda
Lynch were married at South River Meeting-house 29 January 1789.
The following witnesses signed the marriage certificate: Elizabeth
Douglas, Susanna Johnson, Betty Johnson, Elizabeth Caffery, Anna
Lea, Sarah Johnson, Salley Johnson, Rachel Paxson, Lucy Terrell,
Sarah Martin, Robert Hanna, Robert Johnson, John Paxson, William
Betts, Mary Betts, Robert Wright, Wm. Stanton, Catharine Stanton,
James Martin, Edward Lynch, Catharine Hanna, Ashley Johnson, John
Lynch, Wm. Johnson, Chris. Johnson, Zalinda Lynch, Benj. Johnson,
Anselm Lynch, Wm. Stanton, Achillis Douglas, Henry Terrell, John
Hargrove.

STANTON, LATHAM, son of Wm. Stanton and Huldah Butler, daughter of
Stephen Butler, all of Campbell County, were married at South River
Meeting-house 14 September 1797. The following witnesses signed
the marriage certificate: Ann Lay, Rachel Cary, Nancy Johnson,
Susannah Johnson, Mary Lynch, Lydia Johnson, Hannah Fisher, Sarah
Lodge, Tacy Nicols, Cynthia Cary, Elizabeth Johnson, Betty Johnson,
Sarah Johnson, Benjamin Johnson, Humphrey Baugham, Timothy Johnson,
Robert Hanna, Jonathan Johnson, Enoch Robards, Robert Johnson,
Benjamin Hanna, Jacob Nicols, Joseph Bradfield, William Fowler,
Christopher Johnson, Harry Majors, Wm. Stanton, Sr., Pheby Stanton,
Sally Butler, Stephen Butler, Sally Butler, Hepzibah Holloway, Aaron
Stanton, James Stanton, Zacheus Stanton, Jonathan Butler, Wm. Butler,
James Butler, James Staunton Butler, Asa Holloway.

STANTON, ZACHEUS, son of William Stanton, and Sally Butler, daughter of
James Butler, all of Campbell County, were married at Hills Creek
Meeting-house 16 October 1800. The following witnesses signed the
marriage certificate: Mary Bloxom, Sr., Nancy Butler, Sarah Curle,
Elizabeth Pidgeon, Martha Terrell, Susannah Fox, Druscilla Crew, James
Butler, Sr., Jonathan Butler, Wm. Bloxom, Latham Stanton, David
Terrell, Richard Bloxom, Benjamin Butterworth.

STRATTON, BENJAMIN, son of Joseph Stratton, and Amy Curle, daughter of
Joseph Curle, were married at South River Meeting-house 20 January
1796. The following witnesses signed the marriage certificate:
Letitia Wildman, Betty Moorman, Agatha Johnson, Nancy Moorman,
Susannah Johnson, Rebecca Preston, Joseph Stratton, Sarah Curle,
Joseph Curle, Hannah Stratton.

STRATTON, JACOB, son of Joseph Stratton, and Rebecca Curle, daughter of
Joseph Curle, all of Campbell County, were married at Seneca Meeting-
house 12 November 1800. The following witnesses signed the marriage
certificate: Sarah Curle, Mary Via, Hannah Stratton, Amy Stratton,
Dosha Stratton, Betty Wildman, Betty Moorman, Chisy Hubank, Nancy
Moorman, Africa Moorman, Ruth Gregg, Agatha Johnson, Letitia Wildman,
Shady Stratton, Joel Stratton, Joseph Curle, Daniel Stratton,
Abraham Wildman, Richard Bloxom, James Johnson, Benjamin Stratton,
Jonah Wildman, Reuben Moorman.

STRATTON, JOSEPH, son of Joseph and Naomi Stratton, and Dosha Moorman,
daughter of Micajah and Susannah Moorman, all of Campbell County,
were married at Seneca Meeting-house 19 December 1792. The follow-
ing witnesses signed the marriage certificate: Joseph Stratton,
Micajah Moorman, Wm. Johnson, Joseph Johnson, Thomas Johnson, James
Johnson, Richard Bloxsom, John W. Johnson, Thomas Moorman, Abner
Gregg, Moorman Johnson, Ben Schofield, Lemuel Johnson, Charles
Moorman, Wm. Johnson, Wm. Bloxom, Naomi Stratton, Agatha Johnson,
Rachel Johnson, Ann Bloxom, Sally Moorman, Mary Betts, Jane Johnson,
Judith Johnson, Nancy Moorman, Susanna Johnson, Elizabeth Johnson,
Polly Moorman, Rachel Johnson.

STRATTON, MAHLON and Sarah Moorman, of Campbell County, were married at
Seneca Meeting-house 17 October 1798. The following witnesses
signed the marriage certificate: Micajah Moorman, Reuben Moorman,
James Hunnicutt, James Stanton, William Johnson, Joseph Stratton,
James Johnson, Abner Gregg, Ashly Johnson, Druscilla Burgess, Hannah
Stratton, Agatha Johnson, Milley Johnson, Sarah Gregg, Sarah Curl,
Letitia Wildman, Mary Via, Polly Moorman, Rhoda Johnson, Anna Stratton.

TERRELL, DAVID and Molly Anthony, daughter of Christopher Anthony, were
married at South River Meeting-house 25 September 1788. The follow-
ing witnesses signed the marriage certificate: Christopher Johnson,
William Johnson, Ann Fowler, Matilda Lynch, John Lynch, Wm. Stanton,
Joseph Anthony, Wm. Ballard, Jr., Achillis Douglas, Sam'l Terrell,
Robert Hanna, Wm. Davis, David Johnson, Wm. Davis, Jr., Betty Johnson,
Jane Tillas, Elizabeth Johnson, Rebecca Morlan, Elizabeth Tillas,
William Betts, Ashley Johnson, Charles Anthony, Elizabeth Ballard,
Betty Johnson, Rachel Ballard, Elizabeth Douglas, Sally Johnson, Ruth
Johnson, Rachel Paxon, Mary Betts, Sarah Johnson, Susanna Johnson, Mary
Terrell, Lucy Terrell.

TERRELL, EDWARD, son of David Terrell of Bedford County, and Jane Johnson,
daughter of Gerard and Judith Johnson of Campbell County, were married
at Seneca Meeting-house 19 October 1794. The following witnesses
signed the marriage certificate: Micajah Moorman, Richard Blocksom,
Ashley Johnson, Joseph Curl, Moorman Johnson, Thomas Moorman, James
Johnson, Reuben Moorman, Gerard Johnson, Sr., David Johnson, Sarah
Terrell, Susanna Moorman, Susanna Davis, Mary Butler, Gerard Johnson,
William Johnson, Eliza Johnson, Naomi Stratton, Rachel Johnson,
Effey Moorman, Anna Blocksom, Elizabeth Douglas, Nancy Moorman, Jane
Tillas.

APPENDIX A

OVERVIEW OF LEGAL REQUIREMENTS

The following overview of some early relevant marriage laws of the Colony and of the Commonwealth of Virginia is presented with the hope that it will be as helpful to our readers as it was to the writers in gaining an understanding of marriage bonds and their significance.

Throughout Virginia's Colonial period, marriages were valid only if celebrated under the laws of England and according to the Book of Common Prayer. Ministers of the Church of England were at liberty to solemnize marriages under the authority of licenses or under the authority of banns. The consent of the parent or guardian was necessary if either of the contracting parties was under twenty-one years of age.[1]

In the early days of the Colony, all marriage licenses were granted by the Governor, and the marriages could take place only between the "howres" of eight and twelve in the forenoon[2] because the priests and others partaking of the sacraments were expected to fast until after the mass which usually followed the marriage ceremony.[3]

With the growth of Virginia's population, it became impossible for the Governor to be knowledgeable about the personal lives of all those living within its borders. Such knowledge was necessary to prevent illegal marriages from occurring. So in 1661 the General Assembly transferred the authority to issue marriage licenses from the Governor to the clerks of the county courts. This Act required that "all persons desiring licenses for marriage shall first repair to the Clerk of the County Court, and there shall give bond with sufficient security that there is no lawful cause to obstruct the marriage." Upon completion of such a bond the clerk prepared the license.[4] The bond became payable only if lawful cause was found. An example of such "lawful cause" might be that the two contracting parties were too closely related, or that one of them was already married. After issuing the license, the clerk directed it to the officiating minister, while the bond remained on file in the clerk's office. Later statutes identified the clerk in the county where the bride resided as the appropriate one to issue the license.[5]

Under the authority of banns, the announcement of a forthcoming marriage was required in church services on three successive Sundays or Holy Days in the parish where each of the contracting parties resided. Until 1753, however, the bishops and archbishops had the power to dispense with this requirement.[6] Following the ceremony, the marriage was recorded in the parish records.[7] If banns were used, no issuance of a license by the county clerk was necessary; hence no bond was made out and no minister's return was required for the county clerk's marriage register, although an occasional return was made.

In colonial times marriage under the authority of banns was attractive. For example, it was less expensive. Under banns, the minister performing the ceremony was paid five shillings and there were no other legal fees. Under a license, the Governor received twenty shillings (which was £1); the minister received twenty shillings, and the clerk received five shillings for issuing the license.[8]

The formal language of the marriage bond was adopted in 1734 by "Act of the General Assembly made in the Eighth Year of the Reign of King George the Second." This form bound the bondsmen to the ruling sovereign of England in the sum of £50.[9]

During Virginia's change from Colony to Commonwealth, the Fifth Virginia Convention of the Revolution (1776) adopted the Declaration of Rights which guaranteed religious liberty to all men.[10] Four years later, this new religious liberty was reflected when the General Assembly adopted an Act "for encouraging marriages and removing doubts concerning the validity of marriages celebrated by ministers other than the Church of England." Among its provisions, it declared "good and valid in law marriages celebrated and heretofore celebrated" by dissenting ministers. It provided that "Quakers and Menonists" were the only people who could be married without licenses or banns. It required that ministers and also the clerks of the Quaker and Menonist meetings transmit marriage returns to the clerk of the county court within three months after the marriage.[11]

A further Act adopted in 1784 was designed to meet the need for "one general mode for celebrating marriages throughout the State." This Act, which became effective July 1, 1785, provided that not only Quakers and Menonists, but also members of any other Christian society that had adopted similar regulations were permitted to marry without licenses. The Quakers, Menonists and members of such sects were permitted to solemnize their own marriages or be married by mutual consent of the parties openly published and declared in a religious service of their own church. A license was required of all others. Ministers and clerks of the meeting were required to transmit certificates of marriage to the county clerk within twelve months after the marriage and were subject to a fine of £20 if they failed to do so. Also, the county clerk was subject to a fine of £20 if he failed to record the returns.

The 1784 Act stated the qualifications necessary for ministers who were allowed to perform marriage ceremonies, and specified the minister's fee for the service. It also set the fee for the clerk issuing the license, and called for the preservation of a marriage register by the clerk.[12]

In 1792 an Act was passed which stated that " no minister shall celebrate the rites of matrimony between any persons or join them together in matrimony without legal license, or thrice publication of banns according to the rubrick of Common Prayer, if the parties so married shall be members of the protestant episcopal church..." It also stated that it was lawful for any ordained minister to celebrate the rites of matrimony, according to the forms and customs of the church to which he belonged, between persons for whom publications of banns had been made or who had produced a marriage license. It re-enacted the provisions of the Act of 1784 with respect to Quakers and Mennonites.

After the establishment of the Commonwealth the method of issuing the marriage license, the use of the marriage bond and of the parent's or guardian's consent continued as before. While the same form of marriage bond was used, minor changes were made. The bondsmen were bound to the Governor of the Commonwealth, and in the Act of 1792 all monetary sums appeared in terms of dollars; for example, the bonding sum was changed to $150 instead of £50 and the clerk's fine for failing to make returns became $60 instead of £20.[13]

1. 1H 181, 1632.
2. Ibid.
3. Brydon, George M., Virginia's Mother Church, v.1, p.406, (Richmond, Virginia 1947).
4. 2H 55, 1661.
5. 3H 442, 1705; 6H 82, 1748.
6. Letter from the Rev. C. FitzSimons Allison, D.D., Professor of Church History, Virginia Theological Seminary, Alexandria, Virginia, February 1970 Peter Pence Act 1534.
   Lord Hardwicke Marriage Act 1753.
   Ollard, S.L., Editor, "Marriages", pp. 353-359, A Dictionary of Church History, (London, England 1912).
7. 2H 54, 1661.
8. 3H 445, 1705; 6H 84, 1748. These fees were in Virginia money at six shillings to the dollar.
9. King, George H.S., Marriages of Richmond County, Virginia 1668-1853, p.xx, (Fredericksburg, Virginia 1964).
10. 9H 111, 1776.
11. 10H 362, 1780.
12. 11H 503-04, 1784.
13. 1S 130-132, 1792 (new series).

APPENDIX B

OFFICIATING MINISTERS

The 1784 Act of the General Assembly required that a minister performing marriage ceremonies must have already been ordained and in regular communion with the society of Christians of which he was reputed to be a member. He must have taken the oath of allegiance to the Commonwealth, and have posted a bond of £500 payable to the Governor if he engaged in marriages "incestuous, bigamous, or otherwise unlawful." He could expect to be paid five shillings for performing a marriage. He was required to make a marriage return to the county clerk for recording within a period of twelve months after the ceremony, and was subject to a fine of £20 if he failed to do so. Itinerant ministers were denied the "testimonial" which all ministers had to have in order to perform marriages.[1]

The 1792 Act of the General Assembly changed the ministers' bonding sum to read $1500 and the fine for failing to make returns to read $60.[2]

There follows a list of the officiating ministers whose names appear in the original _Register_ in the Campbell County Clerk's office for the period 1782-1810. Their places of residence and their denominations have been included, if known.

Much of the information listed below was gathered from one source.[3] Other sources, used to determine denomination, are also footnoted. Many of these additional sources give considerable supplementary data about these ministers.

Anthony, John, Bedford County, Baptist
Baldwin, Littlejohn (John), Campbell County
Brown, Henry, Campbell County
Chappell, John, Campbell County
Clay, Charles, Campbell County
Cobbs, Charles, Campbell County, Baptist[4]
Dameron, William, Campbell County
Davidson, Samuel, Campbell County, Baptist
Denton, James, Bedford County
Dodson, William Campbell County, Baptist
Drury, Joseph, Bedford County, Baptist
Early, Abner, Campbell County, Methodist Episcopal
Easter (Ester), Matthew (Mathew), Campbell County
Edge, Obediah (Obadiah), Campbell County
Flowers, William, Campbell County, Baptist
Hatcher, Jeremiah, Bedford County, Baptist
Holt, John W., Bedford County, Protestant Episcopal[5]

Hunter, Andrew, Bedford County, Methodist
Hurt, James, Campbell County, Baptist
Jennings, Samuel (Samuel K.), Campbell County, Methodist[6]
Johns, Edmund, Campbell County, Baptist
Kabler, Frederic, Campbell County, Methodist
Kenney (Kenny), James, Campbell County, Methodist, later became Baptist[7]
Kenyon, William, Campbell County
Lacy, Drury, Campbell County
Lasley (Lesley) (Lastly), Menoah (Manoah), Campbell County, Methodist
McRoberts, Arch (Archibald), Campbell County
Macky, Charles, (No information found)
Mahone (Mahon), William, Campbell County
Martin, William P. (William Peters Martin), Campbell County[8]
Matthews (Mathews), Phil (Philip), Campbell County, Baptist[9]
Maxey (Masey), Bennett, Campbell County, Methodist
Meeks (Weekes), Anderson, Campbell County
Mitchell, James, Campbell County, Presbyterian
Mitchell, Samuel, Campbell County, Methodist[10]
Nowlen (Nowlin), David, Campbell County, Baptist
Panell (Pennell), Joseph, Campbell County
Paup (Phaup), John, Bedford County
Warinner (Warriner) (Warner), James, Campbell County, Baptist
Worley, Joshua, Campbell County

1. 11H 503, 1784.
2. 1S 132, 1792 (new series).
3. Adams, W B., undated MSS containing names, place of residence, and denominations (when known) of ministers licensed by the County Courts of Bedford County and Campbell County. Probably prepared in the 1930's. W. B. Adams, a local genealogist, used court records and Pugh's Official Map of Campbell County 1872 in preparing the MSS now on file in Jones Memorial Library, Lynchburg, Virginia.
4. Early, Ruth H., Campbell Chronicles and Family Sketches 1782-1926, p.28, (Lynchburg, Virginia 1927).
5. Blunt, Ruth H. and Blunt, Louise A., "The Little Anglican Church on the Hill," a publication of the Lynchburg Historical Society Museum, v.7, No.1, dated 1969 but issued in 1970.
6. (Cabell, Margaret C. A.), Sketches and Recollections of Lynchburg by Its Oldest Inhabitant, pp. 209, 281-83, (Richmond, Virginia 1858). This book was published anonymously, but the author is known to have been Margaret C. A. Cabell.
7. Semple, Robert B., A History of the Rise and Progress of the Baptists in Virginia, Revised Edition by Rev. G. W Beale, p. 334, (Richmond, Virginia 1894).
8. Christian, W. Asbury, Lynchburg And Its People, p. 100, (Lynchburg, Virginia 1900).
9. Semple, p.280.
10. Christian, p.29.

APPENDIX C

MIGRATIONS OF CAMPBELL COUNTY QUAKERS

During the study of Quaker marriages in Campbell County, curiosity prompted a digression to analyze and chart the Quaker migrations to and from this area.

The importance of the Quakers in the early development of Virginia is unquestioned. In tidewater Virginia they began to arrive in the 1650's; the first Quaker "Meeting" in the area which became Campbell County was established in the 1750's and survived to the 1850's. The Quakers came here, as most frontier people do, because they could settle on good land. They left primarily because, as non-slaveholders, they couldn't successfully compete in the Virginia economy of the early 1800's.

But where did the Campbell County Quakers come from and where did they go? In Bell's book, 33 pages are devoted to "Removals" -- that is, a listing of those who were removed from the rolls of one Quaker Meeting and transferred to another, often in a remote region.

The chart on the next page summarizes and quantifies this in- formation for Campbell County, by decades and by regions. While the data may not be altogether rigorous, the chart goes far to satisfy curiosity about the Quaker migrations, especially the magnitude, route and timing of the immigrations from Pennsylvania and of the emigrations to Ohio. The summary is deemed worth sharing with our readers, as an interesting by-product of the Quaker marriage research.

QUAKER MIGRATIONS TO CAMPBELL COUNTY

DECADE	FROM PENNA. & MD.*	FROM EASTERN VA.**	FROM HANOVER CO., VA.	FROM BEDFORD CO., VA.	FROM MISC. SOURCES	TOTAL
1760's		8	6			14
1770's		3	2		1	6
1780's	13		23			36
1790's	68	19	22	14	6	129
1800's	1	2		11	8	22
1810's		12	5	2	2	21
1820's		1			1	2
1830's			1		1	2
TOTAL	82	45	59	27	19	232

*Via Meetings in Loudoun and Fairfax Counties, Virginia.
No record was found of Quaker migrations to Campbell County via the Shenandoah Valley.

**Via Meetings in Virginia Counties: York, Isle of Wight, Surry, Prince George, Dinwiddie, Charles City, Henrico & Spotsylvania.

QUAKER MIGRATIONS FROM CAMPBELL COUNTY

DECADE	#TO VIRGINIA COUNTIES	TO NO.CAR.	TO PENNA.	TO OHIO	TO VARIOUS	TOTAL
1790's	40	6			1	47
1800's	6	20	47	172		245
1810's				178		178
1820's	1			14		15
1830's					1	1
TOTAL	47	26	47	364	2	486

#To Meetings in Virginia Counties: Fairfax, Surry, Dinwiddie, Henrico, Hanover and Bedford.

I N D E X

Any name which appears on a page may appear more than once on the same page.

And may we urge that you keep in mind the many possible variations in spelling of a name. For instance, we encountered as many as eleven variations for one surname. We have herein indexed separately every name, and each of its variations. This includes first names as well as surnames.

Just before the initial entry of a name, we have grouped and under-scored all variations of the surname which we found in the text. There-after, we have made cross-reference to a spelling variation only when a variant was widely separated in the index from the initial entry of the name; or, when there appeared an obvious error of recording a person under two completely different names.

Abbreviations and symbols,
    key to, 6
Abraham, Robertson, 67
Acree, David, 7

Adams, Addams

Adams, C. S., 21
   David, 7
   Elizabeth, 28
   G., 87
   George T., Jr. Mrs., viii
   James, 28,79
   John, 7,13,23,87
   John, Jr., 13
   Nancy, 87
   Nathan, 87
   Penelope, 95
   Perthenia, 13
   L., 95
   Robert, 44
   Robert, Jr., xiii
   Susannah, 23
   Thomas, F., 7
   W. B., 124
   William, 7,59
Addams, William, 7

Adkins, Abigail, 53
Akers, Ann, 77
   Catharine, 20
   Elizabeth, 87

Akers, continued
   John, 7,59,77,88
   Mary, 59
   Peter, 20
   Ruth, 102
   Sally, 90
   William, 7,77,87
   William, Jr., 102
   William, Sr., 90,102
Akin, Betsy Ann, 79
   Isabella, 93
   Joseph, 7,79,93
   Mary, 93
   Sally, 93
   William, 93
Albemarle County (Va.), xiv
Alexander, Elizabeth, 80
   Esther, 71
   family, 4
   J., 4
   James, 68
   John, 53,56,80,107
   Ro., 17,20,33,71
   Robert, xiv,4,8,15,65,89,90,
     92,94,96,103
   Sally, 65
   Thomas, 7,10,79
   Thos., 10,79
   W., 4,37,52
   William, 61
Alexandria, Va., 122

Alford, John, 7

Aligre, Allegre

Aligre, Ann, 39
    Anne, 39
    Matthew, 39

Allen, Hartwell, 7
Alley, John, 7
    Peter, 7
Allison, C. FitzSimons, The
    Rev. Dr., vii,122

Allmond, Almond

Allmond, William, 7
Almond, Rheubin, 7

Altavista, Va., xii
Alvis, David, 100
Ambrose, Ambrose, 41
Amherst County (Va.), 24,115

Amorett, Armonett

Amorett, Jacob, 8

Anderson, Anna, 103,117
    Frances, 60
    John, 117
    John, Jr., 98
    Mary, 117
    Matilda, 98
    Nancy, 98
    Polly, 99
    Robert, 60
    Sally, 98
    Susan, 57
    William, 45,99

Angel, Angell, Angill

Angel, _____, 11
    Polly, 37
    Rhoda, 37
Angell, Rhoda, 37
Angill, Polly, 37

Angler, Katherine, 95
Anthony, Charles, 110,119
    Chris, 116
    Christopher, 110,112,114,115,
        119

Anthony, continued
    Christopher, Jr., 110
    Elizabeth, 110
    Jno., 98
    John, 37,41,42,77,89,102,
        123
    John A., 35
    Joseph, 119
    Mark, 8
    Mary, 110,113,115,116
    Mary Crenshaw, 41
    Mevory, 112
    Molly, 110,119
    Penelope, 112
    Polly C., 41
    Sarah, 98
    Sarah Tate, 110
    W. B., 41
Appomattox County (Va.), xiv
Armistead, Ann, 66
    Cona, 91
    Elizabeth, 100
    Francis, 91,100
    John, 100
    John S., 66
    Robert, 66,91,100
    Samuel, 76
    William, 8
Armonett, Jacob, 8
Armstrong, Benjamin, 73,91
    Fanny, 73
    Polly, 91
Arnold, Elizabeth, 14
    James, 7
    John, 14,21,43
    Patsey, 7
    Sally, 7
    Susannah G., 21
Arrington, Adler, 8,66,98
    Charles, 8,30,66
    Daniel, 8
    John, 8,30,66
    Polly, 98

Arther, Arthur

Arther, Barnabas, 88
    Sarah, 88
    William, 88
Arthur, Ann, 78,102
    Bonabus, 8
    Charles T., 111
    Elizabeth, 35

Arthur, continued
    Joseph, 103
    Milly, 9
    Sally, 103
    Tabitha, 41
    William, 8,41,78
    Wm., 35,84

Asbury, Nancy, 71
Asher, Elizabeth, 94
    John, 8,86,94
    Sarah, 86
Askew, Anthony, 19,64
    Catherine, 64
    Elizabeth, 19
    Jemima, 64
    Pliant, 64
    William, 8
Austin, A., 4
    James, 8
    Polly, 66
    Simeon, 89
    William, 9

                    B

Baber, Baker, Beaver

Baber, Charles G., viii
    Douglas, 9
    George, 45,91
    James, 9
    John, 3, 9
    Judith, 45
    Nancy, 49,95 (see also
        Patterson, Milly)
    William, 49,58,95

Bagby, William, 9
    William S., 78

Bailey, Baily, Bealey, Baley,
        Baly

Bailey, Betsy, 99
    Elizabeth, 22, 107
    George, 39
    James, 9,19
    James, M., 107
    Jonathan, 9
    Josiah, 110,111,114
    Keziah, 34

Bailey, continued
    Linda Rilly, 93
    Marah, 9
    Martha, 22,44
    Mary, 101
    Nancy, 101
    Nunnery, 9,91
    Robert, 9
    Sarah, 9,31,107
    Savage, 44, 107
    Susannah, 88,110,111
    Temperance, 9
    Thomas, 9,110
    Toby, 9
    William, 9,88
    Yancie, 19
Baily, Nunnery, 9

Baker, Douglas, 9
    Glover, 34
Baldwin, John, 47,123
    Littlejohn, 28,104,123
    Susan, 61
    Susannah, 61
    Zebulon, 9
Baley, Linda Rilly, 93
    Marah, 31
    Poley, 31
    Sarah, 31
    Thomas, 31
    William, 31,93
Ballard, Amos, 110,116
    Barclay, 110,111,115,117
    Barklay, 115
    Byrom, 110,112
    Eleanor, 115
    Eliza, 116
    Elizabeth, 110,112,116,119
    James, 110
    Judith, 110,112,114,116
    Lydia, 117
    Mary, 110,112
    Mourning, 110,116
    Nancy, 110
    Polly, 111
    Rachel, 110,112,113,114,115,
        119
    Sarah, 116
    Susanna, 110
    William, 110,113,115,116
    William, Jr., 110
    Wm., Jr., 119

130

Baltimore, Maryland, xii
Baly, Betsy, 99
    Elebath, 99
Bangham, Benjamin, 10,60
    Humphrey, 60
    John, 35
    Lucy, 60
    Mary, 35
    Tacy, 60
Baptist(s)
    A History of the Rise and
        Progress of the Baptist in
        Virginia (Semple), 124
    Ministers, 123,124
Barber, Charles, 32
    Lucy, 32
    William, 10
Barker, Mary, 82
Barlow, Edith, 98
    Elizabeth, 42
    Jane, 42
    Mary, 34
    Thomas, 34,42,98
    Thos., 42

Barnard, Bernard

Barnard, Benjamin, 11,53
    Eunice, 53
    Timothy, 10,38,53 (see also
        Gardener, Nathaniel, 38)

Barnes, Jas., 17

Barnett, Barnette

Barnett, Anna, 72
    David, 28
    Nancy, 72
    Rachel, 84
Barnette, Timothy, 38
Barns, Samuel, 10

Barnwell, Elizabeth, 85
    Sally, 85

Barrach, Barrack, Barracks,
    Barrick, Barrox

Barrach, Moore, 10
Barrack, Moore, 10
Barracks, Russell, 10
Barrick, Russell, 10

Barrow, Anne, 72 (see also
    Barnett, Anna)
Barrox, Moore, 10
Barton, Elijah, 10
Bass, Elizabeth, 62,100
    Josiah, 68,94,100
    Josiah, Jr., 10
    Peter, 10,67
    Polly, 30
    Rebeckah, 68
Baugh, Bartlet, 23
    Betty, 23
    Elizabeth, 90
    Thomas, 53
    Thos., 53

Baugham, Baughan, Baughn

Baugham, Elizabeth, 113
    Humphrey, 113,117,118
    John, 113
    Lacy, 60
    Lucy, 113
    Martha, 111,113
    Mary, 115
    Mathew, 116
    Tace, 112
    Tacy, 60,113,116
Baughan, James, 19
    John, 112
    Mary, 112
Baughn, Henry, 10
    Richard, 10

Bayer, Boyer, Bowyer

Bayer, Mary, 34

Baylis, John, Jr.
Beachbord, Benjamin, 88
Beale, G. W., 124
Bealey, William, 9
    Wm., 9
Beaver, Judith, 45 (see also
    Baber, Judith)
Beckham, William, 10
Bedford County (Va.), xii,xiii,
    xiv,41,72,80,108,110,111,
    112,113,114,115,116,117,
    119,123,126
Beird, Elizabeth, 18
Bell, James, 11
    James Pinkney, xi,xii,6,109,
    112,113,125

Bell, continued
Mary, 32
Polly, 32
Sarah, 75
Susannah, 75
William, 11
Benagh, James, 90
Bennett, H. E., Clerk, vii
Howard, 95
Berkley County (Va.) [now
W. Va.], 117
Bernard, Benjamin, 11,53
Eunice, 53
Joseph, 11
William, 11
Beteler, Jacob, 12
Betts, Mary, 106,112,113,115,
116,117,118,119
William, 106,115,118,119

Bird, Byrd

Bird, George, 16
Birford, Morning, 28
Birmingham, Betty, 28
Black, Betsy, 54,68,96
James, 11
John, 14,29,31,52,54,56,
64,80,96
Kitty, 64
Mary, 14
Polly, 49,52,54
Sally, 29,56,68
Thomas, 68
Thomas, Jr., 29,68
Thos., 29
William, 11,52,54
Wm., 52
Blackley, Sarah, 116
Blake, William, 11
Blakey, Pleasant, 11
Blankenship, Archibald, 11,48
Benjamin, 11
Edith, 12
Elijah, 11
Henry, 11
Hudson, 11,12,23,53,65,98
Ison, 12
Jesse, 12,23
Levi, 12
Nancy, 98
Obedience, 23
Phebe, 23

Blankenship, continued
Prudence, 65
Zachariah, 12,98
Blankinship, Elizabeth, 48
Hudson H., 48
Leauraney, 53

Blocksom, Bloxom, Bloxsom

Blocksom, Ann, 117
Anna, 119
Ann, Jr. [sic], 117
Gideon,111,117
Mary, 111,117
Mary, Sr. [sic], 117
Richard, 111,117,119
Richard, Jr., 117
Richard, Sr., 111
William, 111
Blossom, Gregory, 36
Blount, Charles, 104
Maria P., 104
Bloxom, Ann, 119
Mary, 117
Mary, Sr. [sic], 118
Richard, 112,114,115,118
Sarah, 113,115
William, 112,114,115
Wm., 118,119
Bloxsom, Richard, 12,76,113,119
Blue Ridge Chapter NSDAR
book sponsorship by, vii
Genealogical Records Comm. of,vii
members of, vii, viii
project of, xi
Regent of, vii
Seventy-fifth Anniversary of,
opp. p. vii
Blunt, Louise Ann Miss , vii,124
Ruth H. Miss, vii, 124
Boaz, Edmund, 12
James, 13,18,84
Russell, 12,81
Bobbit, Humphrey, 12,43 (see also
Bobson, Humphrey)
Bobson, Humphrey (see also Bobbitt,
Humphrey
Bolay, John, 12
Boles, Betsy, 80
Bolling, Archibald, 84
Archibald, Sr., 68
Elizabeth M., 84
Letty, 96

Bolling, continued
    Sarah, 68
Bond, Alice, 110
    Allan, 116
    Benj., 116
    Edward, 116
    George, 12
    Mary, 116
Booker, Peter, 12
Booth, Prudence, 54
    William, 54
Borden, John, 55,69
Bosher, William, 91,103

Botelar, Boteler, Botler

Botelar, Elizabeth, 104
    Sally, 9
    Thomas, 9, 104
Boteler, Henry, 12
    Mary, 81
    Sarah, 81
    Thomas, 81
    Will, 81
    William, 12
    William, Jr., 12
Botetourt County, (Va.), 23
Both, James, 11
Botler, Thomas, 104

Botomes, Bottom, Bottomes,
        Bottoms

Botomes, Mikagah, 65
    Susanna, 65
Bottelar, Mary, 81
Bottom, Martin, 65
    Susanna, 65
Bottoms, Abner, 65
Boudlas, Micajah, 115
Boughton, John, 32,75
    Judith, 75
Bowe, Anne, 73
    Jemima, 73
    Nancy, 73
Bowell, Wm., 104
Bowers, Leonard, 85
Bowes, Russell, 12
Bowles, Lucy, 30
Bowman, Daniel Mrs., vii
    J. J., Mrs., vii
    J. J., Rev., viii

Bowyer, Boyer, Bayer

Bowyer, Mary, 34 (see also Bayer,etc.
Boyer, Adam, 34
    Joseph, 51
    Mary, 34
Bradfield, John, 13,111
    Joseph, 111,117,118
Bradley, Collins, 13
    John, 13,24
    John M., 14
    Joseph, 97
    Judith, 14
    Mary, 14
    Sarah, 29
    Stephen, 13,29
    William, 13,29,104
    Wm., 104
Branch, Fleming, 86
Brent, Elizabeth, 85
Brewer, John, 19
    John H., 13,19
    W. H., 22
Briant, Elijah, 13
Brickard, Mary, 61
Brickeen, John, 13
Brien, Elish, 13
Brien, Ely, 49
Brizentine, Thomas, 13
Brock, Wranny, 13
    Wrenney, 13

Brook, Brooke, Brooks

Brook, Samuel, 13
Brooke, Charles, 115
    Francis, 67
    John, 15,18
    Samuel, 13
Brookneal, Virginia, xii
Brooks, Francis, 67
    James, 13,69
    Jane, 14
    John, 13
    Nancy, 44
    Nelson, 35
    Thomas, 14,35
    William, 14
    Zachariah, 14
Brown, Daniel, 14,79
    Douglas Summers (Mrs. Henry
            Dockery Brown), viii,xii
    Edward, 14,43,89

Brown, continued
    Elizabeth, 33,52
    Henry, 7,8,11,12,13,14,16,20,21,
        26,29,32,37,38,43,46,48,53,
        54,58,59,61,63,66,70,71,76,
        77,79,80,84,85,88,89,96,99,
        102,103,123
    Hubbard, 14,65
    James, 18,20,68,77
    Johannah, 77
    John, 20,33,41,52,56,61,68,77
    John, Jr., 14
    John H., 13
    Joshua, 79
    Judith, 100
    Lewis, 14
    Lucey C., 14
    Lucy, 20,77,79,97
    Mary, 7,33,56
    Mary Arthur Saunders, 14
    Mary Arthur S. or
    MARRYARTHUR S., 14
    Polly, 14,50,79
    Preston, 14
    Quackey, 14
    Ri, 52
    Richard, 100
    Sally, 50,57
    Samuel, 14
    Sarah, 68
    Shadrack, 97
    Will, 7
    William, 14,27,61
Brumfield, Elisha, 15
    James, 15
Brunswick County (Va.), xiv, 33
Bryan, _____, 64
    Agnes, 7
    Andrew, 7
    Andrew M., 34
    Catherine, 23
    Elizabeth, 75
    James, 34,59
    Jane, 28
    John, 7,15,37,94
    John, Jr., 7,15,52
    John, Sr., 23,28
    Morrison, 27,59,81
    Nancy, 86
    Polly, 34
    Robert, 23
    Thomas, 34,82
    William, 15
Brydon, George M., 122

Buckingham County (Va.), 58
Buckler, Henry, 15
Buckner, Elizabeth, 7
    John, 15
    Polly, 79
    William, 15
Bullock, D., 4,20,21,77
    David, 76
    James P., 15,75
    Josias, 20,22,39,52
    Louis, 76
    Nancy, 76
    Patterson, 76
    Patty, 20
    Susanna, 52
Bumpass, Elizabeth, 33
    William, 33,106
Burger, John, 73
Burgess, Betty, 111
    Daniel, 111,117,118
    Deborah, 111
    Drucilla, 110,118,119
    Grace, 117
    James, 15
    John, 111,118
    Jonathan, 111
    Joseph, 111,117,118
    Joseph C., 111
    Joseph, Jr., 111
    Margaret, 111
    Mary, 111
    Polly, 111
    Samuel, 15
    Thomas, 110,111,117,118

Burley, Burnley

Burley, Elizabeth
    Gracie, 45
    Mary, 34
    Nancy, 34
    W. Garsy, 34
Burnett, Betsy, 81
    James, 16
    William, 16
    Wm., 16
Burnley, Nancy, 34
Burns, Polly, 104
Burress, Daniel, 114
Burton, Alex, 51,107
    Alexander, 45
    Elizabeth, 11
    Jesse, 16,51,107
    John, 107

Burton, continued
  Nancy, 107
  Patsy, 51
  Robert, 112
  Robert, Jr., 16
  Sally, 45
  William, Jr., 45
  Will, Jr., 45, 107

Butlar, Butler

Butlar, Sary, 9
Butler, Anna, 103
  Betsey, 37
  Deborah, 111
  Edward, 16,111
  Elizabeth, 104
  Huldah, 118
  James, 111,113,118
  James S., 83, 110,114
  James, Sr., 118
  James Staunton, 118
  John, 16
  Jonathan, 16,37,111,114,118
  Mary, 110,111,112,113,114,
    117,119
  Miley, 32 (see also Butter-
    worth, Milly)
  Nancy, 111,114,118
  Pricilla, 117
  Priscilla, 110
  Sally, 111,118
  Stephen, 111,113,114,118
  Stephen, Jr., 111,114
  Tabby, 19
  Thomas, 10,16
  Toby, 19
  William, 12,64,83,110,111,
    113
  Wm., 64,114,118
Butterworth, Benjamin, 16,21,
  53,110,118
  Betsy, 110,111
  Isaac, 16,18
  Jane, 21,45
  Joseph, 16
  Milley, 32,110 (see also
    Butler, Miley)
  Nancy, 110
  Polly, 53,110,111
  Rachel, 110
  Stephen, 16

Bybe, Bybee

Bybe, Anne, 11
  Edward, 11
Bybee, Benjamin, 16
  Dorothy, 11
  Edward, 25
  Joseph, 16
  Judith, 25
Byrd, George, 16

C

Cabell, Frederick, 17
  George, 17, 41
  John, 17
  Joseph, 17
  Margaret C. A., 124
  W. George, 17
  William, 17
  William L., 17
Cadwalader, Elizabeth, 112
  James, 116
  Jane, 112,116
  Jesse, 110,112
  Jonah, 112
  Mahlon, 112,114
  Moses, 110,112,116
  Moses, Jr., 110,112
  Ruth, 110,112,116
  Thomas, 110,112

Caffery, Caffey

Caffery, Charles, 17,27,41
  Elizabeth, 118
  John G., 76
  Polly, 27
Caffey, Polly, 27
Caldwell, Alexander, 17,59
  Anna Lorry, 94
  John, 17
  Nancy, 60,94
  Oliver, 17
  Polly, 22 (see also
    Clemmons, Polly)
  Sam, 17,22
  Samuel, 17,28,68
  Sophis, 62

Calihan, Callahan, Callihan

Calihan, Mary, 44
Callahan, David, 17
  Elizabeth, 88
  John, 17
  Stephen, 88

Callaway, Calloway

Callaway, Betsy, 17
  Caleb, 17,92
  David, 92
  Doshia, 18
  Elizabeth, 92
  Francis, 18,35
  James, xiii,xiv
  Jas., 82
  John, xiii,17,76
  Joseph, 34,39,69,104
  Margaret, 76
  Nancy, 39
  Polly, 34
  William, 18
Callihan, David, 17
Calloway, David, 92
  Elizabeth, 49
  Frances, 69
  John, 7,51,92
  Joseph, 49
  Sarah, 7
Campbell Chronicles and Family
    Sketches 1782-1926, xii,124
Campbell County, (Va.), 93,110 -
    116,118,119
  courthouse records, xi,2
  courthouse photograph, frontis-
    piece
  early ministers of, 123,124
  first officials of, xiii,xiv
  historical sketch of, xiii,xiv
  marriage bonds of, 7-107
  Quaker (Friends), records of,
    110-119
  Quaker Meeting-houses in, 108
  Quaker migrations to and
    from, 125,126
  present day map of, x
Campbell, Archibald, 43,63
  Clark, 25
  Dicey, 104
  Elizabeth, 43
  Elizabeth Henry, xiii

Campbell, continued
  Ginnet, 63
  James, 18,63
  Jane, 63
  Jenny, 63
  John, 17,18
  Lunaney, 84
  Mary, 36
  Samuel, 18,43,63
  William, 18,96
  Wm., 43
  William (General), County
    named for, xiii

Canady, Cannaday, Cannady

Canady, Pleasant, 43
Candler, Ann, 114
  Daniel, 11
  Henry, 18,48,92,106
  James, 11,110,111,112
  Jane, 47
  John, 18,106,110,114
  John, Jr., 18,112
  John, Sr., 18
  Lucy, 11
  Mary, 21
  Penelope, 12
  Polly, 21
  William, 12,21

Canifix, Canifax, Cannafax,
Cannafix, Cannefax, Canneyfix,
Cannfix, Cannifax, Conifax,
Conifex, Connefax, Connifax

Canifax, Ann, 104
  Rebecca, 102
  William, 18
Cannaday, John, 83
Cannady, Pleasant, 43
Cannafax, Ann, 104
  Ben, 76
  Benjamin, 76
  William, 82
Cannafix, Ann, 104
  William, 104
Cannefax, Radford, 16
Canneyfix, Nansey, 82
Cannfix, Johnney, 82
Cannifax, Anne, 32
  Chesley, 18

Cannifax, continued
Edward, 18
John, 18,32,82
Radford, 18,32
Rebecca, 82
Rebeckah, 82
Rhoda, 12
Susannah, 32
William, 18,82
Cardwell, Robert, 19,42,66
Robert, Jr., 66
Robert, Sr., 19
Sally, 66
William, 19

Carey, Cary

Carey, Jonathan, 113
Carnifax, John, 102
Carnifix, Chesley, 18
Carrell, Delilah, 53
Carroll, Delila, 53
Etheldread, 19
Carson, Betsy, 78
Elizabeth, 40,80
James, 58,78
John, 15,19,80
Mary, 15,58,78,80
Moses, 104
Peggy, 53,58
Robert, 80
Sarah, 78
Thomas, 19,23,78
Thos., 29,78
William, 19,53,58,80,83
William, Jr., 19
William, Sr., 19,40
Carter, Elizabeth A., 59
John, 19,99
John D., 19,99
Pledge, 19
Carty, Elizabeth, 17
Patrick, 17
Carver, Cornelius, 19
James, 39

Carwile, Carwiles

Carwile, Nancy, 26
Carwiles, Jacob, 20,70,99
John, 20

Carwiles, continued
Nancy, 26
William, 20
Cary, Cyntha, 111,113,118
Cynthy, 116
John, 111
Rachel, 111,118
Samuel, 111,113,116,117
Sarah, 111,113
Caswell County, (N.C.), 70
Cave, Dudley, 112
Chambers, Josiah, 95
Chandler, Abraham, 47
Jane, 47
Paton, 104
Peyton, 104

Chapel, Chappell, Chaple

Chapel, Jesse, 20
Chaple, Jesse, 20
Chapman, Benjamin, 20
Chappell, James, 57
John, 13,24,31,35,42,44,49,
56,68,71,74,91,101,123
Charles City County (Va.), 126
Charlotte County (Va.), 39,41,45,
55,91
Cheatham, Bearnet, 45
Bernard, 45
Peter, 33
Robertson, 33,79
Tabitha, 79

Cheek, Chick

Cheek, Anderson, 20
Martha, 89
Chenault, William, 20
Chewning, Harden, 20,36
Chick, Anderson, 20,77

Childras, Childress

Childras, Nancy, 25
Childress, Fleming, 20
Nancy, 25
Samuel, 26
Vaulton, 20
Chilton, Elizabeth I., 78
Judith, 78

Chilton, continued
  Nacy, 38
  Raleigh, 78
  Richard, 78
Christian, Anthony, 42
  W. Asbury, 124
Christy, Elijah, 20
Clark, Alexander, 8,11
  Bennett, 20
  Christopher, 99
  David, 20,72
  Elizabeth C., 72
  James, 20,21,47,53
  Jewell T.,Mrs. (Archival
    Assistant), viii
  John, 20,21,72,74,87
  Judith, 72
  Katharine, 74
  Lucy, 72
  Martha, 20
  Mary, 20
  Micajah, 20,72
  Nancy, 33,67
  Paulett, 21,51
  Polly, 87
  Richard, 20,47
  Robert, 20,21,103
  Sarah, 37
  Thomas, 20,21
  Thomas M., 61,72,111
  Thomas W., 93
  Thos., 21,33
  Tucker, 72
  William, 21
Clarkson, James F., 21
  Thomas, xii, 109
Clay, Charles, 17,25,34,77,
    79,123
  Marston, 21
  Marstone, 37
  Sally, 37
Clayton, William, 21
Claywell, Jemima, 50
  Peter, 9,50,89
  Rachel, 89
  Solomon, 13,21

Clemens, Clemmons, Clemons

Clemens, Gasper, 22
  Samuel, 49

Clement, Adam, 57,77
  Benjamin, 21
  John, 21
  Johnson, 57,77
  Juriah, 57
  Susanna, 77
  William, 21,59,110
Clemmons, Gasper, 22
  Polly, 22 (see also
    Caldwell, Polly)
Clemons, Gasper, 22
Clifton, Jonathan, 22
  Thomas, 74
Clodhopper, Daniel, 83
  Polly, 83
Clopton, A. W., 22
  Abner W., 22

Cobb, Cobbs

Cobb, Charles, 49
  John, 31
  Mary Lewis, 8
  Robert, 8,27
Cobbs, Charles, 7,8,9,10,14,15,
    19,20,22,24,25,29,31,32,33,
    34,35,38,39,40,42,44,47,48,
    54,59,60,61,62,63,65,67,68,
    69,70,71,72,75,79,81,85,86,
    87,89,91,92,97,104,105,107,
    123
  Caleb, 22
  Elizabeth, 65
  Frances, 82
  Frances M., 69
  James, 22
  James H., 22
  Jesse, 22,62
  John, 22,52,65,69
  John B., 22,107
  Martha, 52
  Sally, 69
  Susanna, 31
  Thomas, 22,23,31
  Thomas A., 69
  Thomas, Jr., 23
  Tilghman, 23
  Tilghman A., 23
  William, 107
Cochran, John, 52

Cock, Cocke, Cox, Coxe

Cock, Catherine, 11
  Elizabeth, 51
  Ellenor, 91
  George, 37,51,65,92
  John, 23,54,56
  Martha, 37
  Nancy, 56,92
  Osa, 55
  Rebeckah, 65
  Sarah, 54
  Thomas, 11,23,91
  Thomas J., 40,56
  Thomas, Jr., 23
  Thomas, Sr., 23
  Thos., 91
  William, 37,56,65
  Wm., 23,54
Cocke, Drury, 74
  Drury W., 23,74
  John, 23
  Thos. W., 29
Coffey, Charles, 27
  John, 110,116
  Rachel, 110,112,113
  Sarah, 50
Coffin, Joseph, 116
Coggeshall, Tristram, 88,112,113
Coharn, James, 23
  Thomas, 23
Colbert, Lemuel, 23
Cole, John, 28
  Samuel, 23
Coleman, Berry, 23
  Spilsby, 23
Colewell, John, 22
Collins, David, 24,73
  John, 24
  Peter, 24,59
Colonel Charles Lynch Chapter,
    NSDAR, xii
Colver, Joseph, 25

Condray, Condrey

Condray, Caleb, 24
  Prudence, 11
Condrey, Caleb, 24
  Patience, 36
  William, 24,36
Conely, Caty, 58
Conifax, Benjamin, 11 (see
    also Canifax, etc.)
  Radford, 11

Conifex, Radford, 11
Connefax, Radford, 32,37
Connifar, Benjamin, 24
Connifax, Rhoda, 12
  William, 12
Cook, Benjamin, 24
  David, 15
  Isabella, 17
  Thomas J., 79
Cooper, Joseph, 24,35
  Nancy, 94

Copeland, Copelin, Copeling,
    Coplen, Coplin

Copeland, Mary, 42
  Rachel, 106
  Thomas, 42
Copelin, Elizabeth, 19
Copeling, Thomas, 24
Coplen, Mary, 42
  Thomas, 42
Coplin, John, 43
  Mary, 19
Cornelius, Roberta D. Dr., vii
Covington, Martin, 75
Cox, Absalam, 24 (see also
    Cock, etc.)
  Benjamin, 50,77
  Charles, 24
  Dolly, 77
  James, 24, 114
  John, 24,46
  Littlebury, 24
  Molly, 46
  Nancy, 74
  Sarah, 46
  Susannah, 23
Coxe, Thomas, 21

Craille, Cralle

Craille, Lindsay, 24
Cralle, Lindsay, 24
Crank, Nancy, 80
Crawford, Reuben, 29

Crawley, Crowley

Crawley, Betsey, 86
  Beverly, 24,84
  Charles, 24,25
  Elizabeth, 41

Crawley, continued
    James, 25
    John, 41
Crawly, Mary Eleanor, 88
Creasey, Susanna, 30
Creasy, Fleming, 106
Credell, Mildred, 54
    Nancy, 54

Crew, Crews

Crew, Druscilla, 111,114,118
    Nicholas, 111
Crews, Agnes, 27
    Charlotte, 103
    David, 33
    Elizabeth, 25,39
    Gideon, 25
    Isaac, 27,28
    James, 25,28,92
    Jas., 28
    John, 25
    Joseph, 25
    Josiah, 18,25,39,103
    Josiah, Jr., 25
    Josiah, Sr., 103
    Littleberry, 25,27
    Nancy, 39
    Nicholas, 25,33
    Patsy, 28
    Polly, 18
    William, 18,25,39
    Wm., 18,39
    Wrenny, 25,27,92
Criddle, Keziah, 51
Crider, Henry, 25
Crockett, John, 81
Cropff, Henry, 25
Crowley, Anderson, 20
    Betsy, 86
    James, 25,86
Crump, Thomas, 25,99
Culver, Joseph, 25

Cumbee, Cumby

Cumbee, Charles, 25
    Emanuel, 26
    Margaret, 78
    Nancy, 78
    Peter, 26
    Susanner, 78
    Thomas, 78

Cumberland County (Va.,), 80
Cumby, Emanuel, 26
Cunningham, Anna, 51
    Linna, 51
    Murrell, 12
    Rhoda, 83
    Sarah, 12
    William, 51,83

Curl, Curle

Curl, Archibald, 26
    Joseph, 119
    Sarah, 119
Curle, Amy, 118
    Ann, 113
    Elizabeth, 113
    Hannah, 112
    Joseph, 26,112,113,118
    Rebecca, 112,118
    Sarah, 118
Cyrus, Solomon, 26

D

Dabney, John, 26,43,57,71
    John Q., 89
    Lucy, 89
Dale, Elizabeth, 14
    John, 14,52
Dameron, John, 26
    William, 45,48,60,68,123,106
Daniel, Alexander, 26
    Elizabeth, 16
    James, 26,94
    Jemiah, 48
    Jemima, 48
    John, 27,94
    Josiah, 26
    Leviney, 94
    Mary, 20,48
    Peter, 20,26,48,94
    Peter, Jr., 26
    Peter, Sr., 26
    Richard, Sr., 16
    Robert, 20,26
    Thomas, 26
    William, 26,27

Daun, Dawn

Daun, Jane, 35
    Margit, 35
    William, 27

Davenport, Glover, 15,27
  Wilson, 17,93

Davidson, Davison, Davisson

Davidson, Abner, 27
  Alex, 29
  Alexander, 18,27
  Benjamin, 28
  David, 27
  Elizabeth, 29
  Gabrell, 29
  George, 27
  Isabella, 18
  James, 27
  John, 27
  Joseph, 27
  Lizebeth, 18
  Margaret, 41
  Marget, 41
  Margret, 18
  Nancy, 17
  Samuel, 9,15,18,25,27,38,39,
    41,49,66,79,82,87,95,104,
    107,123
  Susanna, 29
  Rachel, 25
Davis, Annis, 112,114
  Asariah, 27
  Betty, 88
  Biddey E., 84
  Bridget, 84
  James, 28
  John, 28,37,84,115,116
  John, Sr., 112,116
  Lucy, 104
  M., 114
  Mary, 111,112,114,115
  Mathew, 114
  Micajah, 73,113,115,116
  Nancy, 85,111,114
  Sally, 37
  Samuel, 112,114,115
  Susanna, 112,114,117,119
  Thomas, 28,85,112
  William, 112,114,115,117
  Wm., 114,119
  Wm., Jr., 110,114,117,119
  Zalinda, 110,111,112,114
Davison, Alexander, 96
  Benjamin, 28
  James, 17,27
  John, 17,28,41,52 (see also
    Dawson, John, 28)

Davison, continued
  Joseph, 27,28
  Margaret, 41,96
  Nancy, 17
  Samuel, 15,28,96
  Thomas, 28
Davisson, Abner, 27
Dawn, William, 27
Dawsey, John, 28
Dawson, John, 28 (see also
    Davison, John, 28)
  Luanna, 101
Dazelwood, William, 11

Dearing, Deering

Dearing, James, 28
  Milly, 43
Deering, James, 21,43,88,103
  Milly, 43
  Nancy, 103
  Sally, 21
Deison, Charles, 29

Dejarnatt, Dejarnett

Dejarnatt, Walker, 101
Dejarnett, Betsy, 15
  Daniel, 98
  James, 15
  John, 28
  Walker, 28, 101
Dence, Elizabeth Page, 35
Denton, James, 28,36,123
DePriest, John, Sr., 52
  Mary, 21
  Sarah, 52
Derossett, Samuel, 28

Detto, Ditto

Detto, Peter, 72
  Petter, 72
Dews, Reuben G., 29
  Richard, 29
Dibrell, Charles, 29
Dickenson, Edna, 116

Dickey, Dicky

Dickey, Ann, 66
  Edmond, 13
  Edward, 40,65,66
  James, 13,29

Dickey, continued
    Jane, 65
    Jean, 13,65,66
    John, 25,29,40,65,66,85
    Samuel, 13,29,65,66
    Sarah, 40
Dickinson, Austin, 29
Dicks, Agatha, 112
    Nathan, 114
    William, 112

Dickson, Dixon

Dickson, Jane, 22
    John, 22,30
Dicky, Margaret, 13
Dictionary of Church History, A,
    122
Diener, Jacob, 29
    Sarah, 67
Dieson, Charles, 29
Dill, John, 22,29,44
Dillard, Benjamin, 29,74
    James, 29
Dillon, Henry, 17,24,59
    John, 24,59
    Lucy, 59
    Sussannah, 24
    Thomas, 80
Dimney, Edward, 29
Dinwiddie County, (Va.), 126

Dinwiddie, Dinwoddie

Dinwiddie, Anne, 37,105
    Elizabeth, 80
    Frances, 37
    James, 19,80,105
    John, 30,37
    Joseph, 19,30,105
    Mary, 19
    William, 30
Dinwoddie, Jean, 104
Ditto, Peter, 30,72
    Petter, 72
Dixon, Elizabeth, 8
    George, 22
    James, 22,30
    Jane, 22
    John, 30
    Susanna, 8
    Thomas, 30
    William E., 30

Dobins, Elizabeth, 116
    Jonah, 116
    Thomas, 116
Dobson, Lydia, 57
    Nancy, 42
    Polly, 42
    Thomas, 75
    William, 42,57,123
    William C., 57
Dodd, Thomas, 30

Dodson, Dotson

Dodson, William, 31
Dokeridge, Polly, 101
Donald, Sally, 28
Dorman, J. Frederick,F.A.S.G.
    (Editor, The Virginia
    Genealogist), vii
Doss, Agnes, 106
    Ann, 58
    Anna, 106
    Anne, 106
    Hartwell M., 30
    Patsey, 69
Dotson, Elizabeth, 38
Dougherty, Gerard, 46
    Jarett, 30
    Jerard, 30
    William, 30

Douglas, Douglass

Douglas, Achillis, 12,98,110,112,
    113,114,115,116,117,118,119
    Deborah, 111,112,114
    Edward, 22,31,87
    Elizabeth, 110,111,112,113,114,
    115,116,118,119
    James, 22,31,87
    John, 22
    Joshua, 19
    Judith, 113,114,116
    Mary, 111
    Mildred, 98,114
    Polly, 22
    Sarah, 87,115,116
    Wm. Sr., 115
Douglass, Betsy, 110
    Deborah, 114
    Elizabeth, 80
    James, 22
    Jane, 19

142

Douglass, continued
  Robert, 19
  Sarah, 87
Drinkard, Duncy, 31
Drinkwater, Emanuel, 31
  John, 31
  Mary, 101
  Samuel, 31,79
Driskill, Adam, 28,31,70,101
  Anne, 70
  Anney, 70
  Alex., 31
  Alexander, 13,31,38,87
  Daniel, 31,48,67,70,101,106
  Daniel, Jr., 70
  David, 31
  Davy, 101
  Marshall, 31
  Polly, 13
  Richard, 9,31,70
  William, 31
Drury, Joseph, 14,41,45,51,58,
    64,97,105,123
Dudgeon, Alexander, 31,93
  Ann, 7
  James, 31
  William, 32
Dudley, Abner, 32
  Absolom, 32
  Anne, 86
  Armistead, 14,32,86
  John W., Ass't Archivist, viii
  Phillis, 14
Dunn, Richard, 32
  Thomas, 31,81
Dunnavant, Shadrick, 32
  Shadwick, 32

Dupee, Dupuy

Dupee, William, 32
Dupriest, Austin, 97
  Lucy, 97
DuPuy, William, 32

DuVal, DuVall

DuVal, Ann E., 17
  Benjamin, 69
  Lewis, 69
  Sally, 69
  Samuel, 58
DuVall, Ann E., 17

DuVall, continued
  Benjamin, 69
  Daniel, 69
  John, 32
  Marcen, 32
  Mareen, 32
  Sally, 105
  Skinner, 105
Dyer, Elijah, 53
  John, 32

E

Eadds, Edds, Ediss, Eids

Eadds, Jesse, 33
Eanes, Nancy, 33
Early, Abner, 18,32,33,69,71,72,
    75,83,123
  Joshua, Jr., 32
  Mary, 50
  Ned, 32
  Ruth H., xii,124
Easley, Daniel, 117
East, Ezekial, 46
  Isaac, 32
  Joseph, 32
  Sally, 46
  Shadrack, 32
  Thomas, 33,46
  Thos., 46

Easter, Esther, Ester

Easter, Mathew, 123
  Matthew, 17,33,38,42,71,81,90,
    102
Eastins, Charles, 12

Echols, Eckhols

Echols, Elcane, 75
  Elcaner, 75
  Elizabeth, 59
  Moses, 33
Eckhols, Elizabeth, 59
Edds, Anne, 18
  Elizabeth, 16
  Jenny, 65
  Jesse, 33,38
  John, 33,38,65
  Joseph, 18,65
  Polly, 73

Edds, continued
  Sally, 16,18
  Sarah, 38
  Thomas, 18,73
  Thos., 38
  William, 73
  Wm., 73
Edge, Obadiah, 8,13,14,28,30,41,
  44,45,50,58,66,67,78,79,
  123
  Obediah, 26,33,40,77,104,105,
  123
Ediss, Sarah, 38
Edwards, James, 66
Eidson, Barnabas, 33
  Bonibas, 69
  Henry, 55,69,70,76
  Henry, Jr., 69
  James, 33
  Jane, 76
  John, 33
  Joseph, 55,103
  Milly, 70
  Nancy, 69
  Penelope, 83
  Polley, 55
  Sally, 69
Eids, William, 16
  Wm., 16
Eidson, William, 55,70
Elam, Elizabeth, 101
  Frances, 90
  Franky, 90
  Luallen, 33
  Mary, 70
  Obedience, 69
  Patsey, 30
  Richard, 70,90
  Susanna, 30
  Susanah, 101
  Susannah, 69
Elder, Ephraim, 33
  James, 33,67,105
  John, 67
  Martha, 19
  Patsy, 70
  Polly, 19
  Polly M., 25
Eldridge, Ernest
  frontispiece by, vii
Elgin, John, 33

Ellett, Ellet, Elliot, Elliott

Ellett, Elizabeth, 39

Ellett, continued
  Robert, 33
Elliot, Robert, 33
Elliott, David, 106
  Elizabeth, 39
  Katherine [B.] (Mrs.
    Herbert A.), viii
  William, 33
Ellis, David, 34
Elmore, Andrew, 34
Embree, Elizabeth, 110
  Mary, 110
  Moses, 110,116
Encyclopedia of American
    Quaker Genealogy, v.6,
    Virginia, xii
England, Isaac, 34,45
  Joseph, 34
  Titus, 45
Emporia, Va., viii
Enright, O.B.,Jr. Mrs. (Lucile
    Slate Enright), vii
Episcopal Theological Seminary,
    vii, 122
Epperson, Elizabeth, 90
  James L. Mrs., viii
  Joseph, 7
  Little B., 7
  Littleberry, 34,83,85,90
  Nancy, 7
  Phebe, 85
  Richard, 7,34,83,90
  Rosanna, 83
  Rudd, 90
  Samuel, 7
  William, 34
Erwin, James, 110
  Jane, 116
  Magdala, 116
  Magdalen, 110
  Mary, 110
  Samuel, 116
Ester, Mathew, 123
  Matthew, 33,123

Evans, Evins

Evans, Anne, 28
  Anthony, 34,100
  Becky, 79
  Catherine, 15
  Daniel, 15,28,37,97
  Elenor, 97
  Elizabeth, 60
  Ellender, 97

Evans, continued
  George, 34
  Jane, 15
  John, 24,34
  Leticia, 37
  Mary, 39
  Nancy, 79
  Thos., 79
  Thos. R., 28
  Rees, 15
  Riece, 37
  Sampson, 60
  William, 34
Eve, George, 34,36
  George, Jr., 36
Evins, Nancy, 79
Evoute, Joseph, 110

F

Fairfax County, (Va.), 126

Fares, Faris, Fariss

Fares, Phoeba, 58

Farguson, Ferguson, Furguson,
    Furgusson

Farguson, Nimrod, 117
Faris, Benjamin, 93
  Claiborne, 34
  Elizabeth, 24,88
  Frank, 20
  Jesse, 24
  John, 20,23,24,35,48,54,59
  William, 24,35
  William A., 35
  William Amos(s), 35
Fariss, Phebe, 58
Farley, Edward, Sr., 97
  Henry, 97
  Mary, 97
Farmer, James, 35
  Molly, 99
  Thomas, 99
Farris, Benjamin, 88
  Elizabeth, 88
Farthing, Elizabeth, 31
  Fanny, 13
  Martha, 32
  Molly, 26
  Nancy, 26
  Sally, 37
  Thomas, 32

Farthing, continued
  William, 13,26,31,37
  Wm., 13
Fawcett, Marion Asher Mrs., xii

Feazel, Feazle

Feazel, Rachel, 116
Feazle, Aaron, 116
  Barnet, 116
Feddell, Judith, 113
Ferguson, Andrew, 35
  Joseph, 10,35
  Mary, 83
  Robert, 68

Ferrall, Ferrell

Ferrall, James, 34
  Mary, 115
Ferrell, Nancy, 113
  William, 35,60,113

Field, Fields

Field, Andrew, 17,87
  Betsy, 45
  Daniel, 35
  Jemima H., 50
  Margaret, 45,50
  Mary, 17
  Peggy, 45
  Rachel, 87
Fields, Betsy, 50
  David, 35
  Isabella, 68
  Jemina, 50
  Magret, 50
  Marget, 17
  Margret, 54,68
  Nancy, 54
  Patsy, 17
Finch, _____, 28
  Barnet, 35
  Barnett, 49
  Barnit, 35,59,98,102,105
  Barnit, Jr., 105
  Betsy, 27,38
  Bernard, 28,35,105
  Bernett, 38
  Blagdon, 20,27,42,85
  Blagdon, Jr., 35
  Fanny, 27
  George, 16

Finch, continued
  Hannah, 102
  Jemima, 42
  John, 27,35,56
  Martha, 20
  Patsy, 56
  Polly, 16
  Sally, 85,105
  Selah, 59
Fisher, Alice, 116
  Ann, 112,117
  Betsy, 116
  Elias, 112,113,114,117
  Elizabeth, 111,114
  Hannah, 113,116,117,118
  John, 111,113
  Joseph, 112,113,114,116,117
  Joseph, Jr., 111,117
  Robert, 113,116
  Samuel, 20,111,113,114
  Sarah, 116,117
Fitch, Samuel, 35
Fitzpatrick, John, xiii (In the
    Bedford County, Va. records
    this name also appears as
    John F. Patrick)
  Sarah, 54 (see Patrick, Sarah)
Fleming, David, 36
  John, 36
  Nancy, 18
  Samuel, 18,46,103
Flowers, Elizabeth, 92
  Naomi, 36
  Rolin, 92
  Samuel, 36
  William, 8,10,12,13,16,17,19,
    22,27,29,30,35,40,44,50,54,
    56,59,60,63,64,65,66,70,74,
    78,79,81,82,85,88,90,96,97,
    101,104,106,123
  William, Jr., 13,18,25,27,29,
    36,57,61,65,74,78,90,93,95,
    100,104,106
  William, Sr., 84,92
  Valentine, 36
Forbes, John, 82
  Nancy, 82
Fore, Elizabeth, 45
  John, 45,92
  Peter, 36
Forrest, Polly, 90

Forsee, Foshee

Forsee, Daniel, 36

Fosdeck, Geo., 83
Fosdick, Elizabeth, 50
  George, 36
  Lydia, 90
  Sally, 89
  William, 50,89,90
Foshee, Daniel, 36
Fosher, John, 36
Foster, Joshua, 79
  Larken, 24
  Nancy, 58
  William, 58
Fowler, Ann, 89,112,113,119
  Christopher, 12,36
  John, 36,86,89,113
  Jno., Jr., 12,86
  Judith, 86
  Margaret, 87
  Mary, 87,89,115
  Molly, 89
  Nancy, 12
  Polley, 116
  Polly, 112
  William, 12,36,117,118
Fox, George, 26,36
  James, 36
  Margaret, 58
  Richard, 24,36
  Susannah, 24,118
  Thomas, 20,37
Frances, Lucy J., 24
  Lucy Jones, 24
  William, 60
Frank, Thomas, 66

Franklin, Frankling

Franklin, Catherine, 104
  Edmond, 104
  Edna, 106
  Elizabeth, 36,74,90,98,105
  Henry, 37,84
  Heziah, 96
  James, 100,104
  Jane, 36,105
  Janet, 36
  John, 37,84
  Judy,70
  Judy B., 70
  Kesiah, 105
  Lewis, 60,74,96
  Lewis, Jr., 47
  Margaret, 85
  Mary, 74
  Milly, 60

Franklin, continued
  Nancy, 84
  Nancy C., 97
  Nathan, 83
  Owen, 105
  Peter, 37
  Robert, 37,74,98,105
  Sarah, 74
  Thomas, 36,37,60,62,70,71,74,
    84,96,97,106
  Thos., 74
Frankling, Lewis, 47
  Robert, 47

Frasher, Frashure, Frashier,
Frazier, Frazor, Frazer, Freisher

Frasher, Marget, 47
Frashier, Daniel, 37
  Elijah, 37
  John, 37
  Thomas, 37
  William, 37
Frashure, Joel, 38
Frasier, Daniel, 37
  Elizabeth, 50
  Sally, 50
  William, 50
Frazer, Anney, 88
  Henry, 37
  William, 88
Frazier, Anney, 88
  John, 38
  Joseph, 38
  Micajah, 38
  William, 37,88
Frazor, Thomas, 37
Fredericksburg, Va., 122
Freeman, Frank, 12,43,64,83
  Morris, 34,38
Freisher, Sally, 50
  William, 50
Fretwell, Leonard, 38
  Linwood, 38
Friends (See Quakers)
Friends Records, South River,
    Bedford County, Va.,
    Proceedings of Monthly
    Meeting, 1757-1797, Vol.1,
    xii
Frith, Rhoda, 10
Funai, Louis R., Jr. Mrs., vii
Funk, Peter, 17
Fuqua, Elizabeth, 32

Fuqua, continued
  Lavina, 62
  Moses, 24,29,32,62,72
  Nancy, 72
  Obediah, 72
  Sally, 24
  William, 72
Furguson, Peter, 84 (see
    Farguson, etc.)
Furgusson, Peter, 84

G

Galbraith, Galbreath, Gilbreath

Galbraith, Samuel, 17
Galbreath, Samuel, 38,104

Galding, Golding, Galden

Galden, Keziah, 62
Galding, Jacob, 41,66
  Lizbath, 62
Gallagher, Thomas, 22
Gallaway, Benjamin, 58
Gallion, Mitchell, 38

Gardener, Gardner

Gardener, Andrew, 58
  Nathaniel, 38
Gardner, John, 38
  Nathaniel, 38

Garrett, Garrott
  Elijah, 10
  John, 10,55
  Josiah, 39
  Susannah, 10
Garrott, Elijah, 39
  Josiah, 39
Garvin, Elizabeth, 85
  Susanah, 85
Gash, Michael, 39
Gaston, Elizabeth, 104
Gatt, Christopher, 115

Gaulden, Gauldin, Gaulding

Gaulden, Patty, 94
Gauldin, Anne, 91
Gaulding, Elizabeth, 102
  Lucy, 102

Gausney, Gosney

Gausney, Benjamin, 39
Gee, Benjamin, 105
    Jane, 105
    Job, 105
    John, 105
    Sarah, 105
George, Betsy, 83
    Lucy, 12
    Milly, 83
    William, 59,80
    William, Jr., 59
Gibbs, Edward, 32
    Frances, 32
    Francis, 32
    Nancy, 28
    Peter, 32,39

Gibson, Gipson

Gibson, Jane, 10
    John, 23,39
    Patrick, 94
    Sarah, 32
    Robert, 39
Gilbert, Benjamin, 39
    Benjamin, Jr., 39
    Betsy, 15
    Charles, 16,39
    John, 39,62
    Lavina, 48
    Micajah, 39
    Michael, 39
    Rachel, 62
    Samuel, 39
Gilbreath, Anne, 61
Gilchrist, Charles, 39
Giles, Perrin, 40
Gilespie, Charles, 40
Gilinwaters, Kesniah, 107
    Kezia, 107

Gillespie, Gillispie, Gilespie

Gillespie, Charles, 40
Gilliam, Elizabeth, 28
    James, 40
    Nancy, 28
    Patteson, 40
    William, 28
Gillispie, Charles, 40
Gipson, Jane, 110 (see also
        Gibson, etc.)

Glass, Calah, 19
    Cathy, 105
    Caty, 105
    Ceilia, 19
    Charles, 40,105
    James, 40,88
    John, 40
    Nancy, 40
    Mary, 46
    Vincent, 40,46,59,105
    Vincent, Jr.,40
    Vincent, Sr., 40
    Vinson, 19
    William, 40
Glazebrook, Julius, 41
Goad, Thomas, 41
Godfry, Charles, 41

Godsee, Godsey, Godsy

Godsee, Henry, 41
Godsey, Molley, 107
    Polley, 107
Godsy, Henry, 41
Goff, Anne, 51

Goggin, Gogins

Goggin, Elizabeth, 97
    Letice, 30
    Richard, 30,97
    Robert, 41
    Stephen, 30,97
Gogins, Richard, 41
Going, Indah, 29
    John, 73
Goldfinch, John, 75
Golding, Jacob, 41,106
Gooch, Thomas, 41
    Thomas, Jr., 41
Goochland County, (Va.),xiv
Goode, Robert, 41
Goodman, Bartlette, 19
    Gibson, 41
    John, 7,19,41,62,72
    Milly, 62
    Sally, 19
Goodwin, John H., 15
    Micajah, 56,68,82
    Spicy, 68
Goolsby, Arthur, 41
Gordon, Giles, 42
    John, 41
    John M., 42

Gordon, continued
  Judith Ann, 42
  W., 85
Gore, Amos, 91

Gosnall, Gosnay, Gosnell,
    Gausney

Gosnall, Benjamin, 42
  Dawson, 57
Gosnay, Lotty, 90
Gosnell, Benjamin, 42
  William, 42
Gosney, Benjamin, 39
Graham, Elizabeth, 31
  Susannah, 75
  William, 31

Gray, Grey

Gray, Nancy, 13
Grayham, Mary, 75
Green, Thomas, 56
  William 42
Greenwood, Bartlett, 42
  Bartlette, 42

Gregg, Grigg

Gregg, Abner, 117,119
  Ann, 117
  Ruth, 118
  Sarah, 119
  Thomas, 38,40
  Thos., 21
Gregory, Doshy, 32
  Elizabeth Misa, 102
  John, 7,45,48,70,102
  John, Jr., 32,42,48,57
  John, Sr., 32,57
  Mary Ann, 45
  Nelley, 45
  Peggy, 7
  Peter, 42,57
  Richard, 42
  Sally, 70
  Sophia, 57

Gresham, Grisham, Grishaw,
    Greshaw

Gresham, William, 42
Greshaw, Susan Spica, 80
Grewell, Alice, 110
  Timothy, 111

Grey, Nancy, 13 (see also Gray, etc.)
Griffin, William, 77
  Wm.,77
Griffith, Christopher, 23
  William, 42
Grigg, Abner, 111,117
Grigsby, Etchinson, 114
  Etchison, 112
Grisham, Isaac, 42
Grishaw, Elizabeth, 40
  Isaac, 40
  Isaac, S., 80
  Susan Spica, 80

Guthrey, Guthrie, Guthry

Guthrey, James, 55
  William, 42
Guthrie, Henry, 55
Guthry, Agnes, 55
  Henry, 55
  William, 55
Gunnele, Sally, 29

Guttery, Guttry

Guttery, George, 48
  Henry, 106
  James, 106
  Martha, 106
  Penelope, 18
Guttry, Penelope, 18
Guy, John, 21,43

H

Haas, Hass

Haas, Frederick, 43
Haberer, Walter [J.], Executive
    Sect., vii
Hackett, Amy, 72 (see Hatcher,
    Amy)
  Esther, 104
  Isaac, 43
  Joseph, 12,43
  Lucy, 34
Haden, Anthony, 34,39,71
  Benjamin, 9,18,41,49
  Elizabeth, 39
  James C., 43,89
  Jenny, 39
  J. M., 71
  John, 43,71
  John D., 49

Haden, John, Sr., 26
  Lucy, 33
  Martha, 93
  Milly, 26
  Polly N., 49
  Rachel, 71
  Rebecca, 34
  Richard, 33
  Richard P., 33
  Turner, 26

Hains, Haines, Heynes

Hains, John, 43
Haines, John, 43
Hairston, Samuel, xiii
Hale, Nathan, 110,116
  Robert, 54
  William, 43
Haley, Hannah, 86
  James, 12
  William, 86
Halifax County (Va.), 59,91
  93,98,111
Hall, Charles, 43
  Frances Ann, 47
  John, 43
  Martha, 44
  Robert, 47
  Thomas, 43
  William, 43

Halloway, Holloway

Halloway, Abner, 113
  Amos, 113
  Hepzibah, 113,117
  Mary, 113
Hambleton, Benjamin, 43
  James, 44,55
  Susannah, 55
Hamers, Elizabeth, 68
  Rachel, 68

Hamersley, Hammersley, Hammersly

Hamersley, Mary, 71 (see also
    Handsley, Mary)
  Richard, 44
  William, 71
Hamersly, Richard, 44
  Susanna, 7
Hames, Jack, 99
Hamilton, James, 44

Hamlet, James, 44
  Lucy, 44
Hammersly, William, 44

Hammock, Hammond

Hammock, Lewis, 44
Hammond, Lewis, 44
Hamner, Elizabeth, 110,116
Hancock, James, 49
  Leannah, 61
Handsley, Mary, 71 (see also
    Hamersley, Mary)

Hanks, Hawks

Hanks, Abraham, 44,67
  Tabitha, 10
  Thomas, 44,69
Hanley, Betsy, 113 (see also
    Stanley, Betty)

Hanna, Hannah

Hanna, Benj., 113
  Benjamin, 111,113,117,118
  Catharine, 112,113,116,118
  Robert, 110,112,113,115,116,
    117,118,119
  Susannah, 116
  Thomas, 113,116,117
  Thos., 113
Hannah, James, 44
Hanover Co., (Va.), 126
Haraway, Chas., 7
  Eppa, 44
  John, 7
  Polly, 7
Hardaway, Drury, 44
  Lucy Ann, 91

Hardwick, Hardwicke

Hardwich, Leoney, 60
  Leony, 60
Hardwick, William, 44
Hardwicke, Lord, 122

Hargrove, Hartgrove

Hargrove, John, 118
Harlin, David, 35

Harold, Harrold

Harold, continued
  Gillard, 11
  Phelia, 11
Harper, R. Vaughn Mrs., vii
Harris, Benjamin, 16
  Betty, 68
  Charles, 44
  Elizabeth, 16
  Hannah, 116
  John, 16,44
  Martha, 37
  Mary, 116
  Nancy, 16
  Nathan, 26,45
  William, 16,19,37,45,68,99
  Wm., 68
Harrison, Frances I., 78
  Joseph, 45
  Sally, 59
  Samuel J[ordan], 16,45,73
  Samuel Jordan, 45
  W., 45
  Wm., 42
Harrold, Jane, 11
Hartgrove, William, 44
Harvey, Betsy, 44
  Eleanor, 46
  Isham, 45
  Jesse, 25,45,73,77,84,103
  Nancy, 9
  Polly, 53
  Richard, 9,45,53,54
  Sim, 45
  Tabitha, 36
  Thomas, 9
  Thomas, Jr., 45
  William, 48 [sic], 9,36,44,53
Harvie, Jack D., 45
Hass, Frederick, 43
Hatcher, Amy, 72 (see also
    Hackett, Amy)
  Henry, 45
  Isaac, 88
  Jeremiah, 38,123
  Rachel, 117
Hawkins, Benjamin B., 25
  Joseph, 46
  Littleberry, 46
  Mildred, 47
  Richard F. Mrs., Regent,
    Blue Ridge Chapter NSDAR,
    vii
  Robert, 47
  William, 46,47
Hawks, John, 25 (see also Hanks,
    etc.)

Haws, Hawse, Hayes

Haws, Elizabeth, 48
Hawse, L., 100
Hayes, Elizabeth, 48
Haynes, Nancy, 87
  Parmeanas [Captain], 87
  Polly, 110,112
  Ro., 78
  Robert, 78
Hays, John, 46
Hayth, Benjamin, 94
  Patsy, 58
  Polly, 94
  Sally, 88
  Thomas, 58,88,99
  William, 46,58,94

Hazelwood, Hazlewood

Hazelwood, Benjamin, 46
  Richard, 46
  Tom, 24
Hazlett, William, 51
Hazlewood, Thomas, 46,90
  William, 46
Headon, John, 116
Heath, William, 29
Helm, Elizabeth, 61,101
  James, 30,46,61,101
  John, 30,61
  Mary, 30
  Thomas, 104
  William, 61
Henderson, Daniel, 46
  Samuel, 46
  William, xiii

Hendrake, Hendrick, Hendricks

Hendrake, Betty, 112
Hendrick, Bernard, 46,52
  Betty, 117
  Nancy, 46
  Pendleton, 37
  Robert, 46
  Sarah, 117
Hendricks, Bernard, 38
  Elizabeth, 113
Hening, William Waller, 6,122
Hennes, William, 46
Henrico County, (Va.), xiv, 126
Henry County, (Va.), 66,106
Henry, Dinah, 64
  Diner, 64

Henry, continued
James, 99
Patrick, xiii
Spottswood, 107
Henson, Charles, 91
Herndon, Daniel, 46
Edmund, 44,46,53,96
Lucy, 53
Mary, 44,115
Jacob W., 47
Hewston, Peter, 47
Heynes, John, 43

Hicks, Hix

Hicks, James, 36,47
Richard, 47,48
Richard W., 47,48
Higginbotham, Thomas, 103
Hightower, Dickey, 47
Eleanor, 23
Eline, 23
Eliza, 23
George, 23,47,54
Jenny, 54
Richard, 47
Susannah, 91
Hiley, James, 47
William, 47
Hill, Mason, 84
Ruebin, 47
Hill(s) Creek Meeting-house,
xi,108,114,118
Hines, Henry, Jr., 47
J. A., 58
James, 8,47
James, Jr., 58
Wm., 8
Hinge, Ambrose, 47
Hings, Paton, 47
Peyton, 47
Hinshaw, William Wade, xii
Hinson, Charles, 47
Hinton, William, 26,48
Historical Sketch of Campbell
County, Virginia, xii
Hix, Elizabeth, 33 (see also
Hicks, etc.)
F., 46
John, 24,35,48,49,82,83,90
John, Jr., 35,90
Leany, 84
Libby, 90
Martha, 46

Hix, continued
Mary, 84
Rebeccah, 82
Richard, 46
Richard W., 46,48
Sabra, 35
Sarah, 49
Sibbeller, 33,90
Sibby, 90
T., 46
William, 24,33,46,83
Wm., 46
Hockaday, Isaac, 48
Hodges, Charles, 48
Hogan, Betsy, 102
Cora, 102
Emille, 102
Enoch, 102
Milley, 102
Holcombe, J., 100
Sarah, 100
Holder, Elijah, 48
Holesapple, John, 18
Nancy, 18
Philip, 18
Holladay, David, 48
Holley, James, 48,66,74
Holloway, Abner, 116
Amos, 113,116
Asa, 116,118
Hapzibah, 113
Hepsibah, 117
Hepzabih, 110
Hepzibah, 116,118
Isaac, 48,116
Mary, 113,116,117
Samuel, 78
Sarah, 116
William, 113
Holmes, Sarah, 116
Tabitha, 76
Holt, Asa, 48
Betsey, 67
Betsy, 67
Elizabeth, 31
James, 67
John W., 13,19,28,31,32,39,45,
53,54,61,72,82,84,88,90,92,
95,97,123
Leonard, 48
Nancy, 101
Robert, 31,67,101
Hood, Alexander, 48
Anney, 24

Hood, continued
  James, 24
  John, 48,49
  William, 49
Hopkins, Mary, 23
  William, 49
Hopwood, John, 49
Hoskins, Thomas, 49
Howe, Joshua P., 61

Howel, Howell, Howle, Owl

Howel, Charles, 31
  John Thomas, 17
Howell, Lucretia, 72 (see also
    Howett, Lucretia)
Howerton, Elizabeth, 87
  George, 49
  Grief, 59,87
  Willmarthe, 59
  Willmorth, 59

Howeth, Howette, Howett

Howeth, Elizabeth, 41
Howett, Lucretia, 72, (see also
    Howell, Lucretia)
Howette, Elizabeth, 41
Howle, Elizabeth, 21
  John Thomas, 21
Hoyle, Charles, Jr., 85
Hubank, Chisy, 118
Hubbard, James, 49
  John, 40,49
  Nat, 49
  Nathaniel, 49
  William, 49
  William J. Mrs., viii

Hudson, Hutson

Hudson, George, 95
  John B., 49
  Mary, 39
  Sally, 95
  Thomas, 49
  William, 49

Hughes, Hughs

Hughes, Benjamin, 102
  David, 50
  Elener, 25
  Littleberry, 50

Hughes, continued
  Mary Elener, 25
  Emory, 50
  Emry, 24
  Fanny, 102
  John, 50
  Josiah, 75
  Robert, 25
  Susanna, 75
Hughs, David, 50
Hundley, Jane, 7
  Josiah, 22
  Mary, 32
  Teen, 7
Hunnicutt, James, 119
Hunt, John, 50
Hunter, Alexander, 50,54,55,63,
    66,90
  Andrew, 55,89,124
  Ben, 45,50,55
  Benjamin, 45,50
  Elizabeth, 62
  George, 62
  James, 50,62
  John, xiii,35,40,50,55
  Mary, 30
  Nancy, 50,55
  Peter, 50
  Rachel, 35
  Robert, 91
  Samuel, 66
  Thomas, 50,55
  William, 21,51

Hurd, Hurt

Hurd, Patsy, 96
Hurt, Daniel, 75
  Garland, 51
  Henry, 112
  J., 23,64
  James, 7,9,17,23,42,47,48,49,
    51,52,56,61,64,65,67,75,79,
    82,93,94,96,101,102,103,124
  John, 51,64
  John M., 51
  Mary, 75
  Moses, 112,116
  Patsey, 96
  Polley, 96
  Polly H., 64
  W. C., 64
  William C., 64
Huston, Henry, 51

Hutchen, Mary, 95

Hutcherson, Hutcheson, Hutchinson

Hutcherson, Hannah B., 63
   John, 51,65
   Mary, 96
   Nancy, 96
   Polly, 95
   William, 51
Hutcheson, William, 51
Hutchings, Drury, 45
   Rosanna, 45
Hutchinson, Hannah B., 63
   John, 51

Huts, Hutts

Huts, Leonard, 51
Hutson, Sary, 95 (see also
      Hudson, etc.)
   William H., 51
Hutton, Sarah, 110,112
Hutts, Jacob, 51
   Leonard, 51
   Michael, 51
   William, 51
Hyatt, L.T.G. Mrs., vii

                  I

Innis, Harry, xiv

Irvin, Irvine

Irvin, John, 21,51,68
   John, Jr., 68
   Louisa, 51
   Mary Ann, 21
   Polley, 51
Irvine, Amelia, 48
   Christopher, 75
   David, 41,48,75,79,86
   Francis, 86
   Jane, 26
   John, 11,27,93
   John, Jr., 68
   Joseph, 51
   Louisa, 51
   Lucretia, 93
   Magdalen, 79
   Margaret, 75
   Mary Ann, 21
   Mathew, 68
   Nancy, 41,68

Irvine, continued
   Peggy, 11
   Robert, 41,48,86
   Robt., 48,86
   Safiah, 86
   Sally, 41
   William, 51
Isle of Wight County, (Va.),
      xiv, 126
Issenberry, Jacob, 26
   Mary, 26

                  J

Jackson, Isaac, 24,29
   Josiah, 82
   Lewis, 77
   Luckey, 29
   Nancy, 52
   Polly, 49
   Sally, 24
   William 29
James, Christopher, 115
   Daniel, 116
   Isaac, 113
   John, 113
   Rachel, 113
   Sarah, 113,115
   Thomas, 113

Jeanis, Jennings

Jeanis, Tyra, 51

Jenkins, Jinkins

Jenkins, Barbara, 25
   Cary, 52
   Catharine, 100
   Fanny, 52
   Francis, 52
   Joseph, 52,83
   Mary, 52
   Olive, 52
   Robert, 25
   William, 52
   William R., 52
   William Rodgers, 52
   Wm. Rogers, 53
Jennings, Elizabeth, 67
   Jesse, 20,91
   Lucy, 44
   Mackey, R. B., 101
   Pleasant, 101
   Priscilla, 106

Jennings, Samuel, 124
  Samuel K., 54,74,124
  S. K., 29,36,58
  Stephen, 53
  Tyra, 51
  William, 91
Jinkins, Cary, 52
Johns, Ann, 75
  Anne, 100
  Cynthia, 15
  Daniel, 15
  Edmund, 7,8,15,16,17,19,21,22,
    27,28,30,32,34,35,39,40,43,
    49,50,52,54,55,56,57,69,70,
    72,74,75,76,80,81,82,85,87,
    88,90,91,94,98,99,101,102,
    103,105,106,107,124
  James, 90
  Jesse, 65,100
  Jesse, Jr., 65
  Lockey, 65
  Magdaleen, 55
  Mallery, Jr., 73
  Nancy, 43,90
  Polly B., 75
  Sally, 54
  Sarah, 15,55,73,100
  Siller, 78
  Stephen, 52
  Susanna, 44 (see also
    Jones, Susanna)
  William, 52,54,80,90
  William T., 43

Johnson, Johnsone, Johnston

Johnson, Agatha, 111,114,115,118,
    119
  Ann, 76
  Anselm, 114
  Ashley, 76,110,112,113,115,116,
    117,119
  Ashley, Jr., 112
  Benj., 114,118
  Benjamin, 89,101,111,112,114,
    115,118
  Betsy, 75,115,117
  Betty, 110,112,114,115,116,118,
    119
  Caleb, 111
  Charles, 9,12,52,114,115,117
  Chas., 78
  Chris, 118

Johnson, continued
  Christopher, 38,52,53,71,97,
    110,111,112,113,115,117,
    118,119
  David, 52,112,114,115,119
  Elijah, 114,117
  Eliza, 119
  Elizabeth, 9,97,104,112,118,
    119
  Garland, 114
  Gerard, 112,113,116,117,119
  Gerard, Jr., 115
  Gerard, Sr., 119
  Hannah, 77
  Isaac, 52
  James, 15,53,113,114,115,116,
    118,119
  James L., 53
  Jane, 89,113,119
  Jean, 115
  Jepetha, 114
  Jepha, 111
  John, 13,45,53,75,77,99,113,
    114,115,116
  John, Jr., 53,75,99
  John, Sr., 80
  John W., 53,111,119
  Jonathan, 110,111,112,114,116,
    117,118
  Joseph, 53,98,111,112,114,115,
    119
  Judith, 110,111,112,115,117,
    119
  Lemuel, 114,119
  Leroy, 54
  Lucy, 13,114
  Lydia, 110,117,118
  Martha, 89,101,111
  Mary, 101,110,111,114
  Matilda, 111,114
  Micajah, 53
  Micajah M., 53
  Mildred, 112,117
  Milley, 114,115,119
  Millie, 112
  Milly, 53,114,117
  Molly, 114
  Moorman, 53,78,114,119
  Mourning, 112,113,114,116,117
  Nancy, 84,111,114,115,116,117,
    118
  Newberry, 112
  Newby, 111,114,115

Johnson, continued
  Nicholas, 111,114
  Penelope, 110,112,115
  Philip, 52,75,99
  Pleasant, 53,115
  Polly, 78,99
  Rachel, 68,114,117,119
  Rhoda, 15,111,117,119
  Robert, 53,68,110,111,112,
    113,114,115,116,118
  Ruth, 68,113,119
  Salley, 110,114,115,118
  Sally, 45,119
  Samuel, 10,114,115
  Sarah, 110,111,112,113,115,
    116,117,118,119
  Simeon, 53
  Susanna, 53,71,111,112,113,
    114,115,117,119
  Susannah, 111,116,118
  Thomas, 53,76,114,115,116,
    119
  Timothy, 110,118
  William, 39,53,110,111,112,
    113,114,115,116,117,119
  William, Jr., 111
  William, Sr., 111,117
  Wm., 39,111,113,114,117,119
  Wm., Sr., 115
  Zachariah, 53
Johnsone, Christ., 64
Johnston, Ch., 54
  Charles, 54
  Leroi, 54
  Robt. W., 48
  Thomas, 80

Joiner, Joyner

Joiner, Elizabeth, 32
  William, 55
Jonathan, Samuel, 47
Jones Memorial Library (Lynch-
    burg, Va.), viii,124
  Achsah, 81
  Ann, 46
  Anne, 10
  Benjamin, 10,13,53
  Betsy, 92
  Caty, 97
  Charles, 59
  Christiana, 46
  David, 7,35,46,54,82,97

Jones, continued
  Dorcus, 71
  Dorkus, 71
  Dorothea, 40
  Edmund, 47 (mistake for Johns)
  Elizabeth, 17,21
  Frances, 55
  George, 46,53,54,81
  Haden, 54
  James, 54
  Jesse, 50,54,55
  Joel, 54
  Joel W., 54
  John, 24,54
  John S., 55
  Josias, 85
  Judith, 85
  Lockey, 24
  Mary, 55,81,102
  Nancy, 50,92
  Neil, 60
  Oakley, 55,81
  Patsey, 34
  Patty, 32
  Peggy, 97
  Polly, 26
  Publius, 21,24,33,46,55
  Publius, Jr., 69
  Rachel, 42
  Rebeckah, 53
  Rhoda, 92
  Richard, 55
  Sally, 47
  Susanna, 44
  Susannah, 44
  Susanner, 81
  Thomas, 26,34,40,42,44,55,71,
    92,97,107
  Thomas, Sr., 50
  Thos., 29
  William, 55,62,94
Jordan, Betsy, 31
  German, 55
  Sam, 55
  Sam'l, 31
  Samuel, 55,71
  William, 55,92
  William, Jr., 55
  Woodson, 96
Joyner, Elizabeth, 32
  Peter, 32 (see also
    Joiner, etc.)
  William, 55

Jude, George, 31,77,87,101
  George, Jr., 55,77
  Lucy, 101
  Mary Anne, 31
  Sally, 77
  Sarah, 77
Judkins, Charity, 95
  David, 95
  Joel, 95,96
  Rachal, 96
  Rebeckah, 96
  William, 95,96

K

Kabler, Frederic, 124
  Frederick, 53,55,97,103
Keasey, Edward, 56
Keen, Jeremiah, 56
Keesee, Avery, 56
Kelley, Daniel, 88
Kelly, Dennis, 23,56,71,76
  Nathaniel, 56

Keney, Kenney, Kenny

Keney, James, 10
Kennady, John, 47,56
Kennerley, Joseph, 30
Kenney, Hannah, 76
  James, 9,11,12,13,14,17,20,
    21,23,24,25,28,34,35,39,
    45,46,47,49,50,52,58,59,
    60,62,68,70,73,74,76,77,
    79,82,85,86,87,90,94,95,
    96,97,99,101,102,105,124
  Sally, 10
Kenny, James, 10,13,18,32,41
  Sally, 10
Kent, Polly, 23
  Robert, 56
  Robert E., 11
  Smith, 11,52,56
Kentucky, 92
Kenyon, William, 87,124
Kevil, Mary, 41
Key, Betsey, 56
  Elizabeth, 35
  Francis, 94
  Frankey, 94
  Jacob, 13,35,60,94
  Lucy, 13
  Mary, 35
  Milly, 60

Key, continued
  Thomas, 56,60
  William, 56
  Wm., 56
Kidd, Arnold, 56
  John, 58
  Obedience, 58
  Polly, 58
Kimlin, Donald W. Mrs. (Nell
    Gardner Kimlin), vii
King, Abigail, 52
  Elizabeth, 57
  George H.S., F.A.S.G., vii,122
  James, 56
  Jane Henry, 99
  Martha White, 19
  Polly, 37,74
  Polly L., 37
  S., 60,74
  Sackville, 19,47,87,99
  William, 57
King's Mountain,
  battle of, xiii
Kirby, Orpha, 117
  Richard, 117
Kitchen, Thomas, 86
Kivel, Patsy, 12
Kneel, Patsy, 12 (see also
    Kivel, Patsy)
Knock, Denis, 60
Kutzs, Mary, 116

L

Lackey, Leckie, Leckey

Lackey, William, 56
Lacy, Arch, 112
  Archibald, 57
  Drury, 30,72,124
  John, 104

Lain, Laine, Lane, Layne

Lain, Betsey, 48
  David, 58
  James, 64
  Jane, 48
  Polley, 58
  Susannah, 64
Laine, Aaron, 57
  Alexander, 57
  Armistead, 57
  Elander, 17
  Elizabeth, 17

Laine, continued
  John, 48,57,73,79
  Sallie, 79
  William 57
Lamb, John C., 58
  Manson, 57
  Morrison, 57
  Munson, 57
  Patrick, 3,57
  Robert, 57
  Sophia, 48
  William, 42,57
  Wm., 42
Lambeth, Elizabeth, 94
  George, 57
  John, 57
  M., 94
  Meredith, 94
  Washington, 57

Lammond, Lemmond

Lammond, William, 59
Lancaster, James, 57
  Michael, 65
  Thomas, 65
Landers, Anny, 47
  Henry, 47
  Sally, 82
Landis, Elizabeth, 36
  Henry, 36
Landrum, John, 57
Lane, Aaron, 57
  Armistead, 57
  David, 58
  Elias, 58
  John, 57,58,73
  John E. Mrs., xii
  Nancy, 49
  Peachey, 73
  Sallie, 79
  Susannah, 64
Lang, Peter, 40,58
Larrew, Hannah, 110

Lasley, Lesley, Lastly, Leslie

Lasley, John, 58,89
  Menoah, 124
Lastly, Manoah, 124
  Menoah, 124
Lawrence, Frankey, 62
Lawson, Thos., 13
Lawton, Thomas, 58

Lay, Ann, 114,118
  Thomas, 58
Layne, John, 57
  Susannah, 64
Lea, Ann, 113
  Anna, 112,113,118
  Betsy, 115
  Elender, 27
  Elizabeth, 111,113,116
  Gideon, 27,64,112
  Gideon, Jr., 58
  Guideon, 58
  Joseph, 57,87 (see also
    Seay, Joseph)
  Sarah, 57
Leason, Mary Harrison, 81
Leckey, William, 56 (see also
    Lackey, etc.)
Leckie, William, 56
Ledbetter, Joseph, 18,84
  Luraney, 18
  Nancey, 18
  Nancy, 84
Lee, Abner, 58
  Alexander, 58
  Ann, 48
  Anne, 24
  Burrell, 57
  Burril, 58
  Burwell, 21,25
  Elizabeth, 57
  George, 58
  James, 24
  John, 21,25,57,58,95
  John, Jr., 25
  John, Sr., 48
  Levi, 58,59,65
  Miller, 58
  Pamelia, 25
  Polley, 48
  Sarah G., 58
  Shelley, 37
  Stephen, 21, 48,57
  Susanna, 21
  William, 59
  Wm., 16
Leer, Ann, 113
Leeson, Nancy, 25
Leftwick, Thomas, 99
  Thos., 41
Leigh, George, 59
Lemmond, William, 59 (see also
    Lammond, etc.)
Leonard, Robert, 59

Lerrow, Hannah, 116
Lesley, Manoah, 124 (see also
    Lasley, etc.)
    Menoah, 8,10,11,13,14,16,19,
        20,21,24,25,26,27,28,30,
        33,35,36,38,40,41,42,43,
        46,48,51,53,60,61,69,70,
        71,73,74,75,77,78,80,84,
        86,88,89,98,102,103,104,
        105,124
    Menoh, 26
    Polly, 51
Leslie, John, 58
Lester, James, 61 (see also
    Luster, James)
    Joshua, 59
    Miles, 59
    Presley, 59
    William, 59

Lewallen, Lewallin, Lewellen,
    Lewellin

Lewallen, Charles, 59
    James, 59
Lewallin, Charles, 59
Lewellen, Charles, 59
    James, 59
Lewellin, Elizabeth, 97
    Green B., 59
    James, 97
    Sally, 97
Lewis, Alice, 115,116
    Ann, 115
    Corbin, 59,101
    Elizabeth Straughan, 56
    Elizabeth Strawan, 56
    Evan, 110,115,116
    George, 116
    Griffin, 51,55
    Griffin, Jr., 56,59
    Griffin, Sr., 80
    Howell, 71
    Jehu, 115,116
    Jesse, 110,115,116
    Joel, 110,112,116
    John, 60
    Lewis, 60
    Mary, 71,80
    Rebecca, 116
    Sarah, 110,113,116
    Susannah W., 71
    William, 96

Ligen, Ligon

Ligen, Agness, 87
Ligon, Agnes, 87
Liley, John, 60

Lindsay, Lindsey

Lindsay, Margaret, 14
Lindsey, James, 14
    Margaret, 14,42
    Robert, 42,62

Lipcomb, Lipscomb

Lipcomb, John, 60
Lipscomb, John, 60
Listern, Catharine, 40
    Nancy, 40
Listin, Caty, 40
    Susanna, 40
Litchford, Arter, 35
    Arthur, 60
"Little Anglican Church on the
    Hill, The", 124
Littlepage, Benjamin, 15,60
    John, 60
Livingston, James, 60
Lodge, Abel, 60,81,113
    Catharine, 116
    Jacabad, 116
    Sally, 110
    Sarah, 111,112,113,115,118
Lord Hardwicke Marriage Act, 122
Loudoun County, (Va.), 126
Louisa County, (Va.), 38
Lovall, John, 60
Love, Henry, 58
Lovell, John, 106
Loving, Peggy, 100
Loyd, Elizabeth, 79
    Mary, 58
Lucas, James, 60,87
    Jean, 86
    Mildred, 23,48
    Molly, 7
    William, 60
Luke, Faithful, 60
Lunenburg County, (Va.), xiv,92
Luster, James, 61
    Parker, 61
Lynch, Ann, 29,115
    Anna, 110

Lynch, continued
  Anselm, 61,100,118
  Charles, xiii
  Charles, Sr., 96
  Edward, 61,110,111,114,116,
    117,118
  Elijah, 33,61
  Elizabeth, 33
  John, 12,43,80,110,112,113,
    114,115,116,117,118,119
  John, Jr., 98
  John, Sr., 112
  Mary, 110,111,112,113,114,
    117,118
  Matilda, 110,113,118,119
  Nancy, 68
  Polly, 112,114
  Sally, 96,112,113
  Zalinda, 115,116,118
Lynchburg And Its People, 124
Lynchburg, Court records of, xiv
Lynchburg Historical Society
    Museum, 124
Lynchburg, Va., city of, xi,xii,
    xiv, 6,9,15,108,124
Lynchburg, Va., town of, xiv
Lynchburg's Pioneer Quakers and
    Their Meeting House, xii
Lyon, Lydda, 66
  Lydia, 66

              Mc

McAlister, McAllister

McAlister, William, 61
McAllister, James, 61
  John, 61
  Joseph, 61,104
  William, 61
McCamish, James, 61
McCargo, David, 61,106
McCarty, Thomas, 61
McCawley, Edward, 61
McClanahan, James, 62
McCloud, Robert, 62
McCoun, Kiziah, 44
McCown, Thomas, 62

McCoy, McKoy

McCoy, Betsy, 43
  Daniel, 43,67,99
  John, 62

McCoy, continued
  Mack, 62
  Thomas, 62
McCune, Thomas, 99
McDaniel, James, 62
  John, 62
  Lodowick, 36
  Sarah, 82

McDearman, McDearmen, McDearment

McDearman, Nancy, 51
  Thomas, 62
  Thomas, Jr., 62
McDermen, Thomas, 62
McDerment, Nancy, 51
McDowell, James, 67

McGee, Magee, Megee

McGee, Polly, 54
McGehee, Jenny, 84
  John, 84
  Lynch A., 84
  Mathew, 84
McGeorge, Elizabeth, 103
  Lawrence, 103
McGlasson, Barnet, 62
McGrah, Charles, 62
McGray, Charles, 60
McHaney, Cornelius, 98
  Frances, 98

McIvar, McIver, McIvor

McIvar, James, 35
McIver, Catherine, 63
  Daniel, 63
  Elizabeth, 8
  James, 8,30,35,63,78
  James, Jr., 30
  Jane, 35
  Polly, 30
  Sally, 78
McIvor, Daniel, 62
  James, 62

McKay, McKey, Mackay

McKay, Alex.,78

McKenney, McKinney

McKenney, Daniel, 62

McKenney, continued
  George, 62
  John C., 63 (see also
    McMinnimy, John C.)
  Leanah, 13
  Robinson, 62

McKenzie, McKinzie

McKenzie, Milley, 39
McKey, Helen, 78

McKine, McKinney

McKine, John, 40
McKinney, Charles,71
  Dan, 71
  Daniel, 51,62,63
  Dan'l, 63
  Hannah, 51
  Henry, 49,63
  Jeremiah, 62
  Jn., 51
  John, 63
  John, Sr., 49
  Joseph, 63
  Mary, 49,76
  Molly Roberson, 63
  Nancy, 103
  Presley, 63
  Sally, 40
  Vincent, 63
  William, 49,63
McKinzie, Milley, 39
McKoy, Daniel, 99 (see also
    McCoy, etc.)
McMinnimy, John C., 63
McPherson, Daniel, 116
  Mary, 116
  Stephen, 116

McRenels, McReynolds

McRenels, Poley, 82
McReynolds, Arch, 63
  Benjamin, 63
  Elizabeth, 61
  James, 61
  John, 63
  Joseph, 30,63
  Martha, 96
  Mary, 82
  Oliver, 50,63

McReynolds, continued
  Robert, 61
  Salley, 57
  Samuel, 63
  William, 63
McRobert, Arch, 36
  Archibald, 21,43,58,63,105,
    124

M

Mackay, Alexander, 78,88 (see
    also McKay, etc.)
  Helen, 78
  Jane, 78
  John, 62 (see also McCoy,John)
  Mary, 49
MacKey, Alexander, 88
  Catherine, 8
  Jane, 34
  Mary, 49
  Walter, 62
Macky, Charles, 29,124
Macon, Betsy, 107
Macy, Elihu, 116
  John, 117
  Micajah, 116,117

Maddox, Madox

Maddox, John G., 64
  Thomas, 111
Madox, John G., 64

Magan, Magann

Magan, Pleasant, 64
Magann, Pleasant, 64,92
Magee, Rose, 54, (see also
    McGee, etc.)

Magers, Magior, Magor, Magors,
    Majors, Mayors

Magers, Henry, 64
Magior, Harrey, 38
Magor, Philip, 93
Magors, Henry, 64

Mahon, Mahone

Mahon, Dennis, 64
  William, 11,17,19,37,39,45,63,
    64,77,87,90,93,96,124

Mahone, Barnard, 64
  Barnet, 64
  Barnett, 64
  Dennis, 64
  Pleasant, 64
  William, 124
Major, Harry, 38,116
Majors, Elizabeth Harrod, 93
  Harry, 118
  Henry, 64
  Philip, 93
Mallory, James, 111
Maloney, James, 23

Man, Mann

Man, Martha, 76
Manarin, Louis H., Dr.,
    Archivist, viii
Manly, Ancil, 81
Mann, Agga, 54
  Ann, 76
  Betsy, 65
  Elizabeth, 56,58
  Fergues, 64
  Field, 64
  Jaine, 64
  James, 64,65
  Jane, 64
  Joel, 44,64
  John, 64,66
  Martha, 81
  Mary, 12
  Nathaniel, 65 (see also
    Manson, Nathaniel I.)
  Patience, 65
  Patsey, 44
  Rich, 64
  Richard, 54,56,64
  Sally, 44
  Thomas, 65
  William, 65
Manson, Nathaniel, 65
  Nathaniel I., 65
Marcheson, John, 69
Markham, John, 65
Marriage,
  banns, bonds, consents, laws,
    license, validity of, 120-
    122
  Campbell County Bonds, 7-107
  marriage bond, replica of, 5
Marriage Register No. 1, 1782- 2,
  4

Marriages of Richmond County,
    Virginia 1668-1853, 122
Marshall, Ann, 80
  Betsy, 49
  Daniel, 18,31,65
  David, 65
  Hannah, 23,51
  John, 18,23,31,65,78,86
  Mary, 65
  Mildred E. H., 99
  Nancy, 31
  Patsy, 65
  Thomas, 51,65,69,100
  Thomas B., 65
  Thomas J., 65
  William, 31,49,65

Martain, Martin

Martain, Margit, 88
Martin, Andrew, 65
  Ann, 66
  Annaca, 83
  Charles, 55,65,79
  Daniel, 106
  David, 65,79,81,106
  David, Jr., 65,81,101
  David, Sr., 101
  Elizabeth, 72,81
  George, 36
  James, 16,41,66,79,81,89,103,
    110,112,116,118
  Janie, 41
  Jesse, 66
  John, 66,67,79,106
  Joseph, 66
  Josiah, 81,106
  Margit, 88
  Mary, 14,66,79,87,106
  Matthew, 66,72
  Rachel, 41,101
  Salley, 115
  Sally, 89
  Sam, 86
  Samuel, 14,16,51,62,66,86,89
  Sarah, 81,118
  Susanna, 14
  Thomas, 41,52,66
  Thomas, Jr., 66
  Thos., 52
  Wilis, 67
  William, 14,19,66,67
  William P., 12,16,28,32,36,42,
    45,47,53,57,62,72,73,76,77,
    78,85,86,88,91,92,94,95,97,
    98,103,104,107,124

Martin, continued
  William Peters, 10,11,104,
    124
  Willis, 67
  Wm. P., 23
Maryland, xii,126
Masey, Bennett, 124 (see also
    Maxey, Bennett)
Mason, Adin, 67
  Cona, 89
  Elizabeth C., 8
  Fanny, 62
  Francis, 62
  James, 48,67
  Jamima, 75
  Jesse, 33
  Joel, 48
  John, 7,33,67,105
  Juda, 48
  Judith, 48
  Martin, 8,17,75,83,89
  Mary, 50
  Nathan, 67
  Obedience, 60
  Patsey, 105
  Patsy, 69
  Philip, 67
  Polly, 33
  Sarah, 88
  Susanna, 48,49
  William, 48,60,67,69,85,88
  William, Sr., 48
  Wm., 67

Massacre, Massacree

Massacre, Nancy, 28
Massacree, Nancy, 28

Massee, Massey, Massie

Massee, Sarah, 87
Massey, Sarah, 87
Massie, Silvanus, 23
  Thomas, 12

Mathews, Matthews, Mathis,
    Matthis

Mathews, Luckey, 99
  Phil, 124
  Philip, 19,124
  Polly, 94

Mathews, continued
  Suckey, 99
  William, 97
Mathis, Polly, 94
  William, 94
Matthews, James, 84
  Luckey, 99
  Nancy, 103
  Patsy, 33
  Phil, 124
  Philip, 47, 124
  Sally, 79
  Samuel, 103
  Sarah, 79
  Suckey, 99
  Susanna, 99
  William, 25,33,67,99
Matthis, William, 67 (see also
    Matthews, William)
Maxey, Bennett, 42,54,85,124
  James, 68
May, John, 68
Mayberry, Nancy, 47
Mayors, Elizabeth, 93 (see also
    Majors, Elizabeth Harrod)
Mazley, James, 110
Means, Jane, 18
  Robert, 68
Meeks, Anderson, 124 (see also
    Weekes, Anderson)
Megee, Polly, 54 (see also McGee,
    etc.)

Megenson, Megginson

Megenson, Joseph Cabell, 68
Megginson, Joseph, 68
  Joseph Cabell, 68
Mehorney, Andrew, 68

Mennonites, Menonists

Mennonites, 122
Menonists, 121,122
Meredith, Henry, 57
Merriman, Patsy, 78
Merritt, John, 92
Metcalf, Vernon, 112
Methodist Ministers, 123,124
Methodist Episcopal,
    ministers, 123
Micker, Ruth, 116

Mickle, William, 68
Milburn, Andrew, 13
Millburn, Sarah, 111
Millener, Elizabeth, 55
Miller, Ann S., 13
    Catherine, 100
    Elijah, 68
    John, 9,68,103
    Sally, 103
    Susanna, 112,114,115
    Susannah, 9
    Thomas, 107
Milliner, Ann, 111
    Beverly, 111
    Ruth, 111
Mills, Molly, 66
Milner, Beverly, 117
    Dudley, 117
    Ruth, 117
Ministers, officiating bonding
    of, denominations, fees,
    fines, qualifications,
    residence, 123,124
Ministers' Returns, original
    Register of, 3
Minton, Simon, 68
Mitchell, Adam, 68
    Adams, 25
    Arch, 68
    Arthur, 68 (see also Mitchell,
        Arch)
    James, 10,18,25,43,72,96,124
    John, 68,91
    Judith, 43
    Nancy, 25
    Sally, 91
    Samuel, 13,61,68,85,87,104,
        124
    Susannah, 67
    William, 16,68

Mitchem, Mitchum

Mitchem, Littleberry, 69
    William, 69
Mitchum, Littleberry, 69

Moher, Moore, Moor, More

Moher, Christian, 69
Monroe, John, 34,69
    Nancy, 57
    Robert, 57,69

Monthly Meeting (Quaker), 109
Moor, Wm., 68
Moore, Austin, 69
    Barbery, 14
    Benjamin, 44,55,69
    Charles, 69
    Christian, 69
    David, 88
    Elizabeth, 70
    Frances, 74
    Frankey, 59
    Freeman, 20,69
    George, 67,69
    Goodrich, 33,69
    James, 69,80,81
    James L., 14,19,69,70
    Jane, 82
    Jeaney, 82
    Jenny, 69
    John, 26,39,70
    Joshua, 70
    Judith Walker, 24
    Mark, 70
    Mary, 82
    Matthew, 70,105
    Nancy, 19,80
    Olive, 70
    Patrick, 70
    Predhem, 70
    Predum, 70
    Pridden, 70
    Pruden, 37
    Rebeckah, 55
    Rhoda, 105
    Robert, 70
    Sampson, 59,70
    Sampson, Jr., 26
    Samuel, 14,70,82
    Sarah, 26
    Thomas, 21,28,61,70,81,82
    Thomas, Jr., 81
    Thos., 7,69,81
    William, 19,24,26,33,40,55,
        66,67,69,70,71,82

Moorelan, Moorlan, Moorland,
    Morelan, Morlan

Moorelan, Abigal, 116
    Mary Jr., 116
Moorlan, Abigal, 112
    Ada, 116
    Jason, 116

Moorlan, continued
Jonan, 116
Nancy, 110
Rebecca, 112
Rebekah, 110
Moorland, Aden, 112
Ann, 112
Joseph, 112

Moorman, Moremen

Moorman, Abraham, 56,71
A. C., 38
Achilles, 21,46,56,71
Achilles, Jr., 102
Achillis, 10,46,115
Africa, 115,118
Agatha, 114
Agnes, 88
And., 23
Andrew, 21,53,114
Betsey, 71
Betsy, 114,115
Betty, 114,115,118
Charles, 9,12,38,64,114,115,
117,119
Chas., 93
David, 52
David H., 56
Dosha, 112,114,115,117,119
Effey, 119
Elizabeth, 21,92,99
Henry, 29
James, 32,71,84
James C., 71
James, Jr., 80
James, Sr., 57,84
Jas. C., 77
Jesse, 21,71,84
John, 9,71,80
John H., 111
J., Sr., 80
Juda, 28
Judith, 28,46,71
Lucy, 10,21,29,46,84
Lydia, 115
Mary, 33,93,103,117
Mecijah, 52
Micajah, 71,114,115,117,119
Micajah C., 71
Mich, 43
Mildred, 80

Moorman, continued
Milly, 21,52
Nancy, 21,112,114,115,117,118,
119
Patsy, 56,72
Pleasant, 71
Polly, 46,71,115,119
Prudence, 114
Rachel, 16,113,114,115
Reuben, 118,119
Reubin, 112
Rhoda, 114
Salley, 88,115
Sally, 3,9,119
Samuel, 72
Sarah, 117,119
Susanna, 53,117,119
Susannah, 119
Thomas, 9,51,61,72,114,115,119
Thos., 62,83
William, 33,72,78
William, Sr., 71
Wm., Sr., 80
Zaachas, 16
Zach, 32
Zachariah, 114
Morcheson, John, 24,49,89
More, James, 80
Nancy, 80
Morelan, Ann, 117 (see also
Moorelan, etc.)
Jason, 116,117
Nancy, 116
Rebecca, 116
Moremen, Jesse, 21
Morgan, Hugh, 117
John, 44
Moorman, 72
Morison, John, 8
Morlan, Rebecca, 119
Stephen, 116
Susan, 112
Morris, Ambrose, 103
John, 72
Richard, 72
R., Jr., 65
Robert, 101
Sarah, 83,101
Thomas, 104
Morrison, Bryan, 15
John, 25

Morton,
    Joseph, 72
    Josiah, 72
    Richard, 72
    William, 72
Mosbey, Patsey, 35

Moseley, Mosley, Mosely

Moseley, Belinda, 101
    Edward, 100
    James, 72
    John, 73
    Joseph, 73
    Mary Ann, 9
Mosely, James, 42
Moser, Aron, 73
Mosley, James, 16
    Mary Ann, 9
Moss, Harry, 73
    Henry, 73
    Peter, 73
    Richard, 73
Mullens, James, 73
    Joshua, 73
Mullin, William, 12
Murrell, John, 74
    Polly, 12
    Secelia, 89
    Seley, 89
    Thomas, 12,73,89
    William, 73
Myler, Thomas, 73

                N

Napier, Napper, Nappier

Napier, Charles, 43
    Lucy, 43
    Mary, 38
Napper, Hannah, 83
    Milley, 83
Nappier, Mary, 38
Narkete, Eustis, 104 (see also
    Hackett, Ester)
Narples, Elizabeth, 35
    George, 35
Nash, John Red Head [sic], 23
Neal, Susanna, 64
    Thomas, 64

Negro, Negroes, (see also Race)
    free, 12,29,34,38,43,73,80,
        83,64
Neighbours, William, 73
Nelson, Sarah, 104
    William N. Mrs., vii
Nervimon,Joshua, 47
Newel, Jas., 21
New London, (Va.), 34
Newberry, William, 73
Newbury, William, 95
Newman, Henry, 116

Newsam, Newsum

Newsam, William, 73
Newsum, William, 73

Nicholes, Nichols, Nicols

Nicholes, Patty, 92
Nichols, Joseph, 47,64,92
    Margaret Mrs., Deputy Clerk,
        vii
    Nancy, 64
    Patty, 92
    Tace, 112
Nicols, Jacob, 118
    Tacy, 118
Nigby, Elizabeth, 20
Nigley, Sarah, 36

Noel, Noell, Norvell, Nowell

Noel, German, 74
    German C., 74
    Roderick, 74
Noell, Candice, 98
    German, 74
    German C., 81,98
    Jane, 81
    Joice, 81,98
    Roderick, 74
Nolan, Russell Mrs., vii
Norman, Chester R. Mrs. (Elizabeth
    Bailey Norman), vii
    Thomas, 9
Norris, John, 74
North Carolina, Quaker
    migrations to, 126
North, Abraham, 23
    James, 74

North, continued
  Peter, 74
  Thomas, 23,74
  Thomas, Jr., 74
  William, 74
Norvell, Candice, 98(see also Noel)
  Elizabeth, 16
  German C., 74
  Jane, 81
  Reuben, 74
  Will, 16,107
Nowell, Candice, 98(see also Noel)
  German C., 98
Nowland, Mary, 67

Nowlen, Nowlin

Nowlen, David, 124
  Sarah, 50
Nowlin, David, 74,124
  Mary, 67
  Samuel, 74
  Sarah, 50
Nowsom, William, 59
Numan, Rebeckah, 28
  Nimrod, 28
  Zebeckah, 28

O

Oakey, Paul D. Mrs., vii

Oglesby, Oglesvie

Oglesby, Conway, 36
  David, 36
  Edward, 12
  Elizabeth, 25
  Frances, 27
  Jacob, 74
  Kesiah, 12
  Marey, 25
  Mary, 12,95
  Patey, 76
  Polly, 95
  Salley, 76
  Sarah, 92
  Susanna, 36
  Thomas, 82,95
  Thos., 76
  William, 82
Oglesvie, Sarah, 92
  Susanna, 36

Ohio, 126
O'Kane, Henry, 74
Oliphant, Samuel, 110,116
Oliver, Benjamin, 55
Ollard, S. L., 122
O'Neal, Bartley, 75
Organ, John, 75
Original Register (marriage), 2,3,4,6
Our Quaker Friends of Ye Olden
    Time, xi,xii,6,109,112,113,
    125
Overstreet, James, 75
  Nancy, 61
Owen, Harrison, 75
  Phillip, 51
  Robert, 75
  Sally, 51
  Susannah, 51
Owin, Ursley, 51
Owl, Elizabeth, 21 (see also
    Howel, etc.)
  John Thomas, 17

P

Pace, John, 75
Page, John, 75
  Susan, 15
Pane, Magdaline, 48

Panell, Pennell, Pannill, Pinnell

Panell, Joseph, 124
Pannill, Fanny, 74
  Jerh., 47
  Mary, 47
  Morton, 75
  Samuel, 47,74,75,76
  Sarah B.M., 76
Parish of Russell (Bedford Co.,
    Va.), 93
Parker, William, 61,75
Parkinson, Thomas, 83
Parrish, Isaac, 112
  William, 75
Parrott, Agnes, 14
  Ann, 76
  Ava, 76
  Avery, 76
  Eve, 76
  John, 76

Parrum, Perrum

Parrum, Mary, 52
Pate, Edmund, 76
Paterson, Fanny, 49
Patrick, Catherine, 8
  David, 76
  David F., 76
  Edmond, 8
  J., 4,11,76
  John, 8,54
  John, Jr., 7,39
  Sarah, 54 (see also Fitzpatrick,
  William, 50,63,76,86   Sarah)
Patten, Vincent, 76

Patterson, Patteson, Paterson

Patterson, Charles, 76
  Charles G., Jr. Mrs.,vii
  Drussilla, 25
  Fanny, 49
  Jacob, 76
  Jenny, 92
  Joab, 76
  John, 76
  Lucy, 29
  Milly, 95 (see also Baber, Nancy)
  Pamalia, 33
  Tarleton, 92
  Thomas B., 76
  Thomas Bell, 76
  William, 90
Patteson, David, 76
  James, 11,57
  Lander, 29
  Landis, 11
  Littleberry, 29
  Lucy, 29
  Obadiah, 11
  Pamalia, 33
  Sally, 11
  Tarlton, 76

Patty, Paty

Patty, Sarah, 11
Paty, Elijah, 76
  Larry, 24
  Nancy, 24
  Sarah, 11
Paul, Sam, 47

Paup, Phaup

Paup, John, 65,124

Paxon, Benjamin, 110
  John, 112
  Rachel, 112,115,119
  Ruth, 110,116
Paxson, John, 106,118
  Rachel, 118
Paxton, Rachel, 106
Payne, Elizabeth L., 17
  Jammy, 76
  John S., 71,76
  Philip, 17
Peck, William, 41
Pemberton, James, 76,77,84
  Joseph, 100
  Levinia, 100
Pendleton, Judith, 90
Penn, William, 77
Pennell, Joseph, 124
Pennock, Alice, 116
  Hannah, 110
  John, 110,116
  William, 116
  William, Sr., 116
Pennsylvania, 126
Perdue, Frances, 70
  Francis, 74,106
  Isham, 77
  Jerry, 106
  Minto P., 110
  Sally, 70
  Susanna, 110

Perkins, Pirkins

Perkins, Polly, 52,84
  Temple, 16,77
Perrin, William, 77
Perrow, Daniel B., 37
  Elizabeth, 78,103
  Mary, 37
  Mary Ann, 73
  Stephen, 77
Perrum, Mary, 53
Perry, Elizabeth, 43
  John, 43

Petecrew, Peticrew, Petticrew

Petecrew, Janet, 18
Peter Pence Act, 122
Peticrew, Mathew, 90
Petticrew, Janet, 18
  Jenny, 18
  Matthew, 77

Pew, Pugh

Pew, Hannah, 66
Phaup, John, 124 (see also
    Paup, John)
Philadelphia, (Pa.), 118

Philips, Phillips

Philips, John, 42,77
Phillips, Elizabeth, 102
    John, 77, 102
    William, 77
Pidgeon, Ann, 115
    Charles, 117
    Chas., 116
    Elizabeth, 111,117,118
    Hannah, 116
    Isaac, 111,112,114,117
    Rachel, 110,112,113,116
    Ruth, 112,113
    Sarah, 116
    William, 110,112,117
    Wm., 116
Piedmont Photo Crafts,
    Forest, Va., frontis-
    piece by, vii
Pillow, Edith, 67
    Elizabeth, 67
    Joseph, 67,70
Pillows, Agness, 106
Pinnell, Joseph, 76(see also Pannill)
Pippin, Amy, 83
    Oney, 83
Pirkins, Polly, 52 (see also
    Perkins, etc.)
Pitts, Ritchie, 77
Pittsylvania County, (Va.),
    15,20,50,68,75,102
Plummer, Asa, 117
    Grace, 111
    Joseph, 117
Plunkett, Benjamin, 63
    John H., 78
    Polly, 63
Poe, Samuel, 9
Poindexter, John, 27,78
    Joseph, 78
    Reubin, 78
Pointer, John, 78
Porat (?), John, 10
Porter, Francis, 78
    John, 78
    Peggy, 24,102
    William, 78

Portraiture of Quakerism, A,
    xii,109
Potter, Augustine, 11
    Nancy, 11

Powar, Power

Powar, Helen, 34
    William, 34,78

Powel, Powell

Powel, Johannah, 77
    John, 77
    Sarah, 77
Powell, Betsy, 16
    Cornelius, 9,78
    Eliza, 16
    John, 78
    John F., 45
    Rebeckah, 77
    Wiatt, 16
Power, William, 78,79

Prater, Prator

Prater, Thomas, 78
Prator, Thomas, 78
Presbyterian Ministers, 124
Preston, John, 116
    Rebecca, 112,116,117,118
Previt, Patsy, 79
    Rob., 79
Previtt, James, 79
    Joseph, 79
Prewitt, Michael, 28

Pribble, Prible

Pribble, John, 33
    Martin, 79
    Milly, 33
Prible, Martin, 79
Price, Bourne, 79,82,89
    Robert, 76
    Susan, 94
    Susannah, 94
Priest, Enos, 60
Prince Edward Co., (Va.), 11,
    20,72
Prince George Co., (Va.), 126

Prior, Pryor

Prior, Elizabeth, 44
Protestant Episcopal Ministers,
    123
Pruitt, Michael, 105 (see also Prewitt,
    Sally, 105   Michael)
Pryor, Elizabeth, 44
    William, 79
Puckett, Charles, 79
    Clayburn, 98
    Fleming, 79
    Isham, 79
    Nathaniel, 60
    Patsey, 60
    Thomas, 79
Pugh, David, 65,66,79 (see also Pew)
    Hannah, 66,101
    John, 10,79
    Jonath, 65
    Jonathan, 66
    Locy, 65
    Lot, 79
    Mary Eleanor, 25
    Nancy, 20
    Sarah, 66
Pugh's Official Map of Campbell
    County 1872, 124

Pullam, Pulliam, Pullim, Pullium

Pullam, E., 9
    Iseam, 9
    Penelope, 9
Pulliam, Penelop, 9
Pullim, Isham, 103
Pullium, Isham, 103
    Marjory, 103
Purcell, Thomas, 79

                Q

Quaker(s),
    authority on, viii
    marriages of, xi,108,109,
        110-119,121,122
    meeting-houses, xi,108,110-
        119
    meeting(s) of, 108,125,126
    migration chart, viii,126
    migrations of, xi,125,126
    original records of Friends
        Meetings, xii
Quarles, Jane, 94
    Lucy, 43
    Sarah, 43
Quisenberry, James, 80

                R

Race,
    reference to, 3,12,29,34,38,
        43,64,73,80,83
Ractor, Rector

Ractor, Martin, 81
Raeder, E., 96
Raine, John, 80,83
    William, 80
    Wm., 83
Raley, Isaac, 80
Ramsey, Ann B., 58
    Ann E., 47
    Caroline B., 47
    Caroline, D., 47
    Elizabeth Ann B., 58
    Richard H., 58
Randall, Mary, 88
Randle, M., 117
Randolph, Beverly, 80
    Bevly, 80
    Mary, 88 (see also Randall,
        Mary)
Ranig, George, 95
Rankeen, Robert, 80
Ransbarger, Philip, 80

Ratcliff, Ratliffe

Ratcliff, Harrison, 111,114,115
Ratcliff, Mary, 27
    Mildred, 110,111,114,115
Ratekin, John, 80
    John, Jr., 80
    Laurence, 39
    Lawrence, 80
    Martha, 34
    Rachel, 34,39
    Rebekah, 39
Ratliffe, Mary, 23

Rawling, Rawlins, Rollens,
        Rowling

Rawling, John, 86
Rawlins, Albin, 31
    Lucy, 91
    Mary, 59
    Polly, 59

Ray, Wray

Ray, Henry, 61,70

Read, Redd, Reed, Reid, Reade

Read, Edmund, 80
    John, 94
    John Paul, 81
    John T. W., 80
    Josiah, 80
    Keziah, 71
    Obadiah, 81
    Polly, 49
    Priscilla, 69
    Sally, 94
    William, 49,69,94
Reade, John T., 55
Readen, Robert, 81
    William, 81
Reading, George, 25
Reads, John, 20
Ready, Jenny, 67
    Nathan, 67
Realey, Isaac, 80 (see also
    Raley, Isaac)
Reardson, William, 116
Rector, Elizabeth, 31 (see also
    Ractor, etc.)
    Gan, 10
    Jane, 12
    John, 81,106
    Lewis, 81
    Martin, 81
    Rebeckah, 12
    Sally, 10
Redd, John Paul, 81 (see also Read)
Redding, Joseph, 81
    Robert, 81
    Thomas, 81

Reece, Rees, Reese

Reece, Elizabeth, 24
Reed, John, 81
    Kissiah, 71
    Obadiah, 81
    Polly, 49
    William, 49,71

Reede, Reeder

Reede, Elijah, 10
Reeder, Elijah, 10
    Hannah, 13
    Pricilla, 113
    Thomas, 81,113
Reeding, Thomas, 81

Rees, Herod, 82
Reese, Elizabeth, 24
    Herod, 24,59,82,91
Register of Marriages C.C.C.
    (original Register), 2,6
Reid, Clarisa, 45 (see also Read,
    etc.)
    Hanna, 49
    Hannah, 49
    John, 45,82
    Josiah, 80
    Nathan, 82
    Priscilla, 69
    Rebecca, 55
    Theodore, 45
    Thomas, 55,82
    William, 49
Revily, Isaac, 82
Reynolds, Amelia, 57
    Elizabeth, 66
    Isaac, 43,57
    Issac, 96
    James, 82,97
    John, 44,82
    John, Jr., 27
    John W., 18
    Nancy, 96,97
    Rachel, 43
    Sarah, 27
    William, 82
    William M., 68
    William W., 58
Rhodes, Joseph, 116
    Martha, 116

Rhor, Rhorr, Rohr

Rhor, Phillip, 85
Rhorr, Jacob, 85
Rice, Anna, 84
    Ben, 69
    John, 84,91
    Jonathan, 82
    Judith S., 91
    Samuel, 82

Rich, Ritch

Rich, Allain, 13
    Allen, 82
    David, 82
    Nancy, 13
    Nimrod, 13
Richards, Abijah, 113,116

Richards, continued
   Elijah, 110
   Esther, 110,116

Richardson, Richeson

Richardson, Betty, 116
   Dolly, 86
   Elizabeth, 86
   Geo., 86
   George, 74
   Jacob, 14,82
   John, 70,82,114
   Joseph, 116
   Molly, 114
   Morgan, 83
   William, 82
   Wm., 86
Richeson, Morgan, 83
Richmond, Virginia, 6,122,124
Rick, David, 13
Riddy, Mascilda, 24
Ridgeway, Henry, 34
   Samuel, 83
Riggs, George, 83
Ripley, Thomas, 91
Ritch, Alen, 82 (see also Rich,etc.)
Rittor, John, 81
Roach, Joshua, 83
   Sarah, 68
   William, 68
Roark, Phebe, 83

Roberds, Roberts, Robards

Robards, Enoch, 118
Roberds, Benjamin, 83
   Isham, 83
   Patsey, 104
   Ressley, 104
Roberson, John, 84,116 (see also
     Robinson, John)
Roberts, Aisley, 94
   Benjamin, 83
   Edith, 94
   Enoch, 111,112,115
   Feander,118
   George, 112
   Harry, 83
   Henry, 83
   Isham, 83
   Joe, 83
   Johnny, 14

Roberts, continued
   Mack, 33,83
   Matilda, 110,111,112,114,115,
     116,117
   Morris, 33,83
   Patsy, 104
   Sarah, 14
   William, 84
   Winnie, 43

Robertson, Robinson

Robertson, Archibald, 84
   Arthur, 84
   Christopher, 84 (see also
     Robinson, Christopher)
   Colin, 60
   Henry, 77,84
   James, 38
   James, Jr., 19,68,84
   John, 47,84
   Lewis, 9
   Mary, 38
   Nancy, 71
Robins, Margrit, 97
   Nancy, 97
Robinson, Archibald, 84
   Christopher, 84
   Holcombe, 82
   Isabella, 39
   James, 18,39
   Jane, 71
   John, 71,84
   Lewis, 84
   Mary, 38
   Ratchel, 18
   Thomas, 84
   William, 84

Roch, Rock

Roch, Mary, 65
Rock, Charles, 65
   Mary, 65

Rodgers, Rogers

Rodgers, Samuel, 85
   Thomas, 42
Rogers, Nathaniel, 67,83,85,89
   Sam, 42
   Samuel, 67,85
Rohr, Jacob, 28,85
   Phillip, 85 (see also Rhor,
     etc.)

Rollens, Lucy, 91 (see also
    Rawlins, etc.)
Ronalds, Elizabeth, 66
Roper, Frances, 100
    William, 8,61

Rork, Rorks

Rork, Barnard, 85
    Charles, Jr., 85
    Owen, 85
Rorks, Charles, 85
Rose, William, 85
    William, Jr., 85

Roser, Rosser

Roser, Nancy, 40
Rosser, Ambrose, 70,85
    Ann, 70,98
    Betsy, 72
    David, 97
    Fanny, 39
    John, 8,15,85
    Jonathan, 8,39
    Lavina, 40
    Nancy, 24,40
    Patty, 8
    Pleasant, 8,85
    Sally, 8
    Sarah, 70
    Susanna, 98
    Susannah, 98
    Thomas, 85
    William, 8,24,39,40,73,85,
        105
    Winifred, 97
    Winney, 97
Rowland, Robert, 86
Rowling, John, 86 (see also Rawling)
Rowze, Thomas, 86
Rucker, J. Eldon,Mrs. (Bess
    Sydnor Thompson Rucker),vii
Rugus, Newman, 110

Rush, Rust

Rush, Nancy Ends, 83

Russel, Russell

Russel, Ann, 84
    Elanor, 84
    Ellender, 84
Russell, Elizabeth, 30
    James, 12,30,46

Russell, continued
    Mary, 76
    Milton C., viii
    Nancy, 46
    Thomas, 86,97
    William, 46
Russell, Parish of, 93
Rust, Betsy, 83
    Betsey H., 83
    George, 23,61,62,83
    Gion, 99
    Jeremiah, xiv,60
    Nancy, 83
    Rebeckah, 60
    Rustburg, (Va.), xiv,2
Rutledge, Alex, 60
    Oleander, 60
    William, 86

                    S

Saint John, George, 86
St. Clair, James, 10
St. John, Geo., 75
    George, 75
    James, 86
    James S., 86
    Polly, 107
Sanders, Christopher, 86
    Daniel, 86,92
    Daniel J., 86
    Elizabeth, 78 (see also
        Walker, Elizabeth)
    Hannah, 78
Sandifer, Elizabeth, 70
    Samuel, 70
Saul, Samuel, 86
Saunders, John, 86
    Sally, 82 (see also Lander,
        Sally)
Savage, Richard, 75
Schoolfield, Ben, 119
    Benjamin, 86
    David, 91
    Jane, 91
    John, 86
    Samuel, 30,86

Scot, Scott

Scot, James, 87
Scott, Agnes W., 42
    Annie, 60

Scott, continued
    Ann S., 45
    Aphia, 85
    Ashia, 85
    Belinda R., 73
    Charlie, 72
    Elizabeth, 20
    Gabriel, 41,103
    Gabriel I., 76
    Harriett Baughn, 103
    James, 87
    John, 60,72
    Martha, 20
    Martha W., 41
    Matthias, 87
    Matthis, 87
    Sally, 72
    Samuel, 42,45,73,85
    Susanna E., 76
    Susannah, 76
    Thomas, 62,85,87
    William, 41,45,76,87,103
Scruggs, Drury, 39,87
    John, 22
    Langhorne, 87
    Patty, 39

Sea, Seay

Sea, Anna, 110
    Mary, 15
Seay, Agatha, 35
    Joseph, 15,87
    Mary, 15
    William, 87
Semple, Robert B., 124
Seneca Meeting-house, xi,108,
        115,117,118,119
Shackleford, James, 87
    John, 87
Shanault, Benjamin, 95
    Rachel, 95
Shaner, Elizabeth, 70 (see also
        Shearer, Elizabeth)
Shannon, James, 61,87
    John, 75
    Polly, 61
Sharp, Linchfield, 47
Shartil, Sophia, 89 (see also
        Shuttle, Sophia)
Shearer, Andrew, 87
    Anna, 94
    Anne, 17
    Elizabeth, 70

Shearer, continued
    James, 46,56,70,81,87,94
    Jane, 46
    Mary, 56
    Peggy, 81
    Thomas, 56,87
Shelson, Sarah, 97
Shelton, Booker, 74
Shenandoah Valley, (Va.), 126

Shepherd, Shepperd, Sheppard

Shepherd, Samuel, 6
    Thomas, 88
Sheppard, Thomas, 93
Shepperd, Thomas, 88
Sheras, Margret, 47
    James, 88
Sheuster, Philip, 88
Shinall, William, 68
Shinall, Wm., 58

Shouls, Showls

Shouls, Conrad, 88
    Jacob, 20
Showls, Betsy, 97
    Conrad, 88
    Elizabeth, 97
    Jacob, 20,97
    Polly, 20
Shuttle, John, 88
    Sophia, 89 (see also Shartil,Sophia)

Silcock, Siliock

Silcock, Amos, 88
Siliock, Amos, 88
Simmons, Charles, 40
    Reubin, 40
    Ruben, 19
Simms, Albert E. Mrs., vii
Simpson, Elizabeth R., 71
    John, 71
Skelton, Mrs. Harry E., viii
Sketches and Recollections of
        Lynchburg by Its Oldest
        Inhabitant, 124
Skidmore, William, 88

Slade, Sledd

Slade, John, 88
Slaughter, Ann P., 27

Slaughter, continued
  Charles, 15,27
  Eliza, 15
  Robert Horn, 15
Sledd, John, 88
Sleep, Patsey, 67
Smart, E. C., 80
  Edmund, 80,88
  John, 80,88
  Polly, 80
Smith, Charles, 84,111
  Chas., 26
  E., 10
  Elisha, 10
  Elizabeth, 60,61,64,95
  Francis, 88
  Francis, Jr., 88
  John, 73
  Joseph, 88
  Judah, 95
  Lucy, 9
  Martha, 11
  Mary, 64
  P., 11
  Parrin, 67
  Perin, 15,60
  Reuben, 84
  Richard, 55
  Robert, 88
  Sally, 95
  Stephen, 89
  Thomas, 10,48,61,91
  Thos., 48
Smithson, Drummond, 96
  Drummong, 73
  Jemima, 96
  John, 53
  John M., 89,96
  Lucy, 58
  Mary, 14
  Samuel, 89,96
  Tiry, 89
  Tyre, 89
Snead, Evan, 89
  Salley, 116
  William, 89,113
Sneed, Henry, 88
Snoddy, John, 89
  Robert, 34,89
Snow, Daniel, 67,75,89,102
  Elizabeth, 28
  Henry, 89
  John, 11

Snow, continued
  John, Jr., 11
  Judith, 11
  Sarah, 62
  Vincent, 89
Society of Friends,
  Baltimore, Maryland, xi
Solloman, Polly, 28
South River Quakers, viii
South River Meeting-house, xi,
  108,110,111,112,113,114,115,
  116,117,118,119
Sowell, Philip, 89

Space, Speece

Space, Conrad, 89
  Lewis, 100
  Peter, 90
Spalding, John, 79
Spearman, Elizabeth, 58
  John, 59
Speece, Conrad, 73,89
  George, 89
  Lewis, 34,36,100
  Margaret, 73
  Peter, 90
Spence, Conrad, Jr., 49
Spencer, Beverly, 90
  Charles, 52
  David, 34,84,90
  Elizabeth, 84
  Judith, 80,82,84
  Moses, 52,90
  P., 52
  Polly, 52

Spicer, Spiser

Spicer, Martha, 27
Spiser, Isack, G., 27
  Latus, G., 27
Spotsylvania County, (Va.),126
Stanley, Betsy, 113, (see also
  Hanley, Betty)
  James, 90
  John, Sr., 13
  Sarah, 13,113
Stanton, Aaron, 90,113,118
  Andrew, 35
  Benjamin, 115
  Catharine, 113,118
  Hepzibah, 113

Stanton, continued
  Huldah, 111,113
  James, 110,116,118,119
  Latham, 83,111,113,114,118
  Mary, 116
  Phebe, 110,113,115,116
  Pheby, 118
  William, 110,111,112,113,114,
    115,116,117,118
  William, Jr., 116
  William, Sr., 116
  Wm., 113,115,117,118,119
  Wm., Sr., 118
  Zacheus, 116,117,118
Staples, Charles, 64
  David, 14,70
  Elizabeth, 63
  Frances, 106
  Garland, 90
  Isaac, 90
  Jane, 90
  John, 90
  John N., 90
  John U., 90
  Samuel, 90
  Tuck, 7
  William, 63,90
Statutes at Large, being a
    Collection of all the
    Laws of Virginia, The, 6
Statutes at Large of Virginia,
    being a Continuation of
    Hening, The, 6

Steel, Steele

Steel, Alex., 9
  Alexander, 61,63,74,90
  Alexander, Sr., 90
  Arch, 91
  Archibald, 91
  Elizabeth, 63,74,84
  George, 17
  John, 9,61,63,90
  Mary, 61
  Sarah, 9
Steele, Alexander, 90
  Elizabeth, 63
  John, 84
Steen, Abigail, 47
  John, 91
  Thomas, 56
  William, 91

Stemmons, Jacob, 18
Step, Elizabeth, 63 (see also
    Staples, Elizabeth)

Stephens, Stevens

Stephens, Jacob, 9
  Peggy, 9
  Thomas, 91
Stepp, Anne, 15
  Elizabeth, 81,86
  Jinny, 100
  John, 15,81,87
  Joseph, 91,100
  Joseph, Jr., 100
  Mary, 100
  Solomon, 91
Steptoe, Elizabeth Prentis, 54
  George, 54
  J. A., 82,99
  James, 4,54
  Richard, 54
Stern, Francis, 91
Stevens, Elizabeth, 20 (see also
    Stephens, etc.)
  Jacob, 9
  John, 91
  Peggy, 9
  Robert, 9
  Sarah, 74
  Thomas, 91

Stewart, Stuart

Stewart, Henry, 91
  James, 74,93
  John, 91
Stimmons, Jacob, 91
Stith, Benjamin, 68,86
  Catherine, 54
  Elizabeth Buckner, 71
  John, 47,54,91
  John, Jr., 91
  Joseph, 91,92
  Katherine, 54
  Lucy, 91
  Martha, 86
  Polly, 47
  Richard, xiii,xiv,47,54,71,92
  Thomas, 92
  William, 22,92
  Wm., 92

Stoaks, Stokes

Stoakes, Thomas, 92
Stokes, Thomas, 92
Stone, Keturah, 102
  William, 92
  Wm., 92

Storer, Storey, Storry, Storrey,
          Story

Storer, Archer, 92
  Archibald, 92
  Edward, 37
  Elizabeth, 37
  Pleasant, 92
Storey, Archibald, 92
Storrey, Pleasant, 92
Storry, Pleasant, 92
Story, Elizabeth, 37
  Pleasant, 92

Stovall, Stoveall

Stovall, Bartholemew, 77
  Bartholomew, 105
Stoval, Doritha, 18
Stovall, Dorothy, 18
  Elizabeth, 18,91,105
  George, 93
  George, Jr., xiii
  John, 49,92
  Martha, 77
  Nancy, 91
  Penelope, 49
  Terisha, 93
  Territia, 93
  Thomas, 105
Stoveall, George, 92
Straasberry, Ruth, 116
Strange, Elizabeth, 56
  Frances, 106
  John, 72,93
  John, Sr., 93
  Mary, 56,88
  Nathaniel, 72,93,99,106
  Patsey, 32
  Robert, 32,56
  Robt., Jr., 56
Stratham, Love, 44
Stratton, Amy, 118
  Anna, 119
  Ashley, 115

Stratton, continued
  Benj., 117
  Benjamin, 117,118
  Daniel, 93,115,118
  Dosha, 118
  Hannah, 118,119
  Jacob, 118
  Joel, 118
  Joseph, 26,99,112,114,118,119
  Joseph, Jr., 115
  Mahlon, 119
  Mary, 99
  Naomi, 117,119
  Neoma, 115
  Sarah, 26,114
  Shady, 118
Street, Anthony, 93
Strong, Catharine, 62,102
  David, 93
  John, 36
  Mary, 36
  Robert, 44
  William, 76
  Wm., 76
Stuart, James, 31,61,93 (see also
          Stewart, etc.)
Sturman, Elizabeth, 93
  Iriphena, 93
  Valentine, 93
  William, 93

Sublet, Sublett, Sublette, Subley,
          Sublite, Sublitt

Sublet, Mathew, 94
  William, 93
Sublett, Benjamin, 79,93
  George Allen, 93
  Nancy, 42
  Samuel, 93
  William, 93
Sublette, William, 93
Subley, Benjamin, 93
  Samuel, 93
Sublite, George Allen, 93
Sublitt, Mathew, 94
Surry County, (Va.), xiv,126
Sussex County, (Va.), 19

Sutinfield, Suttenfield

Sutinfield, Nancy, 46
Suttenfield, Edith, 26

Suttenfield, continued
    James, 87,94
    Mary, 47,62
    Nancy, 46
Swain, Jeremiah, 58
Swanson, Delores (Miss), viii
Sweeney, Susannah, 58
    William W., Judge, Sixth
        Judicial Circuit of
        Virginia, vii
Swinney, Joseph P., 111

                T

Talbot, Betsy, 15
    Charles M., 92,94
    Chas., 63
    Edmund, 31
    John, xiii,38
    Levicy, 38
    Matthew, 94
    Pleasant, 15,38,63,85
    Polly, 63 (See also
        Talbot, Sally)
    Sally, 63
    William, 92
    Williston, 15,38,63,94
    Williston, Jr., 94

Taleferro, Taliaferro

Taleferro, Roderick, 94
Taliaferro, Roderick, 94
    Rod'k, 93

Talley, Tally

Talley, Benoni Carter, 102
    Carter, 94
    Clabourn, 94
    Clabren, 94
    Doshia, 16
Tally, Doshia, 16

Taner, Tanner

Taner, Susanna, 26

Tankersley, Tanttersley

Tankersley, Ann, 103
    George, 94
Tanner, Benjamin, 8,19,26
    Betsey, 8
    Branch, 94

Tanner, continued
    James, 8
    John, 94
    Mary, 62
    Mathew, 8
    Nathan, 29,40,54,63,70,77,78,
        91,106
    Nathaniel, 40
    Susannah, 26
    Vincent J., 26
Tanttersley, George, 94
Tate, Caleb, 25,94
    Edmund, 29
    Harriet, 29
    Jesse, 8
    Sally M., 29
    Sarah H., 110
    Sarah Henry, 8

Tayler, Tayloe, Taylor

Tayler, Rachel, 16
Tayloe, John, 94
Taylor, Alice, 112
    Archibald, 95
    Charles, 93
    Edmond, 79
    Elizabeth, 59
    Fanny, 93
    George, 95,100
    Hezekiah, 95
    James, 27
    Jane, 73
    Jeremiah, 68
    John, 39,73,79,94,95
    Nancy, 27
    Patsey, 15
    Peter T., 20
    Polly Ann, 20
    Rachel, 16
    Richard, 46
    Spicy, 79
    William, 20,93,95
Teass, John, 43
    Lucy, 43
Teazel, Elizabeth, 112
    Joseph, 112
Teazle, Philip, 112
Telford, John M., 57
    Samuel, 42
Tend, Edward, 110
Tenner, Mary, 116
Tennison, Ann, 115
    Henry, 115
    John, 115

Tennison, continued
  Margaret, 115
  Sarah, 112,115
Teppance, James, 73 (see also Tuppence)
  Patty, 73

Terrell, Terrill

Terrell, Ann, 112
  Anna, 112
  Benjamin, 23
  Betsy, 114
  Betsy Henry, 72
  Charles, 61,96
  Charles L., 96,115
  Chas. L., 100
  David, 70,111,113,114,118,119
  David, Jr., 114
  Dudley, 72,95
  Edward, 58,89,112,119
  Edward, Jr., 58
  Elizabeth, 58,100,117
  Henry, 88,90,95,112,114,115,
    118
  James, 95,96
  Lucy, 112,118,119
  Luis, 61
  Martha, 118
  Mary, 82,89,111,112,119
  Micajah, xiii,114,117
  Micajah, Jr., 112
  Nancy, 104
  Patty, 111
  Peter, 96
  Polly, 61
  S., 58,104
  Sam'l, 119
  Samuel, 43,96,112,114
  Sarah, 112,119
  Susanna, 114
  Susannah, 111
  Thomas M., 96
  Thomas Moorman, 96
  Timothy, 96,104
  William, 89,96
  Winifred, 70
  Winnifred, 70

Terrence, Torrance, Torrence

Terrence, Andrew, 97 (see also Torrence)
Terrens, Aron, 97
Terrill, Charles L., 96
  James, 95

Terrill, continued
  William, 96
Thomas, James, 36
  John, 27
  Milly, 36
  William, 36,57,82,96
Thomkins, James, 96
  Sarah, 77

Thompson, Thomson, Tompson

Thompson, Andrew, 64,101,106
  David, 96,97,101
  Elendor, 64
  Elenor, 56,64 (see also
    Smith, Elizabeth, 64)
  Elizabeth, 64,96
  Ginny, 106
  James, 25
  Jenny, 106
  John, 9,54,56,64,96,97
  Lockey, 9
  Margaret, 64,101
  Margret, 54
  Mathew, 10,96
  Matthew, 97
  Rebecca, 81
  Samuel, 10,96
  Sarah, 86,88
  William, 97
Thomson, David, 96
  Elizabeth, 96
  John, 28,96
Thopson, Mathew, 44
  Nancy, 44
Thorp, Elizabeth, 55,99
  Francis, xiii,xiv,99
  Iran, 25
  James, 97
  Pemalia, 25
  Solomon, 26
  Sophia, 82
Thuratt, John J., 74

Thurman, Thurmon, Thurmond

Thurman, Ann, 86
  Henry, 110
  Ja., 18
  John, 97
  Rhoda, 7
  Richard, 7,97
Thurmon, Ann, 86
  Richard, 86

Thurmond, Sally, 86
Thurston, Marshall, 51
  Pauline, 92
Tidewater Virginia, 125
Tillas, Elizabeth, 119
  Jane, 119
Tillus, Jane, 113
Timberlake, Charles, 33,35,51
  Christopher, 97
  Elizabeth, 110
  John, 10,83,110,117
  Mary, 110,112,114,115
  Mildred, 33
  Philip, 97
  Polly, 10,110
  Richard, 10,16
  Sarah, 16
Timberlick, Charles, 38
  Nancy, 38
Toler, Edmund, 41
  Juley, 41
Tompson, Sarah, 86 (see also Thompson)
Torrance, Andrew, 97 (see also Terrence)
  Joseph, 97
Torrence, Joseph, 18

Tranan, Trunan

Tranan, Anderson, 97
Tranam, Priscilla, 69
  Wm., 69
Traylor, John, 97
  John, Jr., 14
  Robert, 97
Trenor, James, 97
Trent, Elijah, 27,43,74
  Elizabeth, 43
  Fanny B., 52
  Fanny Brent, 52
  Fany B., 52
  Henry, 26,43,74,97
  John, 43,74,98
  John H., 73
  Lucy, 103
  Luraney, 74
  Obediah, 98
  Polly, 74
  Pricilla, 26
  Sally, 27
  Thomas, 90
  William, 98
  Zachariah, 27
Tribble, Isabella, 90
  John, 90

Trigg, William, 10,98
Trower, Robert, 98

Truhit, Truitt

Truhit, Wm., 73
Truitt, Frances Christian, 73
  Nancy, 3
  Nancy W., 57
Trunan, Anderson, 97 (see also
    Tranan, etc.)
Tucker, Thomas, 20,69,99
  Valentine, 59
Tullas, Jane, 115
Tullis, Ann, 117
  Jallis, 117
  Jane, 117
  John, 117
  Martha, 117
  Richard, 117
Tuppence, James, 34 (see also Teppence)
  Susanna, 34
Turley, Betsy, 73
  James, 51,73
Turner, Elizabeth, 31,110
  James, 75,98
  John, 10,98
  Keziah, 72
  Nancy, 31
  Rebecca, 38
  Rebekah, 38
  Robert, 31
  Sarah, 110
Turnley, James, 10
  James, Jr., 10,45
  Ruth, 10

Tweady, Twedey, Tweedy, Twedy

Tweady, John, 98
Twedey, Robert, 98
Twedy, John, 28
  Robert, 98
Tweedy, John, 98
  Joseph, 23,85
  Joseph, Jr., 98,107
  Mary, 23
  Nancy, 85
  Robert, 23,85,98,104
Twopence, Rocksianny, 35
Tynes, Obediah, 98
Tyree, Daniel, 62
  Mildred, 110,112
  Pleasant, 98

Tyree, continued
  Richard, 98,112,114
  Richmond, 99

U - V

Urquart, Walter, 99
Valentine, Winney, 73
Vannerson, William, 99
VanNorth, Margaret, 14
Vaughan, Ares, 67
Vaughn, Nicholas, 99
  Patsey, 15
  Richard, 43
Venable, Abraham, 99
  Jacob, 99
  John, 99
  Mary, 99
  Robert, 99
  Samuel, 100
Vernon, Jonathan, 99
Vest, James, 62,99
  Robert P., 99
  Robert Parker, 99
  Thomas, 24

Via, Vias

Via, Littleberry, 99
  Littlebery, 99
  Mary, 118,119
Vias, Littleberry, 99
Virginia Counties, mentioned
    (28 different counties), vii,
    xi,xii,xiii,xiv,1,2,4,6,23,33,
    38,39,41,44,50,58,59,66,68,72,
    75,80,91,93,98,102,108,110-117,
    119,123-126
Virginia's Mother Church, 122
Virginia State Library,
  Archives Division of, xi,xii,
    108
  Quaker Records, xi,xii,108
  Reference and Circulation
    Section, viii
  Staff of, viii

W

Wabber, Margaret, 24
Wade, Allen, 103
  Andrew, 68
  Edmund, 99
  Henry, 55,92

Wade, continued
  James, 99
  John, 55
  Orenda, 55
  Pearce, 53
  Pierce, 53
  Polly, 92
  Zackfield, 55,92,99
Walden, Charles, 99
  Henry, 56,89
  Jenny, 56
  Lewis, 89
  Pattsy, 89
  Patty, 56
  Polly, 89
  Richard, 100
Walker, _____ (sister of Frances
    Walker), 22
  Benjamin, 60,76,77,102
  Betsy R., 10
  Buckley, 16,60,77,102
  Chapley, 66
  Charles, 38,59,78,100,103
  Edmund, 100
  Edmund W., 100
  Elizabeth, 16,59,78,93
  Fanny, 22
  Frances, 22
  Francis, 22
  George, 100
  Jemima, 77
  Jesiah, 61
  John, 100
  John, Jr., 100
  Kissiah, 14
  Mary, 50
  Nancy, 102
  Sally, 60
  Sarah, 100,103
  Shapel, 100
  Susanna, 59
  Thomas, 78,81,100
  William, 10,50,93,100,104
  William H., 25
  Wm., 78,104
  Wm. H., 100
Wall, Elizabeth, 99
Wallace, Polly, 53
  Sarah, 53
  William, 53
Walls, Mary, 95
Walrond, Benjamin, 40
  Elizabeth, 40
  John, 40

Walsh, James, 100
Walthall, Henry, 22,33,76
   John, 54
   Thomas, 30,62
   Thos., 30
Walton, Elisa, 62
Ward, Henry, 22,100
   John, xiii,23,32,62,68
   John, Jr., 50,68
   Mary, 61
   Robert A., 100
   William, 91

Warinner, Warner, Warriner

Warinner, James, 124
Warner, James, 11,13,20,25,36,42,
   48,55,57,73,78,79,86,89,97,
   98,105,124
Warrand, Donald, 83
Warriner, James, 57,124

Warrick, Warwick, Warwicke

Warrick, Fanny, 13
Warwick, Fanny, 13
   James, 22
   Nancy B., 93
   Sally B., 22
   William, 93,101
Warwicke, Fanny, 13
   James, 13
Watkins, Aaron, 101
   Benjamin, 101
   Elizabeth, 76
   Enoch, 69,101
   Jacob, 79
   Jane, 10
   Mary, 79
   Moses, 10,46,101
   Mosey, 44
   Patsey, 44
   Patty, 44
   Reece, 44,101
   Robert, 22,76,79,101
   Sarah, 46
   Sheran, 90

Watson, Watzon

Watson, Jennie, 99
Watts, E., 72
   Edward, 14
   Elizabeth, 14
   Mary, 14,72
Watzon, Sally, 77

Wayne, Whayne

Wayne, Betsy, 87
   John, 61,87,93,101
   Joseph, 61,101
   Milly, 31

Weaks, Weeks

Weaks, Elijah, 101
Weatherford, Anderson, 101
   John, 101
Weaver, Juday, 82
   Matthew, 101
   Samuel, 55,101
   William, 49
   William W., 55,82,101
   Wilson, 101
   W. W., 55,82
Webb, Betsy, 40
   Daniel, 79
   Edmond, 79
   Edmund, 40
   George, 102
   James, 60
   Jesse, 36,102
   Nancy, 59
   Polly, 79
   Susannah, 103
   Vinestra, 36
   Vinetta, 36

Webber, Weber

Webber, Henry, 21
   John, 77,102
   John, Jr., 102
   Margaret, 89
   Martin, 102
   Nancy, 35
   Peter, 102
   Rachel, 21,50
   Sally, 35
   William, 102
Weber, Adam, 102
   Casper, 50.102
   Catherine,98
   Henry, 48,102
   John, 35,77,102
   John, Jr., 35,102
   Keturah, 36
   Martin, 35,102
   Mary, 35

Weber, continued
  Peggy, 77
  Peter, 36,102
  Rachel, 21,50
  Sally, 35
  William, 35,102
Weedon, Nathan, 104
Weekes, Anderson, 8,100,101,106,
  124 (see Meeks, Anderson,
  124)
Weeks, Elijah, 101 (see Weaks,
  etc.)
Weisenberg, Christian, 35
Welch, Elizabeth, 91
West, Benjamin, 102
  Frances, 49
  Jesse, 102
  John, 49,102
  Letty, 77
  Obediah, 102
  Reuben, 102
  Thomas, 102
  William, 103
Whayne, Benjamin, 103 (see also
    Wayne, etc.)
  Milly, 31
Wheat, Wm., 35
Whelan, Mary, 67
  Rachel, 69
  Rebeckah, 67
  Thomas, 67,69
Whelton, Betsy, 51
  Thomas, 51
White, Anderson, 103
  Benjamin, 68
  Jonathan, 43,88,103
  Richardson, 103
  Uriah, 103
Whitington, Stark, 91 (see also
Whitlock, Thomas, 103   Whittington)
Whitlow, Andrew D., 10
  Andrew S., 103
  Andrews, 103
  Delilah R., 100
  Elizabeth, 11
  Henry, 10,100
  Patsy, 10
  William, 10,100,103
Whittington, James, 103 (see also
Whorley, John, 73   Whitington)
Wiatt, John, 19
  Thomas, 9,103
Wigginton, Benjamin, 103
Wilbourn, Richard B., 103

Wildman, Wileman

Wildman, Abraham, 117,118
  Betty, 118
  Jonah, 118
  Letitia, 114,115,118,119
  Lettia, 117
Wileman, Latitia, 113
Wiley, Wily

Wiley, Bartlett, 78,103
  Lucy, 84

Wilkerson, Wilkinson, Wilkson

Wilkerson, Joseph, 103
  Parson, 103
  William, 104
Wilkinson, William, 104
Wilkson, Parson, 103
Willan, John, 102
  Polly, 102
Willard, John, 79,98
Williams, Anderson, 39,95
  Elizabeth, 39
  George, 104
  James, 104
  Jesse, 111,113
  Luckey, 95
  Matthias, 57,64
  Phillip, 116
  Polly, 12,64
  Reubin, 104
  Roger, 72,104

  Susannah, 57
  Thomas, 104
  William, 104
Williamson, Ann, 48
  Archer, 15,28,34,44,83,98,101,
    107
  Caldwell, 74
  David, 63
  Debrix, 104
  Elizabeth, 48,74
  Francis, 63
  Henry, 48,106
  Mary, 56
  Nathan, 48,57,104
  Nathaniel, 104
  Patsy, 63
  Raymond H., viii
  Rob., 63
  Robert, 15,28
  Sally, 66

Williamson, continued
   William, 34,48,56
   William, W., 45
Wills, Betsey, 22
   Betty, 22
   Euclid, 22
   John, 22
   Katy, 31
   Mina Ann, 22

Willson, Wilson

Willson, Alexander H., 18
   Eley, 66
   Elizabeth, 19
   John, 18,19,33
   John, Jr., 18
   Martha, 18,82
   Mary, 63
   Mathew, 63,96,105
   Nancy, 19
   Peter, 104
   Polly, 89
   Thomas, 104,105
Wilmoth, Betsy, 90
Wilson, Ann, 30,45
   Champion, 34
   Elenor, 66
   Eley, 66
   Elizabeth, 19,63
   Ellender,66
   James, 8,11,51,85
   Jane, 89
   Janey, 105
   John, 29,30,66
   Joseph, 104
   Joshua, 104
   Lucy, 49
   Margaret, 29
   Martha, 18,63,105
   Mary, 33,45
   Mathew, 105
   Peter, 104
   Polly, 89
   Rachel, 30
   Robert, 50,90,105
   Samuel, 101,104,105
   Sarah, 11
   Sinah P., 11
   Thomas, 45,63,104,105
   W. H., 81
   William H., 81
   W. N., 74
Wily, B., 9 (see also Wiley,etc.)
   Bartlett, 103

Wily, continued
   John, 84
   Lucy, 84
Winford, Joshua, 105

Winfree, Winfrey, Winfry

Winfree, Charles, 8,75
   John, 8,75
   Nancy, 75
   Vaul, 75
Winfrey, Susannah, 8
Winfry, Nancy, 75
   Susannah, 8
Wingfield, Josephine B. Mrs.,
     Librarian, viii
Winston, Alice, 17
   Benjamin A., 13
   Edmund, 17
   George D., 17
   Sarah, 17
Winton, John, 22
Wisenbarger, Christopher, 75
   Peggy, 75
Witt, Roland, 105
Wolf, Mary M., 34
Womack, Alexander, 67
   David, 28,105
   Fanny, 62
   Joel, 105
   Matthew, 28
   Polly, 67
   Richard, 62,105
Wood, Edm., 55
   Edmond, 8,85
   Edmund, 85,105
   Edna, 105
   Elizabeth, 55,76,85,105
   Jesse, 55
   John, 8,22,61,76,85,105
   Joseph, 105
   Mary, 67
   Mildred, 61
   Nancy, 85,91
   Patsy, 8
   Paul, 105
   Robert, 105
   Samuel, 106
   Sarah, 19
   Usley, 22
Woodall, Elizabeth, 100
   Jacob, 100
Woodman, Edward, 34
Woods, Patsy, 91
   Robert, 106

184

Woods, continued
Thomas, 106
Woodson, Anderson, 27,104
Elizabeth, 104
Frances, 27
John E., 104
John, Jr., 27
Obadiah, 106
Wooldridge, Buhard, 41
Daniel, 47
Elisabeth, 19
Frances, 26
Francis, 26
James, 47
John, 106
Mary, 47
Polly, 47
Richard, 47
Sally, 19 (see Woolridge,
Elisabeth)
Simon, 47
Virlinchige, 41
William, 19,41
William, Jr., 41
William, Sr., 41
Wooton, Susannah, 42
Worldly, John, 106
Nancy, 106
Raney, 106
Worley, Daniel, 106
John, 106
Joseph, 106
Joshua, 7,25,47,53,54,64,68,
78,93,94,106,124
Moses, 106
Rhoda, 106
Worsham, Charles, 53
Wray, Henry, 61,67,70 (see also
Ray, etc.)
John, 106
Lucy, 37
Wright, Anny, 40
Charles, 16,106
Eliza, 98
Elizabeth, 40,116
George, 64,95,106
John, 16,43,106
Joseph, 112
Mariah, 116
Rachel, 116
Ro., 16
Robert, 16,40,90,95,98,106,
107,113,118

Wright, continued
Robert, Sr., 40
Silvia, 98
Susannah, 16

Wynn, Wynne

Wynn, Ninea, 29
Wynne, Christeana, 22
Christina, 22
John, 86,107
Jones, 91
Lavina, 29
Leviney, 22
Mourning, 91

X-Y-Z

Yancey, Yancy

Yancey, Joel, 76,107
Joell, 107
Yancy, Elizabeth, 107
Robert, 14
Yates, S. Wirt Mrs., viii
York County, (Va.), 126
Young, Joseph, 87
Matthew, 107
Polly Hubbard, 31
Susannah Hubbard, 87
Will, 87
William, 31
William H., 107

CORRECTIONS AND ADDITIONS

Page 17 The fourth marriage from the top should read Dr. George Cabell instead of W. George Cabell.

97 The sixth marriage from the top should read Richard Thurman and Sarah Snelson instead of Sarah Shelson.

89 After entry five, add:

SNEAD, ISRAEL and Nancy Bondurant, bond 23 December 1807. Israel Snead (b) and John Fowler (b).